EDEN PHILLPOTTS ON DARTMOOR

EDEN PHILLPOTTS

ON

DARTMOOR

Kenneth F. Day

FOREST PUBLISHING

First published 1981 by David & Charles (Publishers) Limited

Republished in 2002 by FOREST PUBLISHING, Woodstock,
Liverton, Newton Abbot, Devon TQ12 6JJ

British Library Cataloguing in Publication Data

A catalogue record for this book is available from the British Library.

ISBN 0–9536852–5–X

Forest Publishing

Editorial, design and layout by:
Mike Lang

Typeset by:
Carnaby Typesetting, Torquay, Devon TQ1 1EG

Printed and bound in Great Britain by:
Polestar Wheatons Ltd, Exeter, Devon EX2 8RP

To
my dear wife
DOROTHY
(*'Gift of God'*)

my good companion for forty years,
to whom I owe so much inspiration
and encouragement: who, having now
passed on into the fuller life beyond,
yet remains an abiding presence.

DEO GRATIAS!

Contents

CONTENTS

Foreword

During the early days of World War II, at a time when the London 'blitz' precluded any possibility of visits to the West Country (and to Eden Phillpotts), for my own refreshment I prepared a small typescript anthology of favourite descriptive passages from novels of the Dartmoor Cycle. I sent a copy to Eden Phillpotts, whereupon he replied:

. . . I have just dipped into your anthology and revived many memories of those bygone days when I trod the Moor and tried to make pictures from the wonders spread around me. It was a labour of love on your part to build this little book, and under happier times in the publishing world I think you would find a ready market. Some day when I am sped, you very likely will do so.

(13 February 1941)

Years later, I expanded that slight effort into an anthology of Dartmoor, with his full approval and generous permission:

You are at liberty to quote from my work anything that may be of value to you.

(26 October 1959)

At that time, however, the completed manuscript found but little favour with publishers, and E.P. shared my disappointment that the project remained unfruitful.

The present book, whose scope far outpaces my previous essay, is an attempt to record definitively Eden Phillpotts's remarkable portrayal of Dartmoor. As the work has pro-

9

gressed, I have found that what has gradually emerged is a comprehensive portrait of Dartmoor as seen through the eyes of Eden Phillpotts. In that sense, it is his book rather than mine, and I am content that it should be so.

The title of the book has a twofold meaning; for while it is designed to give expression to E.P.'s wanderings on the Moor in the years of his physical vigour, it applies equally to a recognition of his unquestioned authority on the subject of Dartmoor.

Regarding the illustrations, the portrait of Eden Phillpotts is from an autographed photograph given to us by him in 1950, while the picture of us is from a colour transparency taken by our nephew, John Hibbard; the remainder are from my own photographs.

Finally, I would express my grateful thanks to all those (listed on pages 11 and 12) whose generosity has contributed towards making possible the publication of this tribute to Eden Phillpotts and to Dartmoor; and to The Royal Literary Fund (the official holders of the copyright in all of Eden Phillpotts's works) for their formal permission to quote from his writing.

Longaford,   KENNETH F. DAY
29, Vermont Way,
East Preston, W. Sussex

Foreword to the Second Edition

It gives me great pleasure to know that the *Eden Phillpotts Memorial Volume* has been given a further opportunity of bringing to the notice of Dartmoor lovers E. P.'s incomparable pen-portraits of the Moor to be found within the pages of his Dartmoor Cycle novels.

East Preston   KENNETH F. DAY

Eden Phillpotts
Memorial Volume

Publication of *Eden Phillpotts on Dartmoor* was first made possible through the waiving of author's royalties and the receipt of donations from the following:–

Sir Alec and Lady Atkinson, Belmont, Surrey

Mrs E.M. Borup, London

Mr J.V. Somers Cocks, Abbotskerswell, Devon

Mr Gerald F. Cox, Almondsbury, Bristol

Mr and Mrs Kenneth Day, East Preston, West Sussex

Sir Keith and Lady Falkner, Ilketshall St Margaret, Suffolk

Mr and Mrs J.A. Gillam, Hove, East Sussex

Mrs E. Godfrey, Dawlish, Devon

Mr and Mrs S.G. Hibbard, East Preston, West Sussex

Mr H.M. Jacobs, Sidmouth, Devon

Mr and Mrs C.R. Jefferson, Hove, East Sussex

Miss W.K. Jefferson, Brighton

Mr Colin C. Kilvington, Plymouth

Mr E.W. Luscombe, London

Mr D.R.S. Munday, Plymouth

Mr James Portman, Calgary, Alberta, Canada

Mr W.H. Ransom, St Albans, Herts.

Mr K.J. Rickard, Roborough, Plymouth

Mrs Nicholas Ross (Adelaide Eden Phillpotts), Kilkhampton, Cornwall

Vice-Adml Sir Guy and Lady Sayer, Widecombe-in-the-Moor, Devon

Miss Jean C. Scott, London

The Misses V. and E. Skilling, Ealing, London

Mr F.H. Starkey, Hay Tor Vale, Devon

Mr and Mrs C.B. Taylor, East Preston, West Sussex

Rev C.P. Turnbull, East Preston, West Sussex

Sir David and Lady Willcocks, London

Willis, Faber & Dumas Ltd, London

The publishers of the first edition, David & Charles, also contributed by accepting a reduced financial return on this book.

1
Eden Phillpotts
as I Knew Him

The name of Eden Phillpotts conjures up many aspects of the writer's art; for as novelist, essayist, poet and playwright he contributed regularly to English literature for upwards of seventy years.

Since his death in 1960 his work has unaccountably suffered neglect; and it is my hope that *Eden Phillpotts on Dartmoor* may arouse interest and renewed appreciation in at least one of the facets of his many-sided art—that of the portrayal of Dartmoor in the remarkable series of novels which he collectively referred to as the Dartmoor Cycle.

EARLY DARTMOOR ASSOCIATIONS
In June 1934 I walked Dartmoor for the first time, staying at Powder Mills Farm on the Cherrybrook between Two Bridges and Postbridge. At that time, I did not realise that Powder Mills was to become my regular Dartmoor base for nearly forty years; but I was captivated by the wildness and loneliness of the Moor, its craggy tors, rushing streams and stony hillsides. The region quickly came to exercise its peculiar fascination over me, and it has never let me go during the period of a lifetime. Such was the theatre of Eden Phillpotts's major work—the Dartmoor Cycle of twenty volumes, comprising eighteen novels and two books of selected short stories.

I was already acquainted with several of the Dartmoor novels, particularly *Widecombe Fair*, when in October 1934

I sent to Eden Phillpotts a letter of appreciation of his Dartmoor writings, enclosing a photograph taken from the summit of Peak Hill looking towards Great Mis Tor. His cordial reply—'Best thanks for your valued letter and the excellent photograph. Good of you to send it.'—was the commencement of a regular correspondence and association over the ensuing twenty-six years.

Early in 1935 I secured a copy of the third volume of the Cycle—*The River*—which vastly enhanced my appreciation of the Moor; for that book delineated faithfully so many details of the region that I was beginning to make my own—the area between Western Dart and Cherrybrook. I found therein, vividly portrayed, the detailed landscape of my perambulations: Powder Mills; Two Bridges; Wistman's Wood; Longaford and Higher White Tors, dominating the high ridge of land whose great dun slopes descend westward to the West Dart and easterly into the marshes of Cherrybrook. I lived with *The River*—and I have continued to do so ever since!

KERSWELL

In 1936 I spent Easter on Dartmoor, and on my way home called by appointment at Kerswell. This was to be the forerunner of many similar happy visits in subsequent years. Before describing such occasions, a few words about Kerswell are perhaps appropriate. The mansion (for such it was, though now divided into separate residences) stands on the east side of the A38 road at the southern end of the village of Broad Clyst, 5 miles north-east of Exeter. From the road, nothing could be seen but tall iron gates flanked on either side by a high brick wall. Beyond the gates, the drive passed a lodge on the left and then curved to the right through thick shrubberies, before opening out as the main door on the west side of the house was reached, sheltered by a deep porch in the perpendicular style. The main frontage of the house faced southward over a large garden and fields beyond.

14

The front door admitted to a wide hall, graced by a splendid painting of Eden Phillpotts which, as he said, made him look like a sea-captain. The second door on the right of the hall led into the main drawing-room overlooking the garden. That room was so attractive that after one of our visits I asked my wife Dorothy to set down her recollection of it, and that description follows in her own words:

The drawing room at Kerswell was a delightful blend of pastel colours. The floor was of well-polished pitch-pine parquet, covered with Persian rugs. The window, in the south wall, reached from floor to ceiling and was furnished with curtains of a delicate green, apparently lined with cream net. A comfortable settee and easy chairs were fitted with linen loose covers of an attractive all-over floral design in delicate shades of blue, mauve and pink, and were plentifully supplied with attractive cushions. One of the chairs stood in the deep window recess. On the tall mantelpiece were treasures of many kinds: tiny china dishes about $1\frac{1}{2}$ inches in diameter, and an elaborately chased silver vase holding a generous display of flowers, from which an occasional petal floated down as we talked. An antique inlaid bureau stood just within the door bearing a large framed photograph of E.P. and also a dagger paper knife. Various small inlaid tables were arranged around the room. The walls were lined with pictures; two etchings of Sealyhams, excellently done, were possibly studies of two of Mrs Phillpotts's dogs— for she bred Sealyhams, and had twelve of them at the time of this particular visit. Over the bureau hung an original maritime painting.

OUR DISCUSSIONS WITH E.P.

Eden Phillpotts was a most courteous man: sparely built, which accentuated his height, with white hair and moustache, a long, rather flattish nose and a face which crinkled into the kindly lines of age, his soft and somewhat husky voice at once put the visitor at ease. There was so much to talk about and the time always passed far too quickly. He would tell us many things about his work and his time on the Moor, and was pleased that we followed the scenes of his books. When considering a new Dartmoor novel, he always planned to spend some time in the chosen vicinity and let the story develop naturally. He would walk the area thoroughly and get to know the inhabitants. He would visit the churchyard in a search for local names on tombstones. A story would then commence to form in his imagination until the time came when the invented characters would demand to be set down on paper. He wrote all his books in a characteristic longhand script, and much of the work was done in the open air with the scene he was describing spread before him.

E.P. was a keen field naturalist and made careful notes of any phenomenon that aroused his interest, so that his word-pictures, painted in glowing colours, have the power to induce vividly in the discerning reader's mind a sense of atmosphere, weather and season. In his view, background and atmosphere could not be created: they must be faithfully observed and noted—for they were there for anyone to see! Once, when discussing such little touches of observation, he instanced an occasion when his leathern gaiters had become dusted with yellow pollen, and he expected that he subsequently 'pushed it in somewhere'. We later tracked down the reference to that circumstance in *Sons of the Morning*, in the chapter describing the Moor southward of Cranmere Pool.

During his early years with the Sun Insurance Office, he had once persuaded a London friend to spend a Dartmoor holiday with him. At first glance of the Moor, the friend had exclaimed, 'My God! What a place!' and had immediately returned to town. On one occasion he had taken his great friend Arnold Bennett on to Great Mis Tor, and Bennett had remarked, 'You have chosen a damned fine theatre for your work'. As a young man, E.P. had spent all his holidays on Dartmoor, and had found Dartmoor people much more interesting than people of his own class. Of his character Thomas Otter, in *The Oldest Inhabitant*, he laughingly disclaimed having met in real life quite such a wily old blade. When writing *The Three Brothers* and *The Virgin in Judgment* he had made as his centre the hotel at Dousland, and the hotel at Bridestowe for *The Whirlwind*. In his early days Dartmoor was still very isolated, and 'white witches' might still be found.

The River—naturally our favourite of all E.P.'s Dartmoor books—was written between February 1901 and February 1902. E.P. was then living in Torquay, but his base when on Dartmoor during the period of the book's creation was the Two Bridges Hotel (earlier known as the 'Saracen's Head'), a very comfortable fishing inn. E.P. recalled good times there with the popular landlord Henry Trinaman, known to his numerous friends as 'Trinny'. (Fascinating accounts of the inn at that time may be found in *Countryside Tales from Blackwood* under the respective headings of 'Salmon Days on Dartmoor' and 'Trinny's', both by T.C. Bridges.) During the period when he was writing *The River*, he often walked up the West Dart to Wistman's Wood and wrote a short story there as a relaxation from his major work. For the short story entitled 'Cross Ways' he had specially visited Powder Mills one cold bright February day. E.P. could not now remember why, both in that story and in *The River*, he had designated Powder Mills Farm as 'Cross Ways'. My own surmise is that the choice of title may have been influenced by the fact that the farm stands adjacent to Higher Cherrybrook bridge, the point of intersection of the Princetown to Moretonhampstead highway with the ancient Lich Path, a moorland track running from Widecombe to Lydford. E.P. used to visit the warrener at Wistman's Wood ('a gloomy man') and follow him around in the pursuit of his duties. He had many times taken a cup of tea with the warrener and his wife; they had two small children who used to run about like little wild things. All that now remains of the warrener's lonely home may be found just beyond the northernmost grove of Wistman's Wood, where a few piled stones and fragments of wall mark the little enclosure where the small wooden hut once stood.

Regarding E.P.'s portrayal in *The River* of Nicholas Edgecombe the warrener, L.A.G. Strong has written, in *Eden Phillpotts: an Assessment and a Tribute*:

Phillpotts is too good a novelist to be led by his own philosophy into failure to appreciate the virtues of the other side. The rationalist will denounce superstition, but realism obliges him to honour the integrity of simple faith. To this he at once responds, especially when it is inspired or fortified by a love of nature. The New Testament faith of Nicholas Edgecombe, nurtured by long hours of solitude on the moors, is most sympathetically set down. He lives by his faith, and his dream of Christ, as he lies with a broken leg on Devil's Tor, is related with the glow of imaginative truth. And, in the final chapter, the faith with which he set out is, after a solitary vigil on the moor, confirmed. Once again Phillpotts's sense of character has triumphed . . . Phillpotts is too good a novelist, too deeply interested in human nature, not to honour simple piety when it emerges in good works and kindly dealings. If one could pin him to a text, it would be the one enforced by an example from nature: 'By their fruits ye shall know them.'

That penetrating analysis, made by L.A.G. Strong in 1953, is of great interest to us when read in the light of correspondence exchanged between E.P. and ourselves in 1940 and to which reference is made later in this memoir.

During our visits to Kerswell, we often discussed *The River* and told E.P. how personal we found the book. His comment was that to take a book so seriously was to pay the author a high compliment and to make the book live. Perhaps an extract from a letter to him will most clearly set out our views on the matter:

10th October 1953

Dear E.P.,

It is not easy to say in so many words just how much we enjoyed our call upon you on Wednesday morning. It was a real privilege to talk with Mrs Phillpotts and yourself once again, and one's only regret was that so many things were left unsaid and many subjects untouched upon in a memorable three quarters of an hour.

However, it set the seal upon our brief visit to the Moor to be able to come and talk to you about it: and indeed it is a remarkable thing to spend half a day at Wistman's Wood and on the summit of Longaford Tor reading all the well-remembered bits out of *The River* with the scene spread before our eyes in all its rich autumn colouring, and then the following morning to come and tell you personally of the joy of this experience, and how much the vivid descriptions in *The River* keep alive our mental picture of the Moor when we are at home. This is not to say, of course, that we do not value the other books of your Dartmoor Cycle, but that *The River* covers our Powder Mills region with which we have a peculiar affinity, and will therefore always remain our prime favourite . . . We were delighted to find you in such good health, and shall hope to find you as fit on our next Dartmoor visit. We shall much look forward to your next book of reminiscences and hope that you may yet write of your memories of the 'Dartmoor Cycle' days, of the interesting Moor characters you encountered and your experiences in gathering your material together. This would indeed make fascinating reading.

With our love to you both,
Kenneth and Dorothy

Regarding old Tommy Caunter, who makes his appearance in the foreword to the book of short stories entitled *The Judge's Chair*, E.P. confirmed that there had been an old chap he used to meet and yarn with in the vicinity of Dunnabridge Pound, the location of the so-called Judge's Chair, which William Crossing considered to be really a dolmen. E.P. showed great interest in our visits to a remote ruin above the West Dart known as Brown's House, and that we had found the doorposts still standing bowed in on each other as described in *The Thief of Virtue*. In his early years, most of his explorations had been around Chagford, where he had spent many hours fishing. Dartmoor, as he originally knew it, was a fisherman's paradise.

E.P. had known William Crossing, author of the monumental and indispensable *Guide to Dartmoor* and other definitive works concerning the Moor, and had walked the Moor with him. At that time, Crossing lived in a cottage near Mary Tavy on a very small income as a journalist.

E.P. had no wish again to visit the Moor, preferring to remember it as he had known it in earlier days. His last visit, in the early thirties, had been to South Zeal, near Okehampton, when gathering material for the trilogy *The Book of Avis*. He was, however, always very interested in our journeyings on the Moor. He recalled the scene across Fox Tor Mire towards Cater's Beam with particular affection, and remembered well the wilderness of Fur Tor and the upper reaches of the West Dart. He much disliked the Forestry Commission plantations then beginning to cover many of the lower slopes of Beardown, Lakehead Hill and Laughter Tor; but he accepted our assurance that the slender television mast recently erected on North Hessary Tor had not proved the expected eyesore. He had greatly enjoyed his major work—the Dartmoor novels—and would have chosen nothing better to do, though if he had his time over again he would have tried to write them better. In his early years he had greatly increased his vocabulary by reading the works of De Quincey.

We used also to discuss the work of other authors whom he had known: Thomas Hardy, whose *Far from the Madding Crowd*, *The Return of the Native* and *Under the Greenwood Tree* he agreed were fine books; Francis Brett Young, whose book *The House under the Water* is a great favourite of ours (E.P. recalled that Brett Young had been sent to him for assistance on deciding to abandon the career of a doctor for that of a writer); and his great friend L.A.G. Strong, whose Dartmoor story *Dewer Rides* E.P. much admired.

We would also talk of many other matters—of music, photography and art. He was very appreciative of photographs of Dartmoor which we sent him from time to time.

20

He particularly liked one of piled clouds over Longaford Tor (taken in 1943) which was Plate 39 of *The Dartmoor Scene*, a small book of my photographs with descriptive extracts from various of his Dartmoor novels which was dedicated to him, and to which he contributed a generous and valued foreword.

A CHRONICLE OF OUR ASSOCIATION WITH EDEN PHILLPOTTS
Over the course of the years we received many letters from him. A perusal of this considerable correspondence brings him very near to us, and I cannot do better at this stage than to introduce representative extracts which will allow him to speak in his own words.

In the summer of 1935 I had visited and photographed the fragments of ruined Brown's House, standing in absolute wilderness on the lower slopes of Wildbanks Hill near the source of the Cherrybrook. I sent E.P. a copy of the photograph:

... It is a delight to see that picture of Brown's House. Thirty years have passed if not more since I sat in the little ruin when I was writing *The Thief of Virtue*. And now—in bed with an attack of gout— I can see it again in my mind's eye refreshed by your picture.

(23 August 1935)

At that time, he sent me a personally inscribed and autographed copy of *The River*, in the limited and definitive 'Widecombe' edition.

As already mentioned, my first visit to Kerswell was at Easter 1936, on returning home from the Moor with a friend. When writing to make the arrangement, I had enclosed a mounted Dartmoor photograph entitled by my father:

Thank you for the very fine view of Longaford Tor: a wonderful sky you have got and your father's calligraphy is a joy: most beautiful. I shall be at home on Easter Monday and it will give me pleasure to see you about ten o'clock on that day.

(1 April 1936)

21

The visit was a memorable occasion. E.P. was very interested in our walking, and that we had been on Bellever Tor in a snowstorm. During our conversation, he told us that in his earlier days he had been very keen on fishing; and if he had his time over again he would do many things differently, but that was not now possible. He had a great aversion to schoolteachers with socialistic ideas imbuing children with the notion that it was not necessary to raise a cap or curtsey to an old man like himself; those actions did not harm the children and taught them respect for old age. As a memento of the visit he gave me an autographed copy of *The Book of Avis*—his recently published trilogy comprising *Bred in the Bone, Witch's Cauldron* and *A Shadow Passes*—which he considered 'a good job of work'. The original of the village designated 'Little Silver' in the trilogy was South Zeal; though in earlier books he had bestowed that name on the village of Gidleigh. He invited us to call and see him again when in the vicinity of Devon.

At Easter of the following year I again visited the Moor, this time with my sister and two friends. I had previously advised E.P. of our coming, but he was unwell and unable to see us:

It is a great disappointment not to see you on this visit but I have been exceedingly sick and cannot hope to be 'down house' in a week: Distracting gout and my right wrist and arm out of action. I have wintered very badly and my last book was written with my left hand. I do hope you are going to have good weather. There is snow upon the moors at present, they tell me . . . I shall look forward to better fortune next time you come West.

(23 March 1937)

On our way home, after a very full and exacting weekend, we handed in at Kerswell a little moorland reminder gathered at Cranmere Pool:

How perfectly delightful of you all! Such a kind thought is most precious to me. I am going to send each of you a book to show my

22

gratitude. It won't be so nice as the sprig of heather from Cranmere, but the best that I can do. I am stronger, as you will see by my handwriting. It was wonderful to think you all got to the Pool, but I expect the going must have been pretty heavy in places.

(30 March 1937)

Shortly afterwards, he wrote for some advice regarding a camera for his wife, Robina, and added the following comment:

I motored up to Dunkery Beacon on Exmoor yesterday and had a grand free horizon with Wales and the Severn Sea to the north. A grand placid Moor, but lacking the quality of my precious Dartmoor.

(6 June 1937)

In August I sent E.P. some photographs: in particular, a picture of the Mill Pool near Tenterden that had figured prominently in his only book set in the Weald of Kent (*The Green Alleys*, dealing with the hop industry); and also a new study of the Longaford ridge on Dartmoor. I also told him of my work as an organist:

I much value this glimpse of you at the organ . . . It is delightful to have this picture of Tenterden Lily Pond and the grand line of Longaford and Higher White (Tors) . . . Please in future address me as my young and valued friends always do—no formalities— just 'E.P.' to you.

(17 August 1937)

During October of that year, in very unfavourable weather, I and a friend essayed one of the toughest walks on Dartmoor. Travelling down overnight from Waterloo to Okehampton, we commenced the day by ascending Yes Tor and High Willhayes, the highest points of the Moor, and then struck over the 'fen' to Cranmere Pool. Strong winds and scuds of rain assailed us from all quarters of the compass. From Cranmere we continued southward over Black Hill to the summit of Cut Hill, leaving Fur Tor on our right. The going over the sodden peat-hags south of Cut Hill was indescribable; on the worst stretch it took us an hour to cover one mile. Passing West Dart Head on our left, we made for Row Tor, crossed the infant West Dart under Crow Tor and struggled up the long slope to Longaford Tor; cresting the ridge, we glimpsed in the failing light, a mile distant and 400ft below, our destination, Powder Mills Farm. Never did food and warm shelter seem more welcome! The following day we returned northward via Postbridge, Stannon Farm and the Grey Wethers stone circle under Sittaford Tor. Ascending Great Varracombe to the summit of Whitehorse Hill, we continued over Hangingstone Hill before striking the military track which took us down to Okehampton and the London train. After our return, I wrote up a very full account of the expedition and sent a copy to E.P.:

A great feat for both of you. Must be made of steel! Very best thanks. Rare good reading and a wonderful adventure. Congratulate you both. I value this account much.

(1 November 1937)

The following year, 1938, we undertook another October weekend walk on the Moor, this time from Lydford. We passed up rocky Tavy Cleave and over Standon Hill, crossing feeders of the Tavy and then the infant Tavy itself before ascending the great slopes of lonely Fur Tor. Here we lunched under the lee of the main pile of rocks, out of the searching south-east wind. Through driving mist we then made for Tavy Head and Cowsic Head, thence to Devil's Tor and the tall menhir known as the Beardown Man. We crossed the West Dart at Fox Holes, and passed up the hill to Longaford Tor before descending to Powder Mills. The following day our return route took us in thick white mist up to Higher White Tor, then down to the West Dart and on to Lydford Tor, where the sun broke through. Crossing the River Cowsic, we continued over Blackabrook

24

Head and up to the jagged summit of Great Mis Tor, where we lunched in hazy sunshine. Time was beginning to run short, and we had a hard walk of it through Merivale, across Whitchurch Common and on into Tavistock, where we caught the afternoon London train with five minutes to spare! This walk was duly written up, and a copy sent to E.P.:

Very grateful thanks for these memories—all so fresh and vivid... I have not been very fit of late but hope soon to get out of doors again.

(1 November 1938)

Dorothy and I became engaged in January 1939, and at Easter I took her to Powder Mills and introduced her to many favourite spots. By arrangement we called on E.P. on our homeward journey, and spent a very happy hour with them. Following our return, we sent him some photographs, including one of the site of the warrener's hut at Wistman's Wood:

Grateful thanks for your valued gifts. That is a wonderful picture: the site of the keeper's old cottage. I am most grateful to you and never fail to appreciate your kindly thoughts for me.

(24 April 1939)

We were married on 27 August 1939, and just before that event we received the following:

... I will write later, and meantime I am so glad to hear you marry so soon. May continued peace attend your nuptials.

(23 August 1939)

That was not to be, however, for within a week of our wedding World War II had broken out; and we let him know of our uncertain future plans:

This was very hard on you and Mrs Day, but I do trust any duties that may be demanded of you will not separate you from her very long if at all. It is a horrible catastrophe, but has been steadily blowing up, like a storm, ever since Nazi rule gripped Germany... Let me know what you are doing presently.

(18 September 1939)

25

When acknowledging our letter of Christmas greetings, he wrote:

Forgive me for not sooner writing to thank you for your valued letter and beautiful Christmas gift. Longaford Tor has an undying fascination for me and I like to think you called your home after that interesting Tor.

(2 January 1940)

Following upon that thought expressed by E.P., it is pleasant to record that the name has been retained through two subsequent removals, and continues to apply to our present home.

In March 1940, whilst recovering from an illness, I felt impelled to write to E.P. at some length regarding our happy married life together and our shared Christian faith, together with an appreciation of the final working out in *The River* of the renewal of Nicholas Edgecombe's strong Christian beliefs after a most severe testing-time. (Reference has already been made to L.A.G. Strong's comments on E.P.'s honouring the integrity of Edgecombe's New Testament faith.) We knew that E.P. was a rationalist and, naturally enough, he did not agree with our religious views and said so, in no uncertain terms—in all friendship. This of course made no difference whatever to the relationship existing between himself and us. Part of his reply is quoted:

First let me say how glad I am to know you have recovered from your painful illness and hope you will soon find yourself quite well and strong again. It is also a great satisfaction to know how happy and perfect is your married life in that beauty of shared understanding and sympathy such a union can bring between two hearts that beat as one. For my principles as an artist and as a man, I need only tell you that I have said 'yea' to life as I found it and tried to do the best within my exceedingly limited powers and narrow endowment. Arnold Bennett, in his introduction to my Dartmoor Cycle in twenty volumes, records my methods and the inspiration which made my cycle such as it is. For those who care

26

to find them, my opinions are implicit there. Had they been otherwise, no doubt the work would have been more welcome than it was. In matters of religion I advocate absolute freedom and the right to follow any road in which we may find support and leading. I hate propaganda of any sort, in art or anywhere else.

(10 March 1940)

Having in our acknowledgement made some reference to the Surrey Hills we knew so well, we were very interested in E.P.'s comment:

Best thanks for your valued letter. I used to haunt Leith Hill when I was a lad stopping with relatives at Reigate 60 years ago.

(20 March 1940)

From August 1940 onwards, south-east England began to suffer under aerial warfare that culminated in the so-called 'London blitz'. As the terrifying activity continued to build up, we received from E.P. the following:

I was so glad to hear from you, but terribly sorry to think of all the misery, torment and broken sleep you and Dorothy have suffered. Much I hope this dementia in the part of these fallen people may soon cease when they find we cannot be conquered thus . . . I shall live in hope of seeing you both again in time to come. Bombs fall round about and Exeter has been smitten cruelly but so far we have escaped.

(24 September 1940)

In January 1941 I was appointed organist and choir-master of a Croydon church with a good choir and a three-manual Rushworth organ. That regular weekend commitment, combined with my work in the City of London with a firm of marine insurance brokers (thus in some measure sharing E.P.'s early experiences of employment with the Sun Insurance Office) all undertaken in conditions of constant air raids, fully employed my time, and Dartmoor became but a nostalgic memory. For our own refreshment, I compiled an 'Anthology of Dartmoor'—a small typescript collection of descriptive passages from E.P.'s Dartmoor books. We sent him a copy, together with some comments on our favourite Thomas Hardy novels:

So glad to hear from you and very pleased to think you have an organ of such fine distinction for your art. I always think it is one of the most noble instruments created by man . . . I knew Hardy after he married his second wife. They used to stop with me at Torquay and I used to stop with them at Max Gate. Florence was young then. She was his secretary in those days when his first wife still lived. Thomas Hardy and I differed radically in our outlook on life, and though facile critics were wont to say that I was his disciple, the truth was otherwise. I never read a line of Hardy until after I had written *Lying Prophets* and *Children of the Mist*. The introduction that Arnold Bennett wrote to my 'Widecombe' edition of the Dartmoor Cycle of my work in 20 volumes is the best thing that was ever written about my attitude to life. I have always said 'Yea' to life. Hardy said 'Nay' to it, and at 84, full of years and honours, said it was better not to be born than live. That's where his muddled philosophy got him. Between his heart and his head he seemed to me to go astray. He was not a rationalist but a grand artist.

I have just dipped into your anthology and revived many memories of those bygone days when I trod the Moor and tried to make pictures from the wonders spread around me. It was a labour of love on your part to build this little book, and under happier times in the publishing world I think you would find a ready market. Some day when I am sped, you very likely will do so.

(13 February 1941)

During 1941 we spent a few days with relatives just outside Sheffield, and took occasion to explore the Peak District of Derbyshire—a moorland countryside of white limestone and dark gritstone. I walked the extensive circuit of the steeply escarpmented plateau of Kinderscout and traversed Derwent Edge, its fantastic rock outcrops reminiscent of Dartmoor tors. When writing to E.P. on other matters we reported on that excursion, and received a long and very welcome reply:

28

I was very glad to hear from you and do trust that nothing senseless will be done with you in connection with the War Machine. One hears of such idiocy in connection with individuals and monstrous fitting of round pegs into square holes. War is nothing but an unmitigated evil viewed from every possible standpoint and a direct negation of every decent human hope for the ultimate Brotherhood of Man which both reason and faith in righteousness should bring within the reach of humanity by this time.

I knew the Peak of Derbyshire and remember on one occasion I drove from Sheffield into beautiful scenery quite close to the city. I used to stop with a dead and gone novelist: Robert Murray Gilchrist, who used to live at Holmesfield, and saw scenes of great beauty among the Derbyshire Edges and in the valleys of the Derwent and other rivers. He wrote wonderful short stories of the Derbyshire folk, all out of print nowadays . . .

I do hope and trust that you both keep well under the strain. I find music my prime support and bless the B.B.C. as the only channel now by which I can listen to it. My favourite composer is Mozart, for his joy of life better chimes with my old age than the more tremendous masters. A sublimity of pure human happiness belongs to Mozart and I am not sufficiently educated in the science of music to appreciate many of our eminent moderns . . .

I have no favourite among my serious stories and never read them again. I continue to work hard, since my powers are useless to help us to any useful purpose now, but the publishing trade is smitten gravely and their difficulties extreme. With affectionate good wishes to you both, dear Kenneth, Your old friend, E.P.

(10 October 1941)

For his birthday that year we sent him a Dartmoor picture, and in our letter discussed, amongst other subjects, English composers. We were enthusiastic about the music of Ralph Vaughan Williams:

Thank Dorothy and accept grateful thanks yourself for the exquisite glimpse of my beloved Moor. How like you both to think of such a happy reminder for me. Many a time I have tramped there in the snow, but now I am too old for those delights. I was much pleased with your letter about music. Vaughan

29

Williams I find too difficult for me; but of English composers I love Purcell and Byrd and Bishop the best.

(4 November 1941)

After having been in a reserved occupation since the outbreak of war, I became liable for military call-up in 1942: but being rejected by the Services, I was thereafter free to continue work and music as before, apart from compulsory fire-watching duties in the City of London and at home. In August of that year we managed to spend a few days on the Moor; though by now all northern Dartmoor had become a vast and active artillery range. Just before the holiday, we heard from E.P.:

I am very glad to think you will have a breath of Dartmoor air and see some of the ancient scenes once again. May you have fine weather and gain much benefit from your holiday for I can guess how hard you both work in these trying days. I shall think of you both with much affection . . . I hope to live to see Peace again, and for my years enjoy good health with work and garden. I amuse myself with raising gladioli from seed—a slow process, but I have a batch sowed four years ago which are coming into flower, and I am going to save one for Dorothy and send it to her this autumn. It will be called 'Dorothy' and I will send directions with it. Robina joins me in all good greetings. Let me hear how you got on. We are so sorry not to see you this year, but all locomotion is terribly difficult now.

(7 August 1942)

During our brief stay at Powder Mills we were delighted to receive from him the following:

Your gift and united letter much valued. I fear the weather has turned unfriendly today. Mind the warning flags and run no danger! Yes, indeed, looking up the Western Dart from Longaford was always a delight to me.

(19 August 1942)

In November we wrote to him, as usual, for his birthday:

How good of you both to remember my birthday and send me such a precious remembrance of your dear selves and my beloved

30

TEL.
BROADCLYST 232.

KERSWELL,
BROADCLYST,
DEVON.

24 Aug 1943

My dear Kenneth & Dorothy

I did so enjoy your
delightful letter with its
breath of the Moor & its
white heather. The latter
will be better than colchicum
to help cure an attack of gout
in my arm (happily the left —
me this time) that is at present
incapacitating me.

It is good to know, though
water-logged & not in a
welcoming mood, the old
earth draws you still & I do
hope you will both be much
the better for your tramps upon it.
Be careful to put on dry socks
& stockings when you get back
to 'Powder Mills', for I never

had a pair of boots that could
defy a Dartmoor bog.

Only yesterday, I was refreshing
my eyes with one of your
masterpieces: the big picture
of 'Longaford Tor' you sent
me in 1936. A noble
scene with a fine sky that
always brings the vastness of
the region back to my thoughts.

Best love to you both.

Your old friend,

C.

Dorothy's seedling 'gladiolus'
is duly marked down for future
despatch

Moor. I value these things mightily . . . I am sending your gladiolus seedling very soon, Dorothy. I have dug all my gladioli up with my own hands and don't feel in the least like eighty years old this morning.

(4 November 1942)

In August 1943 we spent a week at Powder Mills, and never saw Dartmoor looking more beautiful, although very wet underfoot and subject to varied weather conditions. The hillsides were purple with heather, and on one or two days magnificent sunlit cumuli sailed across a deep blue sky; ideal photographic conditions of which we made full use! On the morning of the 23 August we climbed Longaford Tor and spent some time on the summit reconstructing scenes from *The River*. I find from my notes that, 'the Tor was very green and grey: away to the NW Cut Hill stood up in bright sunshine, though we lay in deep shadow. Just as we left, however, the sun came out for a short moment and the Moor shone. On our way down to Powder Mills we had the good fortune to find a bunch of white heather.' That day, we sent E.P. a brief account of our activities to date, together with a piece of the white heather; and by return of post we received at Powder Mills the following acknowledgement with its admonitory warning:

I did so enjoy your delightful letter with its breath of the Moor and its white heather. The latter will be better than colchicum to help cure an attack of gout in my arm (happily the left one this time) that is at present incapacitating me. It is good to know, though water-logged and not in a welcoming mood, the old waste draws you still and I do hope you will both be much the better for your tramps upon it. Be careful to put on dry socks and stockings when you get back to 'Powder Mills' for I never had a pair of boots that could defy a Dartmoor bog. Only yesterday I was refreshing my eyes with one of your masterpieces: the big picture of 'Longaford Tor' you sent me in 1936. A noble scene with a fine sky that always brings the vastness of the region back to my thoughts.

(24 August 1943)

After returning home, we sent him a detailed report of all our moorland expeditions over the holiday, which evoked the following response:

I shall very greatly value this delightful gift and follow your footsteps over that familiar ground with deepest pleasure.

(14 September 1943)

During 1944 E.P. wrote to us in detail regarding the treatment of the gladiolus he had previously sent to us— the special variety he had raised and named 'Dorothy'— and he continued:

Yes, I knew William Crossing and remember a tramp over the Moor with him when he was an old man and I still middle-aged. None ever mastered the secret of the blessed place like he had done. He knew the name of every rivulet and rock on Dartmoor and all there was to be said about it . . . I have sent most of my collection of Dartmoor literature to the Plymouth Library, which lost all its books, or nearly all, in the Plymouth 'blitz'. Among the things saved was my original manuscript of *Widecombe Fair*, which I gave the old librarian, who was a friend of mine and an able writer . . . I delight to think your interest in the precious region persists and hope that you may be able to get there next month.

(1 September 1944)

The following month we did manage to escape from London, at that time under constant bombardment from flying bombs and rockets, and spent a long peaceful week-end on the Moor. We visited Wistman's Wood and brought back with us some moss-festooned twigs and acorns from one of the dwarf oaks: and these we sent to E.P.:

Your token from Wistman's Wood has much refreshed me and acted as your beautiful picture of Longaford Tor always does. I often look at that picture when I desire to be cheered, and these relics of the precious wood brighten this grey and stormy morning. I shall plant the acorns carefully in hope to raise a seedling or two, but rather fear they may not be ripe enough to germinate. I am so very glad you were able to get off for a brief holiday and do hope that Dorothy and you have won peace and comfort from the adventure. Dartmoor to me always meant peace of mind no matter what the weather. It brought the trials and problems of life into their true perspective and often helped to solve more personal difficulties than those belonging to my work. I have also eaten my sandwich and smoked my pipe under sturdy little Crow Tor. A bluebell grew on the top of it. With very cordial thanks for this touching and valued thought of me.

(11 October 1944)

Towards the end of that year I conceived the idea of preparing for possible publication a small book of Dartmoor photographs illustrating a moorland walk between Two Bridges and Postbridge, supplementing the text with descriptive passages from the Dartmoor Cycle. On putting the proposition to E.P., he responded with characteristic generosity:

Of course you have permission to use *anything* of mine you care to use. I know there is a short poem somewhere in one of my verse books which might serve your turn and will try to find it.

(25 November 1944)

A few days later, he wrote again:

I have found this modest rhyme in my *Hundred Lyrics* and copied it for you. It is not up to much, I fear, but if of any use to you by all means use it at any time.

(29 November 1944)

The poem, entitled *Dartmoor*, written in his own hand, is a cherished possession. Naturally, it was gladly embodied in the text of the projected book.

Owing to stringent petrol rationing and other travel difficulties it had not been possible to visit E.P. over the period of the war years. Our rare journeyings to the Moor had been made by train, and whilst there our excursions had been limited by the distance our legs would carry us. With the coming of peace, however, restrictions became slightly more relaxed, and during a short holiday in June

1945 we planned to visit Kerswell once again. E.P. replied to our suggestion:

It will be a very great pleasure to see you both again and I beg you will let me know after 18th June which date may be most convenient to you to visit me. To see your collection of Dartmoor photographs will be a treat indeed.

I do trust you will have fine weather, for June has been a melancholy month of sunless days thus far.

It is good to know that those districts under the last great bombardment are at peace at last and I am glad to think that your sufferings are at an end and your dwelling restored to beauty and comfort.

For my own good fortune I cannot be sufficiently thankful. Despite the raids on Exeter and the air port, only three miles distant, we suffered nothing worse than broken windows and no bomb fell on my land. But I am thankful that we refused to depart and that my house was not commandeered, but left to us and only airmen billeted upon us.

May you enjoy peace and genuine rest on Dartmoor; but be cautious, for the waste is still littered with dangerous things, so they tell me.

(12 June 1945)

Having suggested to E.P. a convenient date, we received the following postcard at Powder Mills:

Shall look forward to seeing you both between 2 and 3 o'clock on 27th June. Do hope the weather is continuing fine for you and Longaford and Wistman's Wood stand where they did. I have a wonderful photograph of Longaford which you took in 1936, and another, with gorgeous cloud effects above it, even better.

(22 June 1945)

On the appointed day we hired a local taxi, which conveyed us as far as Exeter. Existing regulations did not permit our driver to take us further than a distance of 25 miles from Postbridge; so he waited there for us, and we had to catch the bus to take us on to Broad Clyst. At Kerswell we spent a delightful afternoon of conversation, and took tea with Eden and Robina, and Eden's daughter Adelaide, an author in her own right who had collaborated closely with her father in various works and who happened to be visiting Kerswell at the time.

E.P. carefully examined the projected book and photographs with congratulatory comments and reminiscences, and at my request expressed himself as very ready to contribute a short preface. We discussed the plays *Yellow Sands* and *The Farmer's Wife*—in E.P.'s view Devon dialect on the stage was but rarely correctly reproduced—a notable exception being the performance of his friend Charles Wreford, the actor, a Devon man, born locally. He thought that at the present time the public did not care for folk-plays. Before going to bed, E.P. liked to read 'shockers', their construction affording him great amusement; and Robina commented that she was always ashamed to request such lurid titles at the local library! We talked about favourite Hardy novels: Robina had been reading *Jude the Obscure* whilst recovering from influenza, and we all had a good laugh at the gruesome ending to that mournful tale. We commented that E.P.'s *Widecombe Fair* was a particular favourite of ours, because one could pick up the book at any time and start reading enjoyably from any given point. E.P. said that after completing *Widecombe Fair* he thought to make an end of Dartmoor books; but he kept on after all.

This pleasant time slipped rapidly away, and it became necessary to bring a most happy occasion to an end. We caught the local bus outside Kerswell gates, rejoined our driver in Exeter, and arrived back at Powder Mills about 7pm. Following our return home, we heard from E.P.:

It was a very great pleasure to see Dorothy and yourself again and I thought it uncommonly kind of you both to make the journey on my account. May your rest on the precious Moor have done you great good. I much appreciated the delight of seeing all those beautiful glimpses of well-remembered Southern Dartmoor and do hope that you will presently get a publisher capable of treating them worthily. Here is a draft of a brief foreword but if it should prove not what you want, or omit any point you might wish me to make, be sure to tell me. It must be only what you and Dorothy approve.

(2 July 1945)

A week later, in reply to a note enclosing for his perusal my draft introduction to the book, E.P. wrote again:

I think your introduction to the book could not be bettered, but I have ventured to delete a few of your far too generous adjectives about my work . . . I shall long to hear that you have got a publisher and a satisfactory agreement with him. To receive the dedication of the book is a very great honour which I much value and still more the friendship that inspired it.

(8 July 1945)

The foreword which E.P. had so willingly contributed included an understanding appraisal of the severe challenge offered by Dartmoor to the landscape photographer, and— as I acknowledged in the introduction—set upon the little book the seal of Dartmoor authority. I am eternally grateful to him for all his kindness and encouragement over that venture.

In acknowledging our usual birthday letter to him, he wrote:

I still have more stories to tell than time left to tell them in. Publication is the difficulty, for each author is allotted no more than his pitiful quota of paper. I do hope Kenneth's book will not be long delayed and will be produced worthily.

(5 November 1945)

Whilst on vacation at Powder Mills the following summer we were delighted to hear from E.P.:

Thank you for your beautiful descriptions of the Moor which made me long to be with you both seeing those beautiful things. I am at present devoting my waning powers to a long poem, the

38

centre of which is Wistman's Wood, so I am much there in spirit; but memory is not so sure a guide as your eyes in a place. However, I consulted the first chapter of my story *The River* to refresh recollection. It will be a very long poem and very old-fashioned, I fear, for the modern, formless verse our poets employ does not appeal to me and I like the old rules and regulations and respect for prosody. If ever it shall be finished and published, count upon a copy.

I am so glad you are getting such grand, thirsty days up aloft and envy you both your splendid pedestrianism. However, your spirit can fly after your legs have lost their power to tramp, and I can still imagine the yellow pollen of the heather dusting my boots in summer and the snow in winter. I remember a wonderful February day at Powder Mills with the frost on the snow that had fallen overnight.

(11 July 1946)

The poem to which he referred—entitled *The Enchanted Wood*—was duly published, and, true to his promise, he sent us an autographed copy for Christmas 1947. In view of the fact that his normal practice was never to reread his stories after completion, it is interesting to note that in this case he turned for inspiration to *The River*, with its comprehensive description of Wistman's Wood and the West Dart valley, in order to recreate in his own mind that wonderful scene: a word-picture that has so often given us mental stimulus and refreshment when far from the Moor.

My book of photographs, entitled *The Dartmoor Scene*, having been accepted for publication by Frederick Muller Ltd, duly appeared in the 1946 Christmas Book Lists. We sent E.P. a presentation copy:

I am much touched to see that you have dedicated your beautiful little book to me and shall always be very proud of it as long as I live. It brings back regions of the Moor for which I shall always entertain special affection for reasons outside my work. The book is beautifully produced and your own introduction quite admirable. I specially liked the mention of my old friend William Crossing—a man you would have loved, who found new things to say about Dartmoor to his dying day. When I knew him, he dwelt in a cottage on Gallows Hill, in the neighbourhood of Mary Tavy. May this work of yours take its well deserved place in the literature and portraiture of the West Country . . . Bless you both, and may the New Year bring to your nature-loving eyes fresh scenes of beauty when you can seek them. It is a year that may bring greater good to the world than at present promises; after 85 years of it, I can still feel that goodness may triumph over evil if Man will only play his part.

(23 December 1946)

During the summer of 1949 we spent a few days at Powder Mills. The Moor basked in sunshine under splendid photographic conditions, and on our return we sent E.P. a batch of new pictures (one of which—depicting the conical mitre of Longaford Tor—is reproduced in this book).

I do appreciate your kindly thoughts and the shape they take. These pictures of Longaford are very fine and the texture and quality wonderful. You always manage to get such a wonderful sky into your landscapes and they bring Dartmoor to my fading memory as nothing else does . . . I detest the efforts of the forestry people to turn the place into woodland and have always said so. I keep pretty active for my age and enjoyed the heat wave very much, though my garden did not and the watering problems were severe.

(2 August 1949)

We were now taking our annual vacations further afield— in North Wales, Yorkshire and Sutherland, in the far northwest of Scotland; but we continued to correspond regularly with E.P. and Dartmoor remained our first love. In the Autumn of 1953, we advised E.P. of an impending visit to the Moor:

It will be a great pleasure to have a glimpse of you both before long, and we shall look forward to it very much. I do hope the Moor will be in cheerful mood to welcome you both again, and Powder Mills as comfortable as usual. Send me a postcard as to exact date and hour when we may expect you. I do trust you are both very well.

(23 September 1953)

TEL.
BROADCLYST 232.

KERSWELL,
BROADCLYST.
DEVON.

11 July 1946

My dear Kenneth & Dorothy,

Thank you for your
beautiful descriptions of
the Moor which made
me long to be with you
both seeing those beautiful
things. I am at present
devoting my waning powers
to a long poem, the centre
of which is Wistman's Wood,
So I am much there in
Spirit; but memory is not
so sure a guide as your
eyes in a place. However, I
consulted the first chapter
of my story 'The River'
to refresh recollection.

It will be a long poem & very old fashioned I fear, for me modern, formless verse our poets employ does not appeal to me & I like the old rules & regulations & respect for prosody.

If ever it shall be finished & published, count upon a copy.

I am so glad you are getting such grand, bracing days up aloft & envy you both your splendid pedestrianism. However your spirit can fly after your legs have lost their power to tramp & I can still imagine the yellow pollen of the heather dusting my boots in summer & the snow in winter. I remember a wonderful February day at Powder Mills with the frost on the snow that had fallen over-night.

Our fete for the R S P C A made £60, but left us very exhausted! With affection from us both

Your ever, your old friend, K.P.

We duly called at Kerswell on our way home, and spent some time with E.P.; and on our return we wrote to him the letter dated 10 October 1953 already quoted in connection with our comments on *The River*, to which he replied:

It was a very genuine pleasure for us to see you both again and I loved to hear of your happy excursion to the old Moor. Your vivid descriptions and your deep understanding of those regions bring the familiar scenes back to me. One always recognised the difference between Dartmoor and Exmoor. The quality and spirit of the two places is widely different and even opposed sometimes. In my little book *From the Angle of 88* I tried to show in the last chapter of it what Dartmoor meant to me. It was good to see you both looking so splendidly fit and well and to think of all the beauty you have garnered in the wonderful pictures you have made of your native land and the skies above it.

(12 October 1953)

During 1954 we removed from South Norwood to Banstead, in Surrey, and E.P. wrote very kindly of our change:

I do trust you have got over the arduous business of changing houses well and settled in comfortably. I would get out of this place [Kerswell] very thankfully if I could, for it is far too expensive for me now and beyond my means to keep going; but my doctor says I am too old to be uprooted. With love from Robina and myself to you both.

(25 August 1954)

In a letter received from E.P. in 1955, he made a revealing comment on the necessity for him to experience at first hand the topography of a projected book:

I have had rather a fight for life this Winter and the intense cold brought many physical difficulties for me; but I am still fairly strong though very infirm now-a-days. I have just finished a new Dartmoor story, but, lacking the power to visit the scenes of it, I do not get that element of reality I used to strive for.

(18 April 1955)

43

In our reply we tried to cheer him:

It must be very difficult to have to rely on memory for the
necessary atmosphere after having for so many years lived in the
closest contact with the scene of your books during their creation.
Nevertheless, the many books written under these ideal conditions
remain always to bring the authentic breath of Dartmoor to all
readers who are prepared to absorb the setting of the stories, while
to a real Dartmoor lover they are absolutely invaluable in re-
creating memorable personal experiences.

We commented again on what the vividness of the word-
pictures and reality of the characters in *The River* had
meant to us over the years, and concluded:

It is a real pleasure to be able to tell you once again something of
what just one of your hundreds of books means to us, and if we
manage to reach Dartmoor in the Autumn for two or three days
we shall hope to see you then.

In September of that year we advised E.P. of a forth-
coming Moor visit, and commented on a book, edited by
Waveney Girvan, that had recently appeared—*Eden
Phillpotts: an Assessment and a Tribute*—to which several
writers had contributed sections: Girvan himself, L.A.G.
Strong, Nancy Price, Reginald Pound, E.V. Knox, J.C.
Trewin, Isaac Foot and John Rowland each concentrating
on a particular aspect of E.P.'s art. We thought the book a
very attractive and comprehensive survey of his life's
work and told him so. We also enquired as to his knowledge
of the origins of the inn at Two Bridges:

Many thanks for your interesting letter. May Summer still have a
few fine days in store for you when you get to Powder Mills. It will
be a great pleasure to us to have a sight of you both next month,
but let me know a few days before your return when to expect you.
I am infirm now but weathered another winter and delighted in
the summer sun and glowing heat. I work daily, but my working
hours have to be short and I am very conscious that what results is
out of date and my values now behind the times . . . I deprecate the

book kind literary friends compiled about me. It is altogether too lavish of generous praise. I am no master, but just a rank and file teller of tales, most of which are already forgotten. I never heard the history of the Two Bridges house of call, but it grew from an unknown little public house into a very popular resort of fishermen and tourists under my old friend 'Trinny's' management. He has long since passed away.

(13 September 1955)

Shortly after our return home, E.P. wrote to us regarding some of the Dartmoor Cycle books we had discussed with him during our visit to Kerswell:

Robina, hunting among my books, has found 3 good copies of the four you wanted and I will despatch them to you tomorrow. They are *Brunel's Tower*, *The River* and *Demeter's Daughter*, and she thinks you would like me to autograph them, so I will do so. It was a great pleasure to see you both again so splendidly fit and well.

(17 October 1955)

When acknowledging our birthday greetings for that year, E.P. wrote:

My weight of years can well be borne when I think of the number of good and valued friends I still have to make life worth living.

(6 November 1955)

We visited Dartmoor again in September 1957, but E.P.'s health was in poor shape and we were not able to see him: so we called at Kerswell and left for him a little bowl filled with heather, whortleberry and sphagnum moss gathered on the Longaford ridge. At home we found two notes awaiting us, one from E.P. and one from Robina. E.P. said:

I am very much touched by your valued gifts and hate to think that you thought of me and were so near us and I was unable to see you. The next time you come to Devon I look forward in hope that we shall meet again . . . I like to think you had sunshine for your visit to dear little Cherrybrook and Powder Mills.

(30 September 1957)

We acknowledged these notes in a long letter describing in considerable detail the topographical events and weather conditions of the holiday, particularly commenting on a day of marvellous lighting and rich autumnal colouring: 'In the early evening I went up on to Longaford Tor and took colour photographs in all directions. It all looked completely unchanged and completely satisfying, and I sat for a long time watching the shadow of Longaford's cone stretching further and further into the valley.' By return of post he responded:

It is wonderfully kind of you to send me this long letter and I have followed your tremendous flying visit to the West with the greatest pleasure and admiration for your amazing energy . . . You seem to have put the whole of little Dartmoor into your pocket and you bring it all back to my mind again so that I can see it with the love of it we share. I have never met anybody with your understanding of form and colour and those subtle transitions that are one of the unique endowments of the Moor.

(7 October 1957)

When we saw him in May 1959, he had just undergone a successful eye operation. Although by now rather bent, and speaking very quietly, his general health was still very good and he still rose at 7.30am and retired at 10.30pm. We reminisced, and he willingly agreed to his photograph being taken in colour. (This photograph appeared at the end of Clive Gunnell's Westward TV film on Eden Phillpotts [1980].) After our return home, we sent him an enlargement, which pleased him greatly, for he acknowledged it appreciatively:

It was a great pleasure to see you both again and to hear that you had enjoyed such fine weather for your pilgrimages on the Moor. You must know every yard of that Quarter of the blessed Moor. And thank you for this very wonderful gift: myself taken in colour. To look at oneself is an amazing experience and Robina is delighted with your portrait and will count it among her dearest treasures.

(3 June 1959)

We visited him once more that year—in October—and that was to be the last time; for his health began to fail rapidly and in November we received a letter from Robina, sent from the West of England Eye Infirmary, Exeter:

You will see Eden is in hospital where he has been for the last fortnight having a cataract removed. His sight had become too bad for him to read and he felt the great ordeal in coming here might be worth it. It is too soon to know the result but so far he has got on quite well. We will write later and give you our news—as yet we do not know when we shall get home. Eden was so pleased to have your letter which I read to him.

(7 November 1959)

We received a note from E.P. at Christmas, obviously written with great difficulty, to which he had added a footnote: 'Forgive writing. I am very blind just now.' We had a further letter from him in March 1960, in which he said, 'Robina and I are both ill but looking forward to recovery'. In May 1960 we heard from Robina:

Eden had a very bad illness in February and March, and though he has made a wonderful recovery he is not too well and not able to leave his upstairs study. However, I hope with summer ahead he will improve.

(9 May 1960)

In July, Robina replied to a letter of ours:

How kind of you to write. I am glad to be able to tell you that Eden is going on well—he had a very bad cold with a most exhausting cough and it pulled him down badly, but he is much better now and thanks you so much for your kind thoughts of him.

(25 July 1960)

The last note we received from E.P. was a message of concern for us in a personal trouble:

My dear Kenneth, We are much concerned to hear of Dorothy's serious illness, and hope by this time all your anxiety will be past. I will write again, as I am blind at present. Yours ever, E.P.

(24 September 1960)

47

E.P. died on 29 December 1960, at the great age of ninety-eight, and we mourned the loss of a very dear friend. We immediately wrote to Robina, who replied:

Thank you both so much for your letter of sympathy and appreciation of my dear husband—he always spoke in affection of you both. My life seems a blank just now and I cannot realise he has left me. Once he knew he would not write again all joy seemed to leave him. His ashes lie on his beloved Dartmoor.

(7 January 1961)

CONCLUSION

We continued to correspond with Robina until her death on 8 September 1968. We also visited her on several occasions, first at Kerswell and later at Candys, Lympstone, near Exmouth, after her removal there. She felt the loss keenly, and movingly referred to E.P. as 'a good companion always'. E.P. had directed in his will that after cremation his ashes should be scattered on Dartmoor; and it was Robina's wish that the chosen site should be the summit of Longaford Tor. Owing to the severe weather conditions prevailing at the time, however, it was not possible precisely to follow that direction, and in the event the ashes were laid elsewhere on the Moor at a spot which cannot now be positively identified. Perhaps knowledge of the actual place is immaterial, for all Dartmoor was E.P.'s workshop and its bosom a fitting resting-place for one who so faithfully captured and transmitted the spirit of the Moor.

For us, E.P.'s death brought to an end a long and valued association; but it is a pleasure to record that we enjoy a regular correspondence with his daughter Adelaide (Mrs Nicholas Ross) and thus maintain the personal link established with E.P. so long ago.

In 1975 Dorothy and I decided to study in depth the eighteen novels of the Dartmoor Cycle—already well-known to us—with special reference to the characters and

The conical mitre of Longaford Tor

Hay Tor from the south-west

Great Mis Tor from the Walkham valley

topography therein delineated. Each novel is set in a particular region of Dartmoor, and all these locations are familiar to us in many years of Dartmoor perambulations.

We were amazed at the results of our research. The full list of major and minor characters appearing in the Dartmoor Cycle totals 434; a wholly invented population (partly drawn from life) so strongly created and so carefully drawn that by the end of our study they had become old and familiar friends.

The topographical examination was similarly revealing, as is shown by our list of Dartmoor features receiving mention in the Cycle novels: tors, hills and moors; rivers streams and pools; towns and villages; inns, farmhouses, churches and ruins; and sites of natural history, prehistoric remains and bridges; many portrayed in accurate detail.

Our research confirmed conclusively our long-held conviction that E.P.'s knowledge of the Moor was second only to that of his friend William Crossing, greatest Dartmoor authority of all time; while his observation and recording of nineteenth-century life on the Moor and his power of evocative descriptions of Dartmoor in all its varied moods can never be equalled or surpassed.

One aspect of the Dartmoor of Eden Phillpotts and William Crossing has vanished: that of a vast region of small, withdrawn rural communities widely separated from one another by rough roads and tracks, empty save for the occasional farmer's cart, or of market-bound herds of cattle and flocks of sheep; a region visited from the outside world mainly by the fishermen and the artist. Over the years, the internal combustion engine has done much to open up that remote area; radio and television have contributed to the breaking down of the old isolation of moorland farms, hamlets and villages; while with the establishment of Dartmoor as a National Park, the Moor has become a playground for many thousands of summer visitors. Yet, in essence, words which I wrote in *The Dart-*

moor Scene are as true as when they were written, over thirty years ago: 'Crowds venture not far from the highways, and the genuine tramper may spend his day on remote tor and untracked moor alone with the wind and the sunshine, the flying rain and the stealthy mist.' May the loneliness and solitude marking 'the crowns and steeples of the inner waste' long remain.

OUR TRIBUTE TO EDEN PHILLPOTTS

As the foregoing memoir will testify, Dorothy and I remember Eden Phillpotts with great affection; a man of integrity, strong in principles, warm-hearted, generous and responsive; an inspired observer of human character and landscape, possessing the gifted imagination and insight to capture fleeting impressions in passages of memorable prose—and poetry.

We are proud to have been able to claim his friendship, and we value beyond measure the privilege of having shared with him for so many years his intense love of Dartmoor; a love which, once bestowed, endures as long as life itself.

> Bright is the ring of words
> When the right man rings them.
> *R.L. Stevenson*

2
A Brief Survey of the Dartmoor Cycle

DARTMOOR! This high granite plateau, over 200 square miles in extent, rises abruptly from the fertile undulations of the county of Devon, in the far south-west of England. It is an austere region, a breeding ground of rivers and the haunt of buzzard and curlew. Strangely-shaped tors surmount the stony ridges stretching to the horizon, and the Moor remains silent and remote, its upthrust surface a frozen sea swept by passing cloud shadows.

In neolithic times Dartmoor was widely inhabited, the many hut circles, kistvaens and stone rows bearing mute witness to a vanished race. In medieval days the Moor became a royal forest, subject to the laws of the chase. Later, in Elizabethan England, miners streamed for tin, and the remains of their blowing houses can still be found on the banks of the rivers. Nineteenth-century industry then turned its attention to the Moor, and the ruins of abandoned peat works and gunpowder mills give point to the old Dartmoor adage, 'You scratch my back and I'll scratch your pocket.' A considerable area of the northern moors has also long been in use by the Services for training purposes, with consequent restrictions at times on the free movement of walkers. Latest of all in time, Dartmoor has been designated a National Park, and that should do much to preserve this highly individual tract of country, to make it more widely known and valued, and to satisfy the essential purpose of a National Park—the unhindered popular enjoyment of a wild and unspoiled countryside, subject only to such restrictions as are necessary to safeguard the proper rights of the inhabitants.

Of the many writers who have sought to capture the elusive atmosphere of Dartmoor, the name of Eden Phillpotts stands pre-eminent. Born in India on 4 Nov 1862, he was the eldest son of Captain Henry Phillpotts, Indian Army officer and political agent. His father dying during his infancy, he was brought to England by his mother. He was educated at Plymouth, and fell under the spell of his beloved Dartmoor early. After leaving school he went to London, where for some years he was on the staff of the Sun Fire Insurance Office, first at the City head office, and then at the West End branch at Trafalgar Square. He became interested in the stage; but finding that he had not the necessary talent to become an actor, he decided to embark on a literary career, which occupied him for the remainder of his long life. He returned to Devon, living first at Torquay and then at Broad Clyst, near Exeter.

At the outset, therefore, consideration should be given to Eden Phillpotts's own tribute to Dartmoor and all that it meant to him, to be found at the conclusion of his brief autobiographical book *From the Angle of 88* (1951):

And now there remains but a single salient that I wish to record: quite literally the mightiest and loftiest, though not the nearest and dearest, of them all. One has to tell of an unfailing ally and partisan in words of devotion worthy such a theme and such a friend.

Dartmoor was already older than her own hills when first we met, for she is an ageless entity and destined to endure long after the last shadows of clouds and men have brushed her bosom and sped to nothingness.

Here was my playground when a child, my workshop as a man for five-and-twenty years; and what a workshop! The great central Devon granites extend for twenty-two miles from north to south, for twenty from east to west—a pin-prick upon the face of the

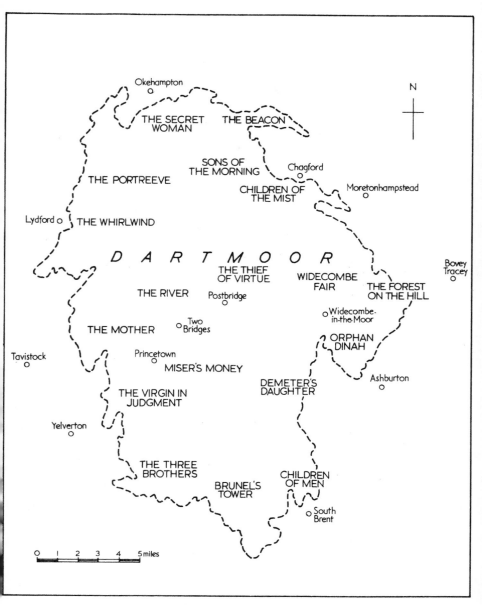

Location of the Dartmoor Cycle novels

island—yet all their world to generations of mankind who have lived and died upon it . . .

Dartmoor, like many another commanding work of Nature, depends largely for effect upon the eyes that view its immensities. It may become an acquired taste, be instantly accepted, or as swiftly rejected once for all. Some say 'yea' to her; some deny any temptation to acceptance; others, from initial indifference, warm into interest and presently flame into love. For me, from the earliest, youthful sense of heightened well-being and happiness— from desire and delight to be taken there and longing to return when taken away—there grew devotion, and the more I understood, the greater it became . . .

Dartmoor is potent to waken all manner of emotions for those in tune with her. Today she may bid you share her hours of ease and contentment, tomorrow prove evasive, musing on secret things, wrapped in thoughts you cannot share. Such moods have given me pause and a sense of loneliness. Lonely indeed I have often been there, yet never abandoned, never lost or wishful to depart . . .

Here, then, was the background of my planning, with its sights and sounds and pageants in view of every eye; but for me there now grew up the foreground of human society that filled it and a demand to seek the relationship and connection between them and their environment . . .

Thus, from being a playground for dreaming and solitude with none for company save my own imagination, Dartmoor grew full of fellow creatures and the challenges of all humanity, while my workshop, with plenty of work to be done, was fortified by their presence. Material never lacked but the need of selection from it often proved difficult. Stories harboured everywhere, now among the folk, their dwelling-place and the Moor around them, now in the chance revelations of old headstones amid their little graveyards, with brief records and inscriptions, when possible to decipher. These would often combine to complement one another and carry on some narrative, where their dates sufficed to tell of possibilities that invention might follow into the realms of story-telling. I never took a plot to Dartmoor for its background, but approached every new scene with empty mind, confident that a story awaited me there.

Work seldom wearied me on Dartmoor, but to be absent always awoke intense longing to return, for I lived more abundantly there than elsewhere, felt less vulnerable, more inviolate, nearer to the elemental things that spelled peace and simplified living.

There remains no more now than abiding gratitude to my spiritual stronghold for an august friendship ever prodigal and generous, yet chastened by regret at my meagre response. But man's molehills cannot repay the companionship of mountains. Dartmoor remains to give of her boundless best for those who seek it, while all that we may do is to acknowledge her benefactions and unite to preserve and ensure her integrity so far as that lies within our power.

As will be seen from the above, Eden Phillpotts's approach to Dartmoor has always been interpretative. In his Dartmoor Cycle—a series of eighteen novels and two books of short stories—written over a period of twenty-five years (1898–1923), the Dartmoor landscape, keenly observed and carefully noted, will be found in the very fabric of their creation. The reader is influenced not only in a general way through the ever-present sense of atmosphere, season and location, but more particularly by wonderful word-pictures of identifiable scenes painted in glowing colours; and these cannot fail to make a profound impression on the Dartmoor lover and evoke a ready response.

For my wife and myself, E.P.'s descriptive Dartmoor writings move us intensely and never fail to arouse vivid memories of great days spent on Dartmoor: of tramping to Brown's House, the Beardown Man and Fur Tor; of red foxes at Wistman's Wood and Fox Tor Mire; of idle days in the Powder Mills valley; of memorable hours on Longaford's summit; of a snowstorm on Bellever; of great thunderstorms and torrential rains; of golden sunsets over the moor-edge; of the stillness of the moonlit Moor.

The eighteen novels which Eden Phillpotts included in the Dartmoor Cycle are all set in localised regions of the Moor, portrayed accurately and in considerable detail—

as I can personally vouch for, after years of close study of the concerned areas 'on the ground'. The books, with their original dates of publication, publishers' names, and respective settings, are as follows:

Children of the Mist (A. D. Innes, 1898)	Chagford
Sons of the Morning (Methuen, 1900)	Gidleigh
The River (Methuen, 1902)	West Dart and Two Bridges
The Secret Woman (Methuen, 1905)	Belstone
The Portreeve (Methuen, 1906)	Bridestowe and Okehampton
The Whirlwind (Chapman & Hall, 1907)	Lydford
The Mother (Ward, Lock, 1908)	Merivale
The Virgin in Judgment (Cassell, 1908)	Sheepstor
The Three Brothers (Hutchinson, 1909)	Shaugh Prior
The Thief of Virtue (John Murray, 1910)	East Dart and Postbridge
Demeter's Daughter (Metheun, 1911)	Holne
The Beacon (T. Fisher Unwin, 1911)	South Zeal and Cosdon Beacon
The Forest on the Hill (John Murray, 1912)	Yarner Wood and Ilsington
Widecombe Fair (John Murray, 1913)	Vale of Widecombe
Brunel's Tower (Heinemann, 1915)	Harford and the Erme Valley
Miser's Money (Heinemann, 1920)	Whiteworks and Fox Tor Mire
Orphan Dinah (Heinemann, 1920)	Buckland in the Moor
Children of Men (Heinemann, 1923)	Avon Valley and South Brent

Note. For publishers' names in these cases where my own copies are of later editions by other publishers I am indebted to Percival Hinton's *Eden Phillpotts: A Bibliography*, as quoted in *Eden Phillpotts: An Assessment and a Tribute* edited by Waveney Girvan (Hutchinson, 1953).

Topographical details figure prominently in all the books and form an integral part of each narrative. The appended list of the principal features and place-names so delineated, together with their respective four-figure Ordnance Survey map references, indicates clearly the comprehensive survey of the Moor to be found within the scope of the Dartmoor Cycle. It should, however, be recorded that for the 'Widecombe' edition of the Dartmoor novels, published by Macmillan in 1927–8, the texts of the novels were carefully revised and in many cases drastically shortened by the author; and many descriptive passages did not survive that revision.

The greatest authority on Dartmoor will always be the West Country writer, William Crossing (1847–1928), for whom Eden Phillpotts had a tremendous regard. The works of Crossing deal factually with a mass of meticulous detail concerning the topography of the Moor, and provide as complete a record of the tors, hills, rivers, tracks and other features as is ever likely to be compiled. Crossing's *Guide to Dartmoor*, which has been referred to as the 'Dartmoor Bible', is a most detailed and accurate book which can never be surpassed, and no one who aspires to know Dartmoor can afford to dispense with it. The wanderer on Dartmoor has good reason to be grateful for Crossing's prodigious labour of love, and, for the benefit of such, reference is made in subsequent chapters to the appropriate excursions detailed in the Guide.

For further information on Dartmoor relating to the period of the Dartmoor Cycle, the following definitive works by William Crossing should be consulted:

The Dartmoor Worker	*Gems in a Granite Setting*
Amid Devonia's Alps	*Ancient Crosses of Dartmoor*
One Hundred Years on Dartmoor	

In dealing with the topography of the novels, it has seemed more convenient to maintain a contiguous pattern of locality rather than to adhere to the order of date of publication of the books. Hence, the regions under study commence with the Vale of Widecombe, continue westward to Postbridge and Two Bridges, and then follow on in a clockwise direction around the borders of Dartmoor. In this way, any overlapping of territory is kept in a closer relationship than would otherwise be possible.

The rendering of the place-names in the chapters which follow and in the list at the end of the book is generally that observed by the Ordnance Survey. Any significant variation appearing in the text of the Dartmoor Cycle is indicated in the list within brackets, while any 'designated' place-name (and by that term is meant an invented name given by Eden Phillpotts to a real place) is shown within quotation marks and brackets. The names of a few places mentioned in the text of the novels do not appear on the Ordnance Survey maps; nevertheless, their position references are duly recorded and may thus be identified. The regions dealt with in the Dartmoor Cycle are covered by the following Ordnance Survey maps:

Scale 1:63,360 (1in to 1 mile)	O.S. Dartmoor Tourist Map
Scale 1:50,000 (approx.1¼in to 1 mile)	O.S. Sheets Nos. 191, 202
Scale 1:25,000 (approx. 2½in to 1 mile)	O.S. Sheets Nos. SX 56, 57, 58, 59, 65, 66, 67, 68, 69, 77, 78

The Dictionary of Characters to be found at the end of this book tabulates names alphabetically grouped in families with brief descriptions, together with a note of cross reference in those few cases where a character in one book is referred to in another.

In the chapters which follow, each book is separately studied, both in respect of the topography of its setting and also concerning the relationship of the characters to that topography. It is hoped that this study of the Dartmoor Cycle—which Eden Phillpotts considered to be his major work and which has undoubtedly contributed significantly to English literature—may prove a useful aide-mémoire for those who already value the Cycle; encourage newcomers to explore for themselves the riches to be found therein; and provide a constantly available evocation of the Moor for all who love Dartmoor and seek its preservation.

3
Widecombe Fair

Widecombe Fair is perhaps the most widely read book of the Dartmoor Cycle. One reason may well be that some of the incidents in the book form the basis of Eden Phillpotts's highly successful play *The Farmer's Wife*. The novel is in some respects a complex one; for it is a narrative of varied events affecting scattered homesteads around the widely-spread village community of Widecombe, which events, nevertheless, are cleverly combined together to constitute a composite record of absorbing interest.

At the close of the nineteenth century, Widecombe was still an isolated and self-contained community; traffic with the outside world was still maintained only by horse and trap or by farm cart; and a journey to Exeter was a notable event indeed! Eden Phillpotts gives us a graphic picture of the fair as it appeared at the period of the story:

Widecombe Fair, while sunk from its ancient glories, yet offered opportunity for local holiday-making; and now, with its return, the life of the hamlet recognised the day from force of habit. The men were relieved of work; their masters also found themselves drifting with the throng of the fair, to see friends, mark what merriment was afoot, loiter a little, drink a little, and investigate the ewes and rams that were offered for sale.

On a sunny morning in early September, few signs indicated that Widecombe intended a revel; but presently appeared men, driving, riding and walking in from outlying villages, and the croak and rattle of heavy wheels was heard. The farm carts came from afar, and in each was a great ram—some with raddled coats; some aged fathers of the flock, gone at the knees and bent at the hooves; some sprightly, brawny, solid masses of flesh, with broad noses, curly fleeces, yellow eyes, and noble chests; the potential parents of another generation.

These great creatures, athirst, panting, and little liking their journey, were lowered from the carts and tethered under the walls of the Church-house, or in the shade of the sycamores that stood upon the village green. The horses that had brought the carts and traps were led to the hedge and fastened there, nosebag on nose; the farmers and labourers congregated together, compared notes, renewed ancient friendships, laughed and chaffed together in good-fellowship of common knowledge and common interest.

The day was hot and the sun was fierce, while on the remote Moor, westerly, darkness brooded and thunder growled from afar before noon; but no threat of possible storm frighted the people, and presently the duns and drabs of the men were enlivened by women's holiday raiment, the flash and twinkle of white blouses and blue, flowery hats with bright ribbons; here a red frock, here a green parasol. When the children were let out of school the music of the fair awoke, and there ran laughter and spread more active movement into the increasing throng . . .

The sky grew darker before evening, and a storm, that had prowled like some hunting beast behind the hills, began to drift closer. The ram sale was ended; the bustle and stir upon the Green were done; the traps and carts disappeared; the horsemen were also gone . . . Heavier and heavier the clouds had risen and piled round the hills, while Widecombe, patient target for many a thunderstorm, waited in the gathering gloom for the lightning and the rain.

Most visitors to Widecombe probably approach the village by the same route as that followed by the orphaned Tryphena Harvey and the lawyer, Mr Blatchford, who had journeyed from Exeter by way of Bovey Tracey. The road climbs steadily from Bovey, and in about four miles reaches the open moorland under Hay Tor—one of Dartmoor's best-known landmarks. Passing beneath Saddle Tor, the road meets the Ashburton road at Hemsworthy Gate; a little to the right stands the stone circle known as Seven Lords' Lands. A short distance further on the road divides, the left-hand branch leading straight to the top of Widecombe Hill and plunging down to the village five hundred feet below.

From the narrative, however, it would appear that either by accident or design the travellers took the right fork, shortly branching left, for that is the road which would take them past Bone Hill Rocks and on to the lower slopes of Bel Tor; and it is from that point that they gain their first glimpse of the Vale of Widecombe:

Across the brightness of afternoon sunshine, a west wind blew bannerets of smoke from the brows of many hills. These vans of vapour were purple in earth's shadow, but grey under the shadow of the clouds above them; and where the low sunshine burnt upon their streamers, they shone a dazzling silver.

It was February; swaling had begun, and Dartmoor's annual cleansing by fire liberated this splendid mass of matter, to fill the lower chambers of the air. With many aerial arches, rolling waves, and glimmering crests, the smoke spanned the depth beneath, where spread the Vale of Widecombe, within its granite cincture of great hills—a dimple on the face of the earth, a cradle under a many-coloured quilt of little fields.

Over the shoulders of Hameldon, the sunshine came slanting amid great shadows, that fell, wine-coloured, from the hills. Light began to ascend and wing out of this deep cup, until only the pinnacles of the church still flamed and flashed rosily above the gathering gloom.

North of the Vale the ground climbed abruptly to the wild heights of Honeybag Tor, Chinkwell Tor, Bel Tor; and upon a lower slope of the last, with their faces turned to the valley, sat a man and a young girl. Upon their left stood the pile of granite known as Bone Hill Rocks, and beneath them, separated from the Moor by a wood of pine and larch, lay Bone Hill Farm, a dwelling with a cheerful face that turned towards the south.

The view, described above, from the eastern rim of the Vale may perhaps best be studied from Bone Hill Rocks, an easy climb from the road across grassy slopes. Straight across the valley, at about the same elevation on Hameldown side, may be discerned Kingshead Farm, the home of Louisa Windeatt, which 'stood highest of all the ring of farms, and the Moor rolled to its outer gate'. As the opposing ridge tends southward, it dips enough for us to be able to see over it westerly to the distant tors of the central Moor. Further to the left, in the depths of the valley, rises the lofty tower of the Church of St Pancras; whilst Southcombe Farm, the home of Tryphena's relatives, William and Grace Coaker and their son Elias, stands on the hillside a little beyond.

We follow Tryphena and Mr Blatchford down the little road towards the village; and as we do so we pass Bone Hill Farm, the home of Peter and Martha Smerdon and their numerous offspring, and Bone Hill Cottages, occupied respectively by Daniel and Joyce Reep and their daughter Margery, and their neighbours Alfred Mogridge, the sexton, and his son Jack. At the Cottages is set the scene of the shooting of Mogridge's carrier pigeon by the dying Daniel Reep. Further down the hill we pass Bone Hill Villa, which we may take to be the original of 'Genoa Villa', the home of Thirza Tapper.

Continuing downhill and crossing a bridge over the East Webburn River, we shortly turn right into the main road at the foot of Widecombe Hill, from whence a brief uphill stretch brings us to the village green. As we climb the rise, we pass a house on the right, now in private occupation, which until recent years was the post office—no doubt the office described as being presided over by Mary Hearn.

Several roads radiate from the village. The road continuing up the valley shortly passes on the left the joint entrance to the lanes leading to Kingshead Farm and to Coombe (which may be taken to be the 'Woodhayes' of the narrative, the home of Young Harry Hawke and his wife Emma) and leads to Bag Park, imagined as the residence of the Squire, Mr Macfarlane. If, however, we turn left, we are at once confronted with the following prospect:

Crossing the village green upon the northern side of the church, Tryphena Harvey and her companion found themselves at the centre of Widecombe. Upon one side of the space wherein they

64

stood rose a lichgate, and springing from it extended an ancient Church House—partly used as dwellings for the needy and partly as a school. Before it ran a heavy porch on granite pillars above cobblestone pavement; beside it lay Widecombe's treasure, a fragment of the village stocks. In the midst of the central square a yew-tree stood, perched on a triple row of granite steps, while westerly appeared the smithy behind a formidable frieze of ploughs and harrows, and the 'Old Inn', a comfortable and ancient house, whose entrance was beneath the level of the road. Here Arthur Pierce was licensed to sell beer and spirits, tobacco and snuff.

If we continue through the village along the road towards Ponsworthy, we shall soon see on our right a very steep lane; and taking that lane we shall pass Southcombe Farm, to which the travellers were making their way. It is well worth while continuing the ascent to the top of the ridge, where, on Dunstone Down, we may obtain another comprehensive view of the vale—this time from its western rim.

On the left skyline rise the rocky heights of Honeybag, Chinkwell and Bel Tors; and further to the right, Bone Hill Rocks. Across the vale the main road down Widecombe Hill 'drops zigzag into Widecombe like a streak of white lightning'; above the line of the eastern wall of the vale project the distant summits of Hay, Saddle and Rippon Tors; beneath follow in succession Top Tor, Pil Tor, Blackslade Down and Whittaburrow. On the great slopes stretching up to those eminences, laid out in their pattern of fields, may be discerned Tunhill, the home of Samuel Sweetland and his sister, and Blackslade, standing 'near a mile from the church in a sheltered and woody nook, flanked by good tilth and crowned with granite, where Whittaburrow clustered against the east'. Blackslade was the abode of Gabriel Shillingford and his daughters. Lower down the hillside, near river level, appear Venton (Uncle Tom Cobleigh and his son and daughter); Chittleford

(Valiant Dunnybrig, his wife and niece); and Lower Dunstone (Abel Gurney and his daughter Nelly).

Returning to the centre of the village, another road is worthy of exploration:

Behind St Pancras Church a road ran away south-east of Wide-combe to Venton, Chittleford and Blackslade under the hills. The way crossed Webburn river at a little bridge, where the stream on her journey through the Vale meandered amid meadows lighted now with the kingcup and cuckoo-flower. A few lengths of granite carried the road across the water, and a handrail of iron protected it. A freshet had lately shaken the foundations of this bridge, and Pancras Widecombe, the stonemason, was working upon it and whistling as he worked. Having passed the bridge, bright Webburn wound through rush flats, amid furze brakes and among little fields to the southern neck of the valley. Thence it plunged into the woods of Lizwell, where larches already glimmered emerald bright against the budding boughs of oak and ash.

If we take that road, we shall shortly cross the little bridge over the East Webburn and pass on our left the Rugglestone Inn, where dwelt the landlord Timothy Turtle and his daughter Sally, beloved of Pancras Widecombe. The Rugglestone—the scene of the 'Riding to Water' incident—stands above the inn and beneath the Moor:

Here stood the famous 'Rugglestone', an enormous mass of granite alleged to weigh a hundred and ten tons. It was a logan, but no hand could rock it, and Mr Turtle, who held a sort of proprietary interest in the boulder, stuck stoutly to an ancient Widecombe saying: that only with the help of the church-door key might the mass be made to move. Two enormous blocks of granite were here supported by a third. They lay on rough ground watered by a stream and littered with stones. The larger logan, whose weathered sides and mossy top faced south, sustained a rowan sapling that sprang up from its midst and sucked life out of the stone. A light of golden-green moss and silvery lichen shone over the mighty boulder; ferns and pennyworts embroidered its face and sides; a tonsure of grass—green in summer, in winter, grey—ascended

Cosdon Beacon from Watchet Hill

The Nine Stones: a neolithic stone circle under the Belstone Tors

(*above*) High Willhayes, Yes Tor, West Mill Tor and Rowtor from Watchet Hill

(*left*) Dorothy and Kenneth Day (27 August 1979)

upon its crown. Beside this master rock stood another, wreathed in a great ivy tod.

Beyond the Rugglestone Inn the farmstead of Venton soon comes into view; the home for many years of that strange and eccentric character, Beatrice Chase (Olive Katherine Parr), a writer of several books about Dartmoor who built there a small Roman Catholic chapel. In the early 1930s, I visited her on several occasions, and well recall her stately manner. John Oxenham wrote a book about her entitled *My Lady of the Moor*, and she liked to be referred to as such (though from our conversation her knowledge of the topography of the Moor appeared to be very local indeed).

A little further on we arrive at Chittleford, about which we are told: 'Chittleford with its adjacencies was itself almost a hamlet, and Valiant Dunnybrig ruled here—a sort of shepherd-king.' Here we turn left and climb up the hill. During the ascent, from a point near the farm road leading to Blackslade and Tunhill, we may obtain a striking backward view over Widecombe—particularly as we saw it on the occasion of our last visit, when a shaft of sunlight brilliantly illuminated the crocketed church tower against the cloud-shadowed bulk of Hameldown beyond. From this point we can see Kingshead Farm across the vale, high on the shoulder of Hameldown.

If we continue to ascend the hill to Cold East Cross, we may then turn left and pass under Rippon Tor on our right, and Whittaburrow and Grey Goose Nest on our left, and proceed as far as Hemsworthy Gate and Seven Lords' Lands, the scene of the fox-hunting incident and the quarrel between Petronell Shillingford and Elias Coaker:

Seven Lord's Lands was the local name for a neolithic hut-circle a mile from Whittaburrow; and hither now the young folk came— to a spot where a stone man's prehistoric home, on lofty ground all tinged with tors, marked a modern boundary and stood at the meeting-place of seven manors.

69

From Hemsworthy Gate, a return may be made to the village down Widecombe Hill, passing on the way the farms of Northway and Southway, both of which receive a brief mention in the book.

Alternatively, we may turn downhill again from the Blackslade farm track; and if we bear left on reaching Chittleford, we shall cross the East Webburn at Lower Dunstone, the home of Abel Gurney, before reaching the Ponsworthy road. Turning right here, we soon see the foot of the steep lane leading to Southcombe, and shortly arrive back in the centre of Widecombe.

An expedition of considerable interest—though not perhaps to the majority of the participants involved—is the occasion of the visit to Grimspound by that organisation founded and led by Thirza Tapper and known as the 'Mothers of Widecombe'. The party climb the slopes of Hameldown above Kingshead Farm, and continue over the great open spaces beyond:

The Beacon on Hameldon is not the summit of that great hill, for north of it the Moor still climbs where the boundary-stones of 'Two Barrows' and 'Single Barrow' lead to 'Broad Barrow', a rush-clad cairn that crowns all. Upon this day of light and shadow the plateau already showed signs of summer heat. For the waste was scorched a little and the ling thirsted. Immense free horizons stretched upon every hand, and the world rolled out vast and dim beyond encircling hills. The air danced over the planes of the desert places, and there was no sound at this height but the drone and buzz of insects on the wing and bees in the heather.

Anon they reached the venerable fragment of a cross nigh the northern slope, and soon stood where the hill fell again under Hameldon Tor. Beneath them now, sunk into a ragged ring, grey Grimspound spread to welcome the party. In the midst thereof stood ruins of Neolithic homes—hut-circles—many so perfect in structure that it needed little imagination to set up again the leathern tent cones that crowned them, and see the smoke curling above the lodge from many a hidden hearth. Due south lay the great main entrance of this fortified village, and due south opened

70

the doorway of each prehistoric home. With cobweb grey they scattered the green enclosure, and the whole venerable village spread at Hameldon's foot in a dimple of the hills.

Here they meet Gabriel Shillingford, his daughter Petronell, Dr Hugh Grenville and Louisa Windeatt, also making holiday; and here the 'Mothers' listen somnolently to Mr Shillingford's learned discourse on the subject of the primeval village.

On the occasion of the picnic arranged by Hugh Grenville on Hameldown for Tryphena and Petronell, when he informs Tryphena of his broken engagement to Petronell, revealing himself in his true colours, and Tryphena recoils from him as 'panting with anger she hastened from him as fast as her long legs could carry her', several references are made to 'The Blue Jug'. This is a boundary stone a little to the south-east of Hameldown Tor.

At the close of the book, the scene depicted from the high road east of the valley is a sombre one; an October impression, contrasting greatly with the bright February picture drawn in the opening chapter:

Far away on the other side of the Vale, loomed Hameldon through the haze, august, stern, touched with amber of fading forests darkling with spruce and pine, swept by long, dead miles of the eagle fern. Sunlight would have wakened all into one harmonious glory of colour, but today Hameldon was wan and sore, and soaked to sobriety by the heavy air; while above, where the mount ascended to the sky, its heights and cairns were withdrawn behind the clouds that rolled heavily upon them.

Widecombe is much visited today, particularly during the summer months; and those who would escape the coach parties and discover for themselves the charm portrayed so vividly in *Widecombe Fair* should go there in spring or autumn. Then, particularly in the early morning or towards sundown, the passage of the years slips away and one may find, in imagination, the lanes and hillsides once again peopled by the diverse and unforgettable inhabitants of Eden Phillpotts's creation, amid the colourful landscapes so surely captured in *Widecombe Fair*.

Crossing's Guide: Bovey Tracey District; Hameldown and the Widecombe Valley. Excursions 83, 84, 86, 87

O.S. Sheets: SX 77, SX 78

4
The Thief of Virtue

The Thief of Virtue is set in and around the hamlet of Postbridge, where in mid-moor the East Dart is crossed by the Tavistock to Moretonhampstead road. Immediately downstream is to be found the most famous pack-horse— or 'clapper'—bridge on Dartmoor, a medieval structure of enormous granite slabs. A short mile north of the village stands Hartland Farm under the tor of that name, the home of the chief character of the story, Philip Ouldsbroom. To the north-east of Hartland, under Stannon Tor, may be found Stannon Farm, the home of Quinton Crymes and his family; and on the south-western slopes of Stannon Tor appear the ruins of an old sheep-fold.

Further still to northward rises the greater height of Sittaford Tor, easterly of which may be discovered the two stone circles known as the Grey Wethers, from their fancied likeness to a flock of grazing sheep. Continuing northward into the valley of the North Teign River, the remote Teignhead Farm, the home of Henry Birdwood, may be reached, standing above the river on the lower slopes of Great Varracombe.

Two miles to the north-east of Postbridge, up Merripit Hill and along the road to Moretonhampstead, is the Warren House Inn, reputedly the third highest inn in England. The landlord of that hostelry was imagined as Gregory Twigg, the Moorman for the East Quarter of Dartmoor. South of the village, the East Dart passes under the clapper bridge and winds under Lakehead Hill and Bellever Tor, eventually to meet the West Dart at Dartmeet.

73

The western skyline is marked by the swelling heights of Broad Down, beyond which may be sought the little ruined dwelling of Brown's House standing in utter desolation on the lower slopes of Wildbanks Hill above the West Dart. That branch of the river then passes under Crow Tor ('Crow' to rhyme with 'now'), the Beardown Tors and the site of the warrener's home above Wistman's Wood on its course towards Two Bridges and the 'Ring o' Bells'.

The Thief of Virtue opens with a magnificent word-painting of summer clouds over Dartmoor; and while the chapter is too long to be quoted in full, an account of the topography of the book would be incomplete without some impression, at least, of the noble skyscape depicted therein:

At midday in summer, shadows, very purple under the ambient splendour of the hour, roamed over Dartmoor, sometimes in thronging companies and sometimes alone. They leapt the rivers, raced the level heaths, and climbed the hills. Upon the sky there worked two separate winds, and each drove its own flock. At lower level advanced the cumuli and threw their shades upon the earth; and above them great lines of transparent but visible vapour, filmy against the blue, sailed in upper zones, and by their direction marked another stream of air . . . In the sunlit, lower strata the full sky pageant culminated. Here cloud-billows like bergs floated along the edge of earth in level lines, wind-steered. Then they approached; their magnitude increased and they bulked enormous . . . The breasts of the rolling legions blazed and faded, blazed and faded again; and their heaviest murk was apparent only, not real. For the least cloud-shadows racing over earth were darker far than the deepest, stormiest stains upon the cloud-cliffs ascending above them. There the darkness was light—the whole sky a relation of great and lesser light . . . The wonder of the clouds diminished, the cumuli humped and dwarfed; there grew increase of density and dimness along their faces and a lessened splendour upon their retreating heads . . . distance at length hid all the wonder of their hearts, until, mildly, gently, as ships on a summer sea, they sailed down to the distant earth-line . . . where sea met sky afar off in the south.

On that glorious summer day, forty-year-old bachelor Philip Ouldsbroom, contemplating matrimony, lies in the heath on Hartland Tor and watches the clouds pass over his head; he then descends the hill into Postbridge to visit Barbara Hext, who keeps the post office and general store. Ouldsbroom's home is pictured as being the tenement farm of Hartland, at the foot of Hartland Tor:

Hartland's ancient fabric stood with white front and roof of thatch among the high-climbing hills by Dart. A squat chimney rose at each end, and the thatch was drawn down over the deep porch. The small windows glimmered from heavy embrasures; the farmyard extended before the door; and at the entrance was a thick, clean mat of red fern. From within came the chirrup of chickens that had run through the opeway and were pecking up crumbs on the blue stone floor of the kitchen. A few garden plants —ribes and a windworn lilac—made shift to live under the windows of Hartland, and the beds that contained them were separated from the rough pavement of the yard by a wall. Behind the homestead sloped a furze-clad hill to granite peaks and ledges, while beneath twinkled Dart, winding through Postbridge and onward under Lakehead Hill.

The little settlement of Postbridge, much visited during the summer months, stands at the centre of a region of great neolithic activity; and, although many of the stone rows, kistvaens and hut-circles were despoiled for wall-building material in the early nineteenth century, much still remains:

Postbridge is more ancient than the road of Roman straightness that strikes through it. Round about are numerous medieval monuments. 'Clapper' bridges and miners' smelting houses, ruined dwellings and symbols of the Christian faith all stand within a walk of the hamlet; while, more ancient yet, though of yesterday contrasted with the stone man's relics, shall be seen a fragment of the Great Central Trackway or Fosseway, which extended from Caithness to Mounts Bay before the Romans landed. Fragments of this ancient, cobbled road still lie northerly of Postbridge, and traverse Dart at a shallow beneath Hartland Farm.

After his call on Barbara Hext, Philip Ouldsbroom continues on his way to visit Quinton and Gertrude Crymes and Quinton's sister Unity at their home at Stannon:

To Stannon farm, beneath the hill of that name, Philip Oulds-broom now turned his steps, tramped the modern thoroughfare of the Moor for a space, then left it half way up Merripit Hill and struck out northerly over the heather. Presently, far beneath him, appeared the little farm. Seen from these lofty slopes, where they extend and form a giant easel for sunset to paint upon, little Stannon lay under its parent hill amid small crofts. The homestead looked like a grey hen with wings outspread above her chickens, for the walls sloped to right and left of the main mass in a manner simple and symmetrical. Dwarfed to a spot appeared the farm under the tor that swept to the sky above it. A brook wound beneath and descended from its cradle of rushes upon White Ridge. Its fountains glittered in a lace of silver that, crossing and recrossing, wove patterns upon the hill, then tumbled into one channel and began their work by carrying sweet water to Stannon.

The ancient sheepfold under Stannon Tor is the scene of Ouldsbroom's successful proposal of marriage to Unity Crymes, and later of Unity's meeting with Henry Bird-wood, with whom she has had a previous understanding:

The ruined sheepfold stood four-square on the western slope of Stannon Hill. Built nearly a hundred years ago, at the time when many enthusiastic spirits discovered Dartmoor and dreamed dreams of prosperity to be dug from her bowels or garnered on her breast, it adds one to a long list of futile enterprises and lies forlorn among the hills—historic evidence that even the toil of a Scot may miscarry. Down the midst run parallel rows of great stones, and at the eastern extremity still stand the roofless remains of a dwelling-house. The place was burned down long ago; a little girl perished in the fire; and her harmless, small sad spectre still haunts her home, according to the fable of the folk.

The above details are confirmed by Crossing in his exact description of the sheep-fold (Excursion 45): he states that it 'was burnt down between 1820 and 1830, when, it is said, a child perished in the fire'.

The disappointed suitor, Henry Birdwood, and his man Ned Sleep occupy the solitary Teignhead Farm, far from any road and served only by a rough moorland track:

From the soaking heights of Siddaford, above the Grey Wethers, there spread northerly a mottled desert patched with darkness of heather on a ground of livid and dead grass. This wan covering brightened in the bogs, where sedges perished in red death and spread dark, ruddy stains, as though blood had flowed out there. The land rolled desolate, water-logged, spiritless even to Cosdon's rounded shoulders heaving to the north. Under Unity's eyes in the cradle of Teign, where it now extended beneath her, stood the home of Birdwood—the loneliest inhabited dwelling upon Dartmoor, but not beyond the beat of death. A little reclaimed land stretched round about, and the house showed no larger than a great moss-grown stone flung here long since and now welded into the hillside.

After the marriage of Unity Crymes with Philip Ouldsbroom, she continues to see Henry Birdwood from time to time: and after her son Martin is born she meets Birdwood at a pre-arranged spot on the Moor, when a disclosure vital to the progress of the narrative is revealed to the reader:

Unity went upon the high Moor with her child three months after it was born, and walked slowly by the valley of Dart to an appointed meeting place . . . Where the river bends back to the west under Broad Down she found a little familiar holt upon the hill-side. Here a few great boulders fell together and made a penthouse against rain and wind. From the mouth of it the valley subtended and great declivities rolled round about. The place was familiar to Unity, though she had not visited it for many months. That she was expected might be seen, for some one had spread the little chamber with fresh litter of fern . . . Around her were the first shy buds of May, and above her a stormy sky broken and cleft with sun gleams. The more usual phenomenon of shadows upon light was reversed, and splashes of brilliant light roamed instead through ambient darkness. In gleaming patches, like great golden birds, the splendour passed. It flashed in the river valley, climbed the hills, winged onward to their crests and ridges, and so vanished again. But darkness was the note of the day; the wind brushed the song of the river fitfully upon the ear; the cleeves were calling to the rain.

The arrival on the scene of the boy 'Tiger', a twelve-year-old runaway from the workhouse at Okehampton, provides an opportunity for reflection on human loneliness:

There is no loneliness in nature, and of Dartmoor it can never be said that it is empty. But watch some road, stretching inexorable mile on mile across the heath, and mark a solitary figure creeping along it. Then large loneliness is swiftly felt, as a quality of the human addition, not the place. Such a figure proceeded on a summer day by no road, but across the heavy ground above Broad Down. It crawled, a mere atom, to the crest of the hill, and there, panting footsore and hungry, flung itself down and fixed enquiring eyes upon the valley beneath. The little object was a boy, and he had travelled fifteen miles across the heart of the Moor, to find himself utterly exhausted above Postbridge. Now his anxious eyes looked ahead and instantly brightened. The troubled countenance of his red and freckled countenance changed to happiness, and he rejoiced. 'Golly—houses!' he said, and instantly rose again to begin the descent to Postbridge.

I well remember sharing Tiger's sense of relief, when, returning from my first expedition to Cranmere Pool, on a sweltering July day, I finally crested Broad Down and glimpsed my destination far below.

In his Dartmoor writings, Eden Phillpotts on more than one occasion comments on the softening influence imparted to a landscape by the east wind:

On a day in August the Moor had receded, grown dim, and taken upon itself the enchantments of the East wind. Detail departed from distance, and the waste swept ridge on ridge and hollow upon hill, in semblance of grey and silver clouds, that rolled upon the sky, so that they might not surely be separated from it. The wind, with most delicate vapour, most tender tones of pearl and azure, wrapped heath and granite in a milky lustre, robbed the sternest rock-mass of its contours, and leavened the waste with the medium of its own opalescent colour. The lesser furzes took it, and the heath; the boulder was bluer for it, and the fading splendour of the fern more dim where the brake spread upon the hills. Colours swam together at the touch of this Orient breeze, and a melting, diffused quality of mingled tints was manifested through all things.

The heat was tempered. A fret of sunny foam drifted along above the cloud-banks, and into the air beneath Hartland Tor ascended feathers of earth-born smoke from fires in a field. They rose in fulvous columns, then bent together westerly, thinned, lost their own sulky hue and took the colour of the day upon their vanishing volume.

It is recounted that Philip Ouldsbroom and Tiger go cutting peat at the peat cutting under Arch Tor; and after a description of the peat beds we are told that:

Round about the land sloped upward from this bottom, and to the north Archerton's flat crown of stones capped a gentle hill.

The tor referred to as Archerton Tor is actually Arch Tor, which stands on a low ridge above Gawler Bottom, down which valley a stream flows towards the East Dart, parallel with the main road from Two Bridges. Archerton is the name of a homestead standing a short mile north-north-east of Arch Tor.

On one occasion Martin and Tiger penetrate the Moor to the heart of the inner loneliness, seeking for a particular plant which grows on Dartmoor only on the shattered flanks of Fur Tor, rising in remote grandeur westerly of Cut Hill:

A rare day of ineffable splendour crowned Dartmoor, and to the seeing eye, even upon this desert was displayed a vision wonderful —a dream of life mating with matter, and of the protoplasmic element flying, swimming, growing, ripening, multiplying, and displaying its eternal miracle upon the bosom of the sun- supported earth. The colour was a cloudless noon in August; the forms were familiar hill and stone-capped tor, broad marsh and glittering stream, roaming herds and flocks scattered widely upon the undulating land. The earth and the fullness of it rolled out glorious, ridge on ridge, to the transparent blue of the horizon . . . Now Martin hunted over the wild shoulders of Fur Tor and stopped twice to survey the scene spread round about him. Infant Tavy glittered to the west, and suddenly, turning his eyes therefrom back to the shattered granite by his way, he found what he was seeking and marked the Mount Ida whortleberry gemmed with scarlet fruits.

From time to time visits are made by various characters to the Warren House Inn, a small hostelry standing exposed to the elements at a height of 1,400ft on the north side of the road from Postbridge to Moretonhampstead. South of the inn the ground falls away across the grass-covered excavations of the old Vitifer and Golden Dagger tin mines:

Gregory Twigg, grown elderly now, but otherwise unchanged, gazed from the door of his home into a wet and stormy gloaming toward the end of December. Before the 'Warren House' there stretched wide spaces where once tin miners had worked; and more than this dreary, broken region of rotting mounds, dry watercourses, and deserted machinery could not be seen, for the air was full of a shouting storm-wind and of driving clouds that shut out all things save the water-logged foreground.

After Unity Ouldsbroom's death, Philip spends a great deal of his time roaming the Moor alone; and whilst doing so, he discovers the ruins of Brown's House and the eminence of Crow Tor—two features which are to play an important part in his latter days:

On a day when the world was white with frost, all roseal under the risen sun, Philip went out into the Moor . . . He went up over Broad Down, then turned towards the west and tramped heedless along, for the earth was hard as iron, and might be traversed with safety anywhere save upon the quaking hearts of moss-clad bogs that never froze . . . Near the upper waters of West Dart, upon the breast of a lonely hill, Ouldsbroom passed by a ruin, known as 'Brown's House' . . . Then, crossing Dart and holding forward by the hither hill, he came upon Crow Tor, and stopped there. The great mass stood sharply up, and at its feet was a frozen pool . . .

On a bog-foundered slope above the gorges of Dart in mid-Moor stands Crow Tor, and seen afar from beneath Wistman's Wood, ascends as a prominent landmark among the hills. In form, at this remote range, it suggests some mighty saurian or hump-backed snail, creeping aloft from its lair in the marshes; while observed at hand, the tor presents an irregular, huge mass of granite piled forty feet above the earth, cleft, torn, and weathered from base to crown. Upon one side the ledges overhang heavily and shut the sky from any who walk beneath them; the summit mounts northerly of this pent-house; and in the midst of the mass is a little plateau of vegetation, dwarfed almost to a carpet by its elevation and the ceaseless pressure of great winds . . . Chance flowers, little to be expected, lift their nodding chimes in the late spring; for a colony of bluebells flourishes aloft upon this vantage ground above the world, and make a scented company, unseen, unknown, where they nod and dance to the buffet of vernal winds.

During a brief stay on Dartmoor in the autumn of 1944, my wife and I visited Crow Tor, where we had our lunch in the wind and the sunshine, surrounded by green and tawny moors with fluffy cumuli passing rapidly overhead. We duly reported our excursion to Eden Phillpotts, which called forth from him the following comment: 'I have also eaten my sandwich and smoked my pipe under sturdy little Crow Tor. A bluebell grew on the top of it.'

The day before Martin and Minnie return from their honeymoon, Philip sets out on a fishing expedition, and revisits Brown's House:

Above West Dart this ruin stands, at the top of a little square fosse, once sharply marked, but now sinking back into the heath again. A bank, flung up to make a barrier between the dwelling and the Moor, was scarcely grave-high now. It stretched grass-clad along to where, upon the northern side, ran fragments of piled stones. The fabric of Brown's House was already reduced to stumps of shattered masonry. The entrance might yet be marked, and two slant doorposts of granite still stood there and bowed in upon each other. The space round about showed no sign of ancient culture, and all that remained of the building revealed fragments of one chamber alone. Three broken walls encompassed it; the fourth was gone. Far beyond sight of human activity Brown's House had stood. Absolute wilderness rolled and rose and sank again to the high horizons on every side of it. To the north ascended a green hill, and its crest was lost in fog that crept stealthily along. Now it thinned, now thickened suddenly, now broke again. Beneath were great ranges of marsh stretching from the brink of the river, and over them, set so closely that they whitened the bog like a thin fleece of snow, spread the silvery tassels of cotton-grass. Southerly, fronting the ruin, there swept that great range of hills whose summits ascend above Wistman's Wood and culminate at Crokern nigh Two Bridges; while to the west ascended Rough Tor, Devil's Tor, and the sweep of the Bear Down hills. Here came Philip from fishing, sat among the fallen stones and ate his bread and meat. About him fed a little herd of Scotch cattle, shaggy, black, and dun; above him a curlew wheeled and uttered its short alarm bark of three shrill notes.

As already recorded, in 1935 I sent Eden Phillpotts a photograph of Brown's House, which I had taken on my second visit to that remote spot. Perhaps his comment may be conveniently requoted:

It is a delight to see that picture of Brown's House. Thirty years have passed if not more since I sat in the little ruin when I was writing *The Thief of Virtue*. And now—in bed with an attack of gout I can see it again in my mind's eye refreshed by your picture.

Continuing domestic difficulties at Hartland bring Philip to the characteristically extravagant resolve to rebuild Brown's House and to spend his remaining days at that sequestered dwelling. In the narrative, this duly comes to pass, though such a rebuilding is pure fiction, and the two slant doorposts of granite still bow in upon each other, as I have seen them on periodic visits. Crossing informs us that:

From what I have been able to gather it never became what its builder intended it to be. The work of enclosing the land around it was never completed, and consequently, instead of becoming the home of a settler, it was suffered to fall into decay.

In the twilight of his age, Ouldsbroom continues for two years or so at Brown's House, and visits Hartland but rarely. Once, while Martin is away from home, he returns and spends two days with Minnie. 'He talked of Two Bridges, and the cheerful company there; he had found a new friend in one Nicholas Edgecombe, a warrener, who dwelt in a house as lonely as his own at Wistman's Wood.' Nicholas Edgecombe, it may be recalled, is the chief character in *The River*.

On one occasion Philip spends a day fishing with Tiger who is now married to Mary French:

A great storm had raged on the first night of March. A red, humpbacked moon went down over the Moor edge and some keen, clear hours followed. The wind freshened hourly and, after midnight, veered south of west and blew a whole gale. The homesteads shook from the thrust of it, a dozen trees fell at Postbridge. Torrents from a black sky heralded dawn and morning came on a shouting wind under grey sheets of rain. Already floods thundered to the valley at the first return of light; but Tiger knew Philip too well to break the appointment. The sky blew clear by seven o'clock, and before eight he was off to the head-waters of South Teign, there to meet the old man. He carried ample food provided by Minnie, together with his own rod and creel.

Later in the day, Philip and Tiger decide to visit the dying Gregory Twigg at the Warren House, and make their way from the South Teign River to the inn over Hurston

Ridge, passing on their route Furnum Regis, the scanty remains of a tin smelting-house, described by Crossing in Excursion 21.

As he approaches the age of seventy, Philip's failing intellect conceives the wild plan, which he duly puts into execution, of taking Martin's son Wesley to Brown's House by stealth, and refusing admission to all; but the faithful Tiger at last persuades Philip to allow him to return the child to his mother. That mission being accomplished, Tiger returns to Brown's House at dawn to find the house empty and Philip missing. After a two days' hue and cry on the Moor, Martin finds Philip's dead body lying on his favourite haunt of Crow Tor:

Riding at sunset of the second day, Martin came aloft to the steep valley of West Dart. At hand stood Crow Tor, and he dismounted and approached it. His purpose was to climb the rocks, if possible, and survey the hills round about with a telescope, which he had borrowed for this search.

Upon the crown of the tor an evening wind played faint music and touched the stones to melody . . . Beneath it, stretched along, lay Ouldsbroom on his face. He had sought his haunt, climbed to his familiar eyrie under the rampire of the tor, and lain down and died there . . . A shining bed in the whortleberry and green grass persisted for some hours to mark the place of passing; but leaf and herbage were restored anon. They lifted themselves again and sprang up to the call of the life within them. Then that silvery depression disappeared, as the sleeping lairs of flocks and herds vanish when they rise up at dawn and go upon their way.

One clue only dates the story. When Martin is ten years of age, Tiger arrives on the scene at the age of about twelve. At that time, Philip Ouldsbroom brings news to Post-bridge of the suicide of Mark Baskerville, the bell-ringer, in the belfry of the church at Shaugh Prior. That occurrence is a major incident in *The Three Brothers*, and reference to the ensuing chapter of that novel discloses the year as 1889. From that fixed point may be calculated the approximate dates of other events from details scattered throughout the narrative, and the imagined period of *The Thief of Virtue* may therefore be assumed to be approximately 1877 to 1906.

Crossing's Guide: Postbridge District. Excursions 44, 45, 46; also 5, 11, 19, 20, 21

O.S. Sheets: SX 58, SX 67, SX 68

5
The River

Perhaps I may be allowed to revert to our already declared interest in *The River*. For many years the circumscribed region portrayed in this book has been our own particular haunt on Dartmoor. We have been intimate with characters and narrative for the whole of that period, and have had the inestimable privilege on many occasions of discussing the book with the author. For us it was a wonderful thing that we could spend an afternoon on the summit of Longaford Tor, reading all the well-remembered passages with the actual scene spread before our eyes in all its rich colouring, and then on the following morning visit E.P. at Broad Clyst and talk with him of the joy of that experience. To be able to tell him just how much the book meant to us was a unique pleasure; and a prized possession is an autographed original edition of *The River* from his own bookshelves.

The book depicts the hamlet of Two Bridges and the high lands flanking the upper reaches of the Western Dart—the titular stream—westward to the River Cowsic and eastward to the Cherrybrook. The Beardown Tors crest the western ridge, while the eastern ridge ascends north from Crockern Tor towards the granite cone of Longaford Tor above Wistman's Wood, before curving gently north-north-east to culminate in the cairn on Higher White Tor.

The area may well be surveyed from Longaford's grassy summit—our favourite vantage point. Southward the view extends across Dartmoor's central depression in a great semicircle from Hameldown (north-north-east) to North Hessary Tor (south-west). On a clear day many features mentioned in *The River* may be identified: Bellever and Laughter Tors, the valley of the ruined powder mills and Powder Mills ('Cross Ways') Farm, Lower Cherrybrook Bridge, Smith Hill ('Cherrybrook') Farm, its thatched roof like 'a lonely bee-hive', the beech avenue at Prince Hall (the site of Merryweather Chugg's cottage), Two Bridges Hotel (the 'Ring o' Bells') and Beardown ('Bray') Farm in its grove of trees on the hill.

To the west we look down on Wistman's Wood in the deep trough of the West Dart valley, and up the great slopes beyond to the Beardown Tors. Just beyond the northernmost grove of dwarf oaks may still be found a few piled stones marking a little enclosure, all that now remains of the warrener's lonely home. The wooden dwelling depicted in the frontispiece of the first edition of *The River* (1902), and mentioned by Crossing, has long since vanished from the scene.

Beyond the curving river valley the desolation to the north-west and north extends to Devil's Tor, Row Tor and the distant dome of Cut Hill. Here we view the inner loneliness so beloved by Eden Phillpotts; his comment in a letter of 1942 (already referred to) may be recalled: 'Yes, indeed, looking up the Western Dart from Longaford was always a delight to me'. Finally, we look towards neighbouring Higher White Tor, and our survey is completed.

The River opens with a splendidly extended and colourful description of the West Dart valley and Wistman's Wood:

But there is a region near her sources where the river winds under huge hills crowned and scattered as to their grassy undulations with stone. The high lands clamber round about to a wild horizon that is roughly hurled upward in mighty confusion against the sky; and from the deep channels of the river's passage her music lulls or throbs at the will of the wind, and wakes or ceases suddenly as the breezes blow. Here beneath the conical mitre of Longaford Tor, in Dartmoor's central waste and fastness, she sweeps along the fringes of a primeval forest. Upon the steep foot-hills of the tor, crooked, twisted, convulsed by centuries of western winds and bitter winters, like a regiment of old, chained, and tortured ghosts, stands an ancient assemblage of dwarf oaks: that wonder of the Moor named Wistman's Wood. Grey lichens shroud each venerable bough, and heavy mosses—bronze and black—drip like wet hair from the joints and elbows of the trees, climb aloft within a span of the new year's leaves and fruit. In the deep laps of these shattered oaks, where rot and mould have built up rich root-room, grow whortleberries that hang out red bells in spring and ripen their purple fruit beside the acorn harvest in autumn; ivy strangles the sturdy dwarfs; the chaos of fern and boulders from which they grow swallows their fallen limbs and carcases, but still they endure and still stoutly obey the call of the seasons. Their amber buds cast sheath at each new-born April; their lemon catkins powder the leaves again in May; . . . and the second spring of the oak annually bedecks each leafy crown with rosettes of carmine foliage that glow against dark summer green . . . Then, the last leaf fallen, this forest sprawls in hibernal nakedness, like a grey web flung over the sere or snow of the wintry hills . . . Here, at least, these two immortals—the stream and the forest—continue to survey each other through the centuries, and, still flourishing in the proper polity of green wood and living water, preserve a melodious and eternal tryst with time.

And so the scene is set, and we are introduced to Nicholas Edgecombe, the warrener, engaged in spinning copper rabbit snares:

Upon a day when autumn was at hand, and the foliage of the trees already turned to warmth and ripeness, there appeared a man beside the confines of the wood, and this human figure struck the highest note of colour in that great scene. Sunlight leapt suddenly along the heights above Dart, huge cloud shadows climbed the eastern hills; and in the midst, where planes of light and shade, green grass, chocolate peat and grey stone mingled upon the slopes and valleys of Longaford Tor, there glowed sudden harmonies of ruddy hue . . .

Blue smoke rose from the chimney of Edgecombe's cabin, . . . a hundred yards distant upon the hillside. It was no more than a square hut of timber under a tar-pitched roof—a solitary spot in the wide desolation . . .

The man was not lonely, for he believed the New Testament, and its message glowed and burned within him, even as its story peopled his nights and days with solemn figures that seemed proper to that waste . . . He figured the Lord as tempted of Satan on Longaford Tor, imagined the fiend as sweeping away in a purple cloud shadow, fancied that the Saviour's robe without seam was shining afar off, when the sunlight touched some distant, upstanding menhir into likeness of a man.

We follow Edgecombe and his young friend Teddy Merle, from 'Bray' Farm, as they set off and climb eastward to the great ridges of the land where, 'immediately beneath them, cast in a semicircle upon the hillside, extended an amphitheatre of stones piled and tumbled together in utmost confusion'. That hollow is locally known as Withybush. From this vantage point they look over the great basin of Cherrybrook towards the old powder mills, observe a distant puff of smoke and hear the report of a gun. Under cover of the stone wall cutting the hillside Edgecombe stalks the poaching Timothy Oldreive, apprehends him on the lower slopes of Higher White Tor and confiscates the gun, which he takes to his master, Farmer Snow, of 'Cross Ways' Farm.

The action then moves to the 'Ring o' Bells' at Two Bridges. The memory of the late 'Granfer' Worth, of Two Bridges, went back to the days when the little inn there—the original of the 'Ring o' Bells'—was called the Saracen's Head and was kept by a woman named Smith and her two sons. He told me that the old inn was taken by Henry Trinaman and subsequently enlarged into the Two Bridges Hotel in 1893. The little tavern was incorporated into the present hotel buildings and can be easily identified as the central section which embodies the main entrance. The interior on the ground floor, however, has been completely altered from its appearance at the period of the story. E.P. remembered good times at that comfortable fishing inn around the turn of the century, where the popular landlord was known to his numerous friends as 'Trinny'.

The 'Ring o' Bells' (and its landlady, Betty Bradridge) features on many occasions in the book, providing opportunity for the reader to become acquainted with the local characters. The wisdom of the grizzled water-bailiff, Merryweather Chugg, the oddities of Sorrow Scobhull and the amusing conversation of minor worthies all add an authentic touch to the narrative. The impecunious Mark Trout was drawn from life. He was George French, the ostler at the Two Bridges Hotel, who lived with his large family in a small cottage at Beardown Lodge, now converted into an outbuilding. He eventually lost his life through falling into the Dart one dark night as he was crossing the bridge after leaving the inn. We knew one of his sons, Tom French (brother-in-law to our friend George Stephens of Powder Mills) who worked for the Duchy of Cornwall—which includes within its estates vast areas of Dartmoor. Tom was undoubtedly an original of one of the little children described as attending Mrs Merle's Christmas party at 'Bray' Farm. Sorrow Scobhull, that strange figure with a haunting dread of Dart, was, so E.P. told us, a composite of several real characters he had encountered on the Moor.

Three miles north, close to the summit of Devil's Tor, stands the lonely menhir known as the Beardown Man, according to Crossing nearly 11ft high and about 8ft in girth. It is to that remote spot that Edgecombe sets out on a trapping enterprise:

The sun shone very brilliantly, and at the upper end of the valley, above the mass of Crow Tor, where it rose above chaos, like some amorphous monster of old, barren moors under great light rolled upward to the northern horizon . . . The warrener pushed for that desolate elevation known as Devils Tor, gaining which, he sat down with his face to the south and rested a while. The spot was singular, and the hill itself crowned with no irregular peaks and turrets like its neighbours. Instead, masses of flat granite covered it, like the dome of some huge bald skull thrust upward through the earth. Close at hand appeared a stone hero's most solitary grave, or the granite memorial of some forgotten form of God-worship. Here stood the Bair Down Man, a lofty menhir that wrote humanity upon the wilderness, and linked the lonely wayfarer with his kind . . . The huge Bair Down Man, visible for many miles against the skyline, always woke a pleasant interest in Nicholas Edgecombe. Now, casting down his gun and his rabbit traps, he strolled to the stone, and walked round it, as was his wont upon the rare occasions of a visit . . . He turned, sat upon the flat head of the tor, lighted his pipe, gazed awhile over the vast expanses of country spread before him, and then, going to his work, descended towards masses of rock that formed a natural burrow, and began setting his wires in the rabbit tracks.

The crown of the hill now rose between Edgecombe and the birthplace of the little Cowsick river. Here was a water-torn region of deep channels cut in the peat, of deep gullies, morasses, and huge rush beds, where the streamlet shone in its many-coloured cradle of sphagna mosses, and twinkled away rapidly to gain volume and speed on its tumultuous course.

It is at that remote spot that Edgecombe has the misfortune to sustain a broken leg as the result of an encounter with a white bull. Here he lies helpless all night long; here he is discovered by Hannah Bradridge and Mary Merle engaged in a whortleberry-gathering expedition; and from here he is carried across the Beardown Tors to 'Bray' Farm, the home of Mrs Merle and her family, where he is nursed back to health. Later, Nicholas completes his convalescence at the 'Ring o' Bells'. Over this period, he has become strongly attracted to Hannah Bradridge.

Mrs Bradridge goes to visit Timothy Oldreive at 'Cherrybrook' (Smith Hill) Farm, which stands on the right bank of the Cherrybrook, a short distance above

Lower Cherrybrook Bridge on the Ashburton road. On her way home, she calls at Merryweather Chugg's cottage at the entrance to Prince Hall avenue. No trace of the cottage now remains, but a walled enclosure on the left of the entrance clearly indicates where a lodge once stood, and that enclosure may therefore be identified as the site of Chugg's home.

Edgecombe decides to build an altar, or cairn, on Devil's Tor to record the saving of his life there; and Mary Merle, learning of that project, determines to visit the spot and try and meet him at this work:

She climbed northward over the huge waste spaces of Bair Down, passed the cluster of tors that surmounts it and, setting her face steadily to the Moor, ascended at length to the flat head of Devil's Tor, upon the fringe of those morasses that stretch hence to the heart of the inner loneliness.

Mary discovers Nicholas engaged upon the completion of his self-imposed task; and later accompanies him on the homeward journey. As they traverse the Beardown ridge, Edgecombe's cabin comes into view:

Presently he stopped a moment and looked down at his house, a mile distant and far below on the other bank of Dart. Upon the side of green Longaford it stood, a spot; and to the right, Wistman's naked forest spread like spiders' grey webs woven along the hills. Above, rising from wilderness of shattered granite, piled in heaps and flung to the four quarters in savage chaos, towered the conical head of the Tor; while aloft a clear sky already darkened to night.

In the chapter entitled 'Longaford Tor' appears a detailed and evocative description of the great scene subtended from the summit of Higher White Tor:

From Two Bridges northward extends a line of little mountains into the moor, and upon Higher White Tor, the culminating peak of this brief chain, shall still be found some eight or nine megalithic fragments of an ancient trackway. From undulations of grass and heather upon its southern slopes the stones stretch aloft irregularly towards the crown of the tor; and Nicholas Edgecombe, when he tramped that way, would oft of set purpose pursue this venerable road and speculate on what manner of men aforetime came and went here amid the unchanging hills . . .

Before turning homeward he had gone out of his way to mount Higher White and think awhile in the upper air it pierced . . . From the crest where he stood the land fell abruptly to deep turfy hollows scattered with granite. Then, beneath a coat of sere grass, warm in tone against streaks and patches of snow, the slopes levelled gradually into great marshes, where water glimmered and acres of sedge, ruddy in death, brightened the basin of Cherrybrook with their prevailing hue. From these fens the plover called, and, rolling easterly, the huge bulk of Hameldon loomed along the sky with a darkness that was yet lighted in opposition to the westering sun. The furrowed face of it might be read like an open book, for its heather-clad and snow-clad bosom was a palimpsest, written and re-written, erased and corrected by Time and his children. Into the mists of the south this hill extended, and beyond it, sun-kissed and hazy, stole forth those remote ramparts of Dartmoor that face toward the sea. There Hey Tor, Saddle Tor and lofty Rippon lifted their heads, and, beyond them easterly, Buckland Beacon's abrupt descent marked the bed of Dart. Yar Tor and Bench Tor and Sharp Tor likewise appeared upon a nearer plane, for the air was crystal with unshed water, and all things were magnified by invisible moisture. Beneath his uplifted vantage ground the warrener beheld Bellaford and Laugh Tors, shrunk to molehills; then a pearly snake of light told of Cherrybrook's course, and, westerly, Holne Ridge and Avon Head and Cater's Beam glowed against the sky, mighty, mysterious, unbroken by any stone.

As the sun began to sink, all the earth was dipped in grey, and the ridges and hollows, where snow still shone, gleamed ghostly, or glowed with faint rose while the sky awakened into evening splendour. Over the distant sea a nimbus of storm-cloud ascended upon the wind, and in the higher air, full of pure light above the sunset red and gold beneath, sped signs of change, where the whips of a great storm flung out their silver thongs before an aerial tempest that swept the upper chambers of the sky. Beneath, at earth level, soft breezes still blew, and in their fitful rise and lull, Edgecombe heard rivers crying of the rain.

Half a mile distant Longaford's strange mitre of earth and stone stood outlined, and, gazing thither, the warrener found his eye send a sudden message to his heart. A woman stood upon the apex of the tor and looked about her. At that distance she was little more than a dark speck crowning the elevation; yet Nicholas knew her well enough, for his sight had a long range. Now he leapt to his feet, shouldered his gun, and made haste to meet her ... Ascending the scarp of the tor, Edgecombe reached her side, where she sat in a natural chair of granite. The stone was furnished with soft mosses; grass and ferns grew in the clefts of it, and, rising upward like a sceptre, sprang a foxglove from the bygone summer.

Here occurs the scene of proposal of marriage and acceptance that overjoys the man. Subsequently, many meetings take place at Wistman's Wood, where Nicholas at times wearies Hannah with his total absorption of the Bible narrative. Following upon their lover's quarrel, Hannah visits Ashburton on her mother's business, and walks the twelve miles home, crossing Holne Bridge and New Bridge and passing Dartmeet. In the gloaming she meets Edgecombe on the long empty road between Lower Cherrybrook Bridge and Two Bridges, where they are reconciled to each other:

In the lift and lull of the wind, from where the river ran over little falls between sheets of still water, its music came and went. Now the melody was distinct with the clean, sharp ripple of tumbling and foaming water; now it faded to a whisper as the breezes died; now it was quite lost upon her ear as the wind waxed high again and played his proper music on the ancient harps of the grass and the granite.

It is on the bank of the West Dart below Beardown Hill that Mary Merle hints to Nicholas that all is not well with his courtship of Hannah, and later, by his cabin at Wistman's Wood, she expresses full contrition for her action.

In the early morning of Edgecombe's wedding day, the scene at Wistman's Wood is evocatively described:

In the early dawnlight of his wedding day, while yet the sun was behind the hills, Nicholas stepped forth; and, looking upward, he saw the morning stars ere they vanished into the blue. A clear and unstained sunrise burst upon the world like music, set earth's pure veil of moisture glimmering under the crystal air, and gathered up the valley vapours as they ascended to the sun. Roseal mists wreathed Longaford's crown like a halo, and adorned the spot where love was first breathed between the man and woman; then they vanished away to the invisible pavilions of the rain. Edgecombe's cabin still stood within the purple shadow of the hills; his breath made a cloud about him and told how impatient autumn, before her hour, shall sometimes be seen stealing stealthily at dawn over the upland world while yet August reigns. But the sunshine touches her, and she gathers her cold gauzes to herself, and vanishes for a little longer.

Later that morning, as Nicholas makes his way down the valley towards Two Bridges to join the wedding party at the inn, he is met by Teddy Merle with a note from Hannah explaining that she is already married to Timothy Oldreive; and on that hot August day his world crashes in ruins around him. In the evening he crosses the Moor to 'Cherrybrook' Farm prepared to exact vengeance, but the sight of the obvious misery of Hannah and Timothy alters his purpose, and he retreats to the seclusion of Wistman's Wood.

Mrs Merle's party on Christmas Day at 'Bray' Farm, including as guests Mark Trout and his numerous children, proves for Nicholas 'a bright spot shining out of gloom'; and in the early spring following, Edgecombe has some conversation with Hannah when they meet by chance on Bellever Tor:

On a day in early spring, the world from Bellaford Tor was draped in the east wind's mantle. Milky hazes wrapped the horizon and washed the Moor with pale light, through which Dart glimmered like a metal thread and wound amid her marshes, her hills and naked woodlands. Larks shrilled in the pale sunlight and plovers called. The wind sang drily in the dead rushes on the hill-top, and above, great separate clouds were scattered in a long procession from east to west. At the zenith only they revealed their true proportions, but rising and receding they huddled into pearly masses and vanished behind the haze. Higher yet, on a plane above the cumuli, long white streaks of freezing vapour stretched southward and obeyed another current of air. Their true motions were so slow as to be invisible to any but a patient watcher. Little colour touched this great scene. The sky was pale and winter had doffed no part of her raiment, for beneath northern-facing walls and in sunless hollows her sere robe revealed ermine fringes of snow. Contrasted with this virgin whiteness, the dead sedges and grasses seemed almost warm in tone. The horizons were all vague and grey; only beneath the sun, now at meridian, earth and sky melted together in liquid vapours of pale, misty gold.

Fire sent forth great clouds of smoke upon the waste, and running ripples of flame crept along before the wind. Behind them extended a gloomy mantle of ash and char; before them streamed their banners of smoke. These spring fires, or 'swaleings', had been deliberately lighted that furze and heather might perish, and the grasses, thus relieved, prosper for flocks and herds.

Sorrow Scobhull, who has a morbid dread of Dart, spends leisure on a summer's day gazing into the river as it traverses the deep valley below Dartmeet, near the Eagle Rock:

Shelves of granite, cracked and riven, here sloped to the stream, and their interstices were filled with little sallow saplings and flowering plants. Immediately beneath lay a salmon pool and beyond it ascended steep banks much torn and rent by floods. Uncovered roots climbed and twisted like silver snakes within this chaos of shattered stone, naked earth, lush grass and fern . . . The crowns of the boulders were grey and apple-green, splashed with ebony lichens and mellowed with mosses and hepatic plants that grew darker of colour towards the rock-bases and became almost black where the river lapped them. Above the banks, tier upon tier, rose oak and ash, birch and larch in ascending planes that shone beneath the vertical glory of the sun. But their underwoods knew not of this noon splendour. Only dawn and red sunset searched their secrets and found a horizontal pathway to their dim hearts. Now was the hour of the forest crowns, and they basked in the blaze. The birch shone in a trembling and lucent veil of tiny leaves, and through its robe ran tracery of bough and branch deep set in the web of shining green; but the oaks collected their light in dense sheaves and galaxies that glowed massively against the delicate, bright hazes of the finer foliage . . .

The lonely gorge was soaked in light, and its concourse of huge rock-faces and abrupt boulders made a new harmony where Dart flashed over stickles and waterfalls, or rested in placid backwaters, or dived by hidden channels beneath the over-lapping rocks. Everywhere bright sunstars in the river flashed upon the shore, to wake riparian shadows with sudden fire and touch each grain of quartz in the granite to a shining gem.

On the same day Nicholas meets Hannah by appointment outside the little cave at Pixie's Holt, above the West Dart near Dartmeet, 'where sunshine twinkled like golden money in a netted purse of shadows'. On two occasions I have searched for Pixies' Holt, but the whole hillside is now so thickly covered with gorse and scrub that I have so far not been successful in locating the exact position of the little cavern and its grove of sycamores. I believe that I have been looking too far to the west, for my friend John Reynolds of Cherrybrook tells me that its O.S. reference is 668730. On the hillside I have, however, particularly noted that 'through one rift in the woodland eastward, the Ashburton road was visible as it climbed upward from the river beneath'.

The main road between Two Bridges and Postbridge is the scene of the serious talk between Merryweather Chugg and Nicholas—whilst riding in the market cart—on the subject of Mary Merle; of whom, we are told 'a pleasant expression, telling of temperamental goodness, marked her countenance'. Chugg alights and goes down the Cherrybrook, whilst Nicholas, having put up his horse at 'Cross Ways', tramps over the Moor to Wistman's Wood to ponder upon the relationship between himself and Mary.

Lower Cherrybrook Bridge, on the road to Ashburton, is the venue of a conversation between Jacob Vosper, head man at 'Bray' Farm, and Timothy Oldreive—'where little bats fluttered and uttered shrill squeaks about Cherrybrook Bridge'.

At Two Bridges, Mark Trout and Sorrow Scobhull meet upon the bridge by the 'Ring o' Bells' in the dusky light of dawn, and set off to walk to Tavistock together:

At peep of day in a sleepy hour towards autumn great hazes hung over the land, and the eastern tors towered very dark against the morning. Dartmoor stretched grey under a drenching dew, and a steam arose from her ponies, where they roamed with shining hoofs and marked each his track upon the glimmering heath . . . Dawn touched Dart, and she blushed faintly along her silver ways. Beneath the old bridge a framework depended to keep the cattle from straying out of their pastures by means of the river bed; and now these hurdles, swaying to the morning wind, splashed in the water.

As they mount the hill they see, in the mists hanging dense above the Cowsic valley, Mary Merle gathering mushrooms. After sun-up, Mary meets Nicholas, also on his way to Tavistock by way of the Beardown clapper bridge. They sit down together at the confluence of the Cowsic and the West Dart; and Nicholas, his mind now made up, asks Mary to marry him:

They found such a spot as he desired, where the lesser streamlet ran into the greater, and where the risen sun, casting a glory between the folds of the hills, touched the river with dawn light, clear and warm . . . They sat facing the east. Mary's face glowed and her bright eyes flashed in the sunshine. At their feet Dart sang to the morning and a broad shallow widened from a little fall. First the water trembled away from beneath the foam, then it rippled onward netted with red and gold; and finally all fret and strife smoothed away, it ended in the peace of the pool. Here a rising fish shattered the reflection of the bank and the sky. Mingled images from earth and air swam together at the little trout's splash; then they trembled out again and grew defined as the water settled to stillness. Rush and thistle, nodding grasses and purple meadow scabious were reflected in the river; and far above, the newborn day alighted like a golden bird upon each granite peak.

One sultry morning, Timothy Oldreive sets off with his baby son to work in the peat cuttings 'where they stretched along the waters of Cherrybrook near their junction with Dart'. A tremendous thunderstorm gradually builds up over the central Moor, and breaks on Cut Hill:

He looked towards the storm-centre and saw that upon Dartmoor a tempest had already fallen. The crowns and steeples of the inner waste were blotted out and unnatural night hurried from the north. A livid radiance spread upon the skirt of the darkness, where rain already fell. Then the sky split, and forked lightnings, leaping from the zenith to earth and back again, ripped up the heart of the storm and crossed its awful cloud-chasms with a network of fire. Thunder jolted and bellowed and made the earth vibrate to every peal . . . The heart of the storm had moved to the south-east; already the rain decreased and a pale light, from which the tors crept forth, stretched across the central Moor; while the thunder sank to a murmur dimly heard in the louder tumult of the river.

Torrential rain floods the rivers and streams; and Nicholas, passing by the peat cuttings, hears the child's cry and rescues it from the rising waters.

On an autumn day of great splendour, Mary Merle makes holiday, and sets off to spend a long day with Nicholas as he goes about his work on Wistman's Warren; and she is overjoyed when he asks her to discuss the date of their marriage:

Conversation now flowed like a river, and, walking upon air with her soul intoxicated, Mary moved beside her lover. They passed beneath Longaford's stone mitre, and presently stood above the huge plain wherein old, ruined powder-mills lay scattered and Cross Ways Farm appeared. Cherrybrook's course could be observed almost from her springs to her confluence with Dart.

Sorrow Scobhull finds Edgecombe working on the side of a hill near Two Bridges, and tells him with great urgency that Oldreive has attacked Hannah beside Bawker's Pools, on the West Dart below Prince Hall bridge. The warrener runs to the spot, and in the fight that ensues, Edgecombe sustains grave injuries, while Oldreive is drowned in the river. Edgecombe is taken to Prince Hall, where he is nursed by Mrs Chugg and Mary Merle; and here, Hannah, now a widow, visits him in his weakness.

The final scene takes place on Crockern Tor, where, long before, Edgecombe had met Oldreive at the Devon tinners' old judgement seat on the summit. Nicholas, found not guilty in his trial for manslaughter and now restored to full health and strength, is still unable to distinguish between love and duty regarding Hannah and Mary, which:

hid their true aspects, and it seemed to him, sorely distressed between them, that duty was transformed to love and love to duty. Finally he could no more part them. They mingled in a maddening figure that pointed both to Cherrybrook and to Bray Farm.

He spends an October day on Crockern Tor, and endeavours to resolve his problem:

Upon the morning of Sunday, Nicholas set forth into the Moor that he might seek there that direction he craved. To Crockern Tor he passed along, where nightly rains under a morning of pure azure glittered around him. It was as though a mist had been caught out of the air, spread upon the waste and woven thereinto with sunbeams. The dawn light mellowed many a league of sere grasses until earth's habit shone like cloth of gold upon the shoulders of the hills against blue gloom and rosy fore-glow in the western sky. Opulence of tone, intense purity of each great colour-wave marked that crystal hour; only the granite, peeping grey from red fern and rusty heath, lifted prisms of quartz to the direct sun-rays, and, discovering their rainbow secrets, scattered them separately.

Now Edgecombe marked the ascending smoke that rose from solitary cots and homesteads in the plain beneath him. As each lifted the incense of a human hearth to the morning, he thought of the hands that had lighted it, and the women on their knees by every gathering flame. He knew all of them, for he stood at the centre of his world. The smoke spires rose lazily, and, mingling, drifted eastwards before a gentle wind. Their thin, opaline cloud softened the clean glory of the hour. Where cottages clustered the vapour thickened, but upon the wide, desolate places, over the river valleys and great peat beds, it fined to a delicate and sunlit gauze before the wind.

Nicholas saw the smoke spring from Bray Farm in its grove of beech trees on the hill of Bair Down; then, turning his eyes towards the east, he marked the thatched roof of Cherrybrook, just visible, like a lonely bee-hive far beneath. From thence, too, a thread of smoke arose . . .

The smoke above Bray Farm rose grey against the western sky; the smoke from Cherrybrook curled blue as heaven into the brilliance of day . . . Noon passed, and the sun rose to his low meridian, then turned westward . . . When the sun sank to setting and made a golden mist of the western hills, it was Cherrybrook that retreated into darkness upon the fringe of another night, and the farm in the trees that glowed and shone.

And at the last his eyes are opened, and he comes to recognise 'that same sublime figure he had once imagined as moving in these solitudes—the Master he had obeyed and presently rejected. Now He was returned, and with a countenance scarcely changed.' Nicholas descends Crockern Tor, and, standing on the highroad beneath, he witnesses a spectacle which we have often experienced when at Powder Mills:

Vastness of dominion and transparent purity of light marked that sunset spectacle. Westward the blue sky faded into green, then

101

brightened to pale gold. Each great hill took the purple shadow of its neighbour; each tor and lofty cairn beamed tenderly with rosy fire, then sank and died away into the oncoming gloom. Impartial night folded to her soft bosom both distant homesteads, so that Cherrybrook and the farm upon the hill alike became invisible. All things grew featureless and vanished. Earth drank up darkness to satiety, then, rolling eastward upon her starry pillows, slept.

At the foot of Crockern Tor Nicholas makes his final choice between the farm in the valley (and Hannah), and the farm on the hill (and Mary); he lays his absolute and unconditioned faith before the throne of that Man-God he had chosen; and sets his face to the farm upon the hill.

A breath of frost twinkled upon the earth that night, where the Moor—mother of rivers—bared a wintry breast to the young moon, and watched in peace beside the cradles of her babes. Under elemental silence all animate life was suspended; the unclouded air slumbered unfretted by any breath; far away infant Dart alone made a murmuring and cried to her sister. Their springs were a mirror for heaven; because where these lesser waters wakened, starlight moved upon the face of them and wound a tendril of pure silver into their tremorous beginnings. And thus the secrets of the everlasting universe mingled with each new-born fountain as the river leapt to her destiny from the heart of that uplifted land.

Finally, something might be said about the supposed period of the story. Many years ago, Eden Phillpotts told us that it was assumed to have happened about the time the book was written. Both the internal and external evidence, however, would suggest that the period was somewhat earlier; and whilst the argument is too detailed to be set out here, one is led to the conclusion that the four-year period of the narrative may be imagined to run from 1889 to 1893.

'CROSS WAYS' AND 'THE JUDGE'S CHAIR'
Eden Phillpotts's portrayal of the region of *The River* would

be incomplete without reference to two of his volumes of short stories—*Knock at a Venture* (1905) and *The Judge's Chair* (1914).

The short story *Cross Ways* appeared in the first-mentioned book (and also in a much later collection entitled *They could do no other*). Eden Phillpotts told me that he wrote the story, set within the old ruined powder mills on the Cherrybrook, during the period that *The River* was in preparation. For that purpose he made a special visit to Powder Mills one bright February day (13 February 1901) when frost was on the snow that had fallen overnight. At that time the powder mills had already ceased working, but the little granite huts in the Cherrybrook valley still held much sulphur and machinery. The mills ceased working in 1896, but the machinery was not dismantled and removed until 1932.

It is appropriate, therefore, to include E.P.'s contemporary impression of the old powder mills:

There is a desolation that no natural scene has power to invoke. High mountains, huge waste places and rivers calling make us feel small enough, not sad; but cast into the theatre some stone that marks a man's grave, some ruined hut or roofless cottage, some hypaethral meeting-place or arena of deserted human activity, and varied emotions rise.

Such an arena, spread on a scale unusually spacious, may be found in the central waste of Dartmoor, nigh Postbridge. Here, where marshes stretch, all ribbed with black peat cuttings, between the arms of Dart, where Higher White Tor rises northward and the jagged summits of lesser peaks slope southerly to Crockern, there lies a strange congeries of modern buildings rotting into dust and rust at the song of a stream. Even the lonely groves that shield these ruins are similarly passing to decay; but many trees still flourish there, and under the shadows of them, or upon the banks of the Cherrybrook that winds in the midst and babbles its way to the mother-river, lie remains of vanished industry. Now only a snipe drums or a plover mews, where some short years ago was great hum and stir of business and a colony of men engaged upon dangerous toil. Rows of whitewashed buildings still peep from the dark grove or stud those undulating hillocks that tend moorward beyond it. Tall grey chimneys rise here and there, and between certain shattered buildings, linking the same together, great water-wheels appear, thrusting forth shattered spokes and crooked limbs and claws. They slumber half in gloom, like fossil monsters partially revealed. Moss hides the masses of their petrified bones; huge liverworts clothe their decay, and hart's-tongue ferns loll from their cracks and clefts, and thrive in the eternal twilight beneath them. Once twin pairs of grinders turned here, and the last aspect of these is even more uncouth than that of the water-wheels that drove them. Their roofs are blown away and the rollers beneath are cased in rust and moss. Willows and grasses and the flowers of the waste flourish above their ruins; broom, dock, rush, choke the old water-courses; crowfoot mantles the stagnant pools: all is chaos, wreck and collapse. For here spreads the scene of a human failure. Its secret may still be read in old proclamations hanging upon notice-boards within the ruins, and telling that men made gunpowder here . . .

Darkness, fretted with white moonlight, was under the fir trees; the Moor stretched dimly to the hills in one wan, featureless waste; an owl cried from the wood, and one shattered chimney towered ghostly grey over the desolation. Quaint black ruins, like hump-backed giants, dotted the immediate distance, and the river twinkled and murmured under the moon.

In the foreword to *The Judge's Chair*, Eden Phillpotts records a personal experience of Laughter Tor and of the Judge's Chair, a cromlech set within the walls of Dunnabridge Pound:

It was a day in high summer . . . Heat danced on the tors, and the lonely heights of the Moor were swept with a fine, transparent haze. The wind drove gentle grey shadows over the hills and valleys, but sharp definition lacked from earth: all things looked distant, and only the roads were clear—the stark, white roads, that stretched out straight and stern, dipping at the undulations to lift again and hold steadily on, reappearing, disappearing, until they vanished, like white threads drawn through some sudden gap or over the far off horizon.

On Laughter Tor I stood and marked the Bair Down range and the high peaks crowned by Longaford's cone. Beneath me roamed East Dart, and upon the west broke Great Mis Tor, like the peak of a ragged cloud. Here and there a copse lay upon the expanse and stretched in a dim smudge of darker green above the scattered granite and dun herbage. Under Crockern the tin miners' meeting-place of old, there spread a cluster of trees, and Prince Hall's plantations stretched nearer at hand, with West Dart throwing a silver loop about them. Beneath me lay the tiny homesteads of Dunnybridge and Brownberry, and now in the tremendous heat I sought their shelter that I might find a patch of shade among their walls.

Rising from a stone where the sun-scorched whortleberry made a cushion, I descended to the great enclosure of Dunnabridge Pound—'The Duchy Pound' beside the highway. Near the gate which communicates with this ancient croft shall be found one of the mediaeval memorials of the Moor: the Judge's Chair—a relic of the old mining days, a granite throne, which tradition affirms stood once on Crockern Tor for the President of the Stannators' hypaethral parliament. Now it has been erected against the dry-built wall of Dunnabridge Pound, and, whether a worthy object of antiquity or no, affords welcome resting-place for the wanderer who is aware of its existence.

The Judge's Chair consists of a great pent stone, supported by upright masses of granite, while beneath, for a seat, lie two more granite blocks. It faces north, and its living footstool is of grass and buttercups. Nothing can be seen but the stony drift-pound, the granite walls, and the sky above; nothing will be heard but the lowing of kine, the cry of a curlew, or the song of a lark.

Crossing's Guide: Princetown and Two Bridges District. Excursions 4, 5. Hexworthy District. Excursion 41. Postbridge District. Excursion 46

O.S. Sheets: SX 57, SX 67

6
Miser's Money

Three miles south of Two Bridges lies the great moorland hollow of Fox Tor Mire, gathering-ground of rivers. To reach that remote region from Princetown, we take the minor road known as Castle Road and, passing Tor Royal, within two miles we reach a point where our way bears to the left and descends into the valley to the small one-time tin-mining settlement of White Works. From this vantage point a comprehensive view of the setting for *Miser's Money* may be obtained, so faithfully recorded in the first chapter of the book:

In mid moor there is a great plain ringed round about with hills. One hog-backed ridge blocks the southern horizon and the majestic outlines of Cater's Beam, unfretted by tor or forest, describe a gentle arc upon the sky; while northerly the land climbs again, and beneath it subtend the grazing grounds, peat cuttings, and waterlogged flats of Fox Tor Mire. The region glitters with little tributaries that flow to Dart, for Swincombe River, Nun's Cross Brook, the Strane, and Fox Tor Gulf Stream all run through the Mire.

This huge cup of jade exhibits scooped sides fretted with granite. Herein can a whole thunderstorm expend itself, or both foundations of a rainbow foot. Mists wander over its streamlets and break in waves of colourless light upon its sides; the Mire will often disappear under the grey sheets of a Dartmoor downpour; and in hard winters it lies beneath a pelt of snow, that reduces its immensity, dwarfs its details, and makes Cater's Beam look like a mighty polar bear. There is little high colour at any time. Sobriety characterises its tones, as restraint marks its contours. Even in August, when the lesser furzes glow and ling light washes the waste with delicate rose and pearl, dim green and grey persist among the gloomy passages of black and broken earth. Only at clear dawns and sunsets will Fox Tor Mire sound its highest colour song, brim with delicate and transient brightness, shine through all its granite reeves and clitters, and blush over its moss bogs, where the sphagna glow ivory white, emerald green, and wine purple.

Upon either brink of this great basin and separated by the miles of it flung between, there stand human dwellings. To the south-east fragments of Fox Tor farmhouse still rise; whilst at the other point of the bow, where the hill descends from Nun's Cross to the south-west, habitations cluster together at the hamlet of White Works and stare out across the Mire upon the ruin over against them. A group of fallen walls and perished outbuildings, of which no more than the foundations remain, mark the grey spot in its desert of green where once stood Fox Tor Farm.

To our right an extremely rough track leads to Nun's Cross and the now deserted Nun's Cross Farm, a short mile away over an intervening ridge of moorland; across the Mire a flash of sunshine may pick out the medieval monument of Childe's Tomb, while the site of Fox Tor Farm is revealed by a small green patch on the great dun slopes of Ter Hill. (That farm was a central feature of Eden Phillpotts's *The American Prisoner*, a book not included in the canon of the Dartmoor Cycle.) Glimpses of distant horizons appear only to east and north-east, respectively towards the border heights of Hay, Saddle and Rippon Tors, and the tors standing guard over the upper reaches of the West Dart—Longaford, Higher White and the Beardowns.

Continuing down the hill, we cross the little granite bridge carrying the road over the Devonport Leat, when all that remains of White Works comes into view. At the imagined time of the story all tin mining had long ceased, and the characters in the narrative (the sole remaining inhabitants of the hamlet and mostly related to one another) were chiefly engaged in farming. On our left stand the Black Houses, a block of three commodious cottages, imagined as the homes of Mary Worth and her family, and of her sister Sarah; whilst a little further down the hill, on the right, is the site of Nathan Mortimer's farmhouse:

The only new dwelling in White Works . . . was a square house faced with stucco and crowned with blue slate—an unlovely erection that had taken the place of one more picturesque but less comfortable. This business-like abode stood in a green croft over which geese grazed and cackled mildly together. Below, a grassy road wound into the little meadows and turf-cuttings that comprised the farm. It was a Duchy property. Evidences of the vanished mines persisted here, and Nathan Mortimer had piled great, dry-built walls of granite round the old adits, where they opened upon his fields.

As recently as 1966 I took photographs of the empty farmhouse, known as Knighton Lodge; but since that date it has been thrown down by the Duchy of Cornwall (the largest Dartmoor landowners) and already the tumbled remains give to the site an impression of antiquity.

The farmhouse of 'Strane Steps' is more difficult to identify: but there can be little doubt that the home of Charles and Jane Pascoe was envisaged as being the house, known as the 'Count House', which stood on the left adjacent to the termination of the road. The ruins which still remain reveal that it was a substantial dwelling:

The old tenement farm of the Pascoes was the most considerable dwelling at White Works and the only one not already mentioned. It lay a little beyond the hamlet, among its own fields. The land belonging to it surmounted the ridge behind and flowed down northerly upon the other side. It was called Strane Steps, after a ford over the little river immediately beneath it . . . Strane Steps farm-house had a wide, whitewashed, homely face that pointed east. It peered with eyes that blinked at dawn from under heavy thatches. The walls were two feet thick and impervious to cold or heat, so that the dwelling maintained an even temperature, even as its master did. Above it ascended two Scotch firs with weatherbeaten heads and red stems, that leant towards each other as though for common support. Alder bushes and whitethorns made a splash of bloom beside the house; grass meadows ascended behind it.

Nun's Cross Farm, the reputed home of the miserly David Mortimer, to which reference has already been made, was, we are told, originally built of earth and stone beside Nun's Cross, but had been subsequently improved upon; and that David had lifted the place to higher prosperity, erected a stout, stone house, and used his first home and birthplace for a cattle byre. As regards its situation and appearance:

It faced the sunrise and looked down over a chaos of rough ground into the distant Mire below. Dry-built walls of granite surrounded the farm, and a small pent-house of wood framed the front door. Within, a spartan severity marked every chamber. To a visitor the house appeared empty of furniture and not only devoid of any adornment and luxury, but wanting in bare necessaries also. This, however, was not the case, for David had triumphantly proved what constituted necessaries and what did not. He had eliminated every convenience that it was possible to live without. The huts of the old stone men were hardly barer than Nun's Cross Farm.

It is of interest that William Crossing records that in reality Nun's Cross Farm was enclosed by John Hooper in 1870; that he knew Mr and Mrs Hooper well; and that at the beginning of this century a modern dwelling house took the place of the quaint little thatched cottage erected by Mr Hooper.

The cross from which the farm took its name, the largest and most famous of the Dartmoor crosses, is so described:

There are two orders of ancient human monuments on Dartmoor: the pre-historic evidences of man's earliest occupation and the mediaeval remains that date from Tudor times. The Neolith has left his cairns, pounds, and the foundations of his lodges; to the mediaeval stannators do the ruined smelting-houses bear testimony, with many a ridge of broken granite, where once the miners streamed for alluvial tin. The Christian symbol also occurs, roughly wrought in granite on wild heaths and lonely hills, to mark some place held sacred, to indicate an ancient path, or guide the wayfaring monk of old on his bleak journey by the Abbot's Way. Of these, the most notable relic is Siward's Cross, or Nun's Cross, by which more familiar name the moormen know it. Once the memorial was thrown down and broken; but bygone antiquaries set it up again and clamped the pieces together with iron. It stands now seven feet high, with stumpy arms and weathered front, whereon to the time-worn granite cling lichens grey and gold.

Most of the action of the book takes place within the immediate vicinity of White Works. One graphic little picture is worth recording—that of David Mortimer moving his flock from one grazing area to another:

David Mortimer, on his old piebald horse, came up through the great plain of Fox Tor Mire behind a hundred sheep. Like a galaxy of stars the new-shorn creatures twinkled upon the green waste, and when they became too scattered a sheep dog flashed out—long and lean—to bring them together again. The farmer was driving his flock to another 'stroll', south of Nun's Cross, and presently, as he ascended the hill within sight of his own house, he came upon Barry Worth cutting rushes . . . The day was hot, and the air danced over the great heath in a tremor of colourless light.

One of the few instances when the action of the book moves further afield provides an unforgettable picture of a wild autumn morning on the western slopes of Dartmoor. Barry Worth is driving his young cousin Anstice to Yelverton on the occasion of her abortive elopement to marry Barry's brother, James:

Great autumn rains had fallen, and more had yet to fall. Morning hope of fair weather was drowned before noon, and to-day the cloud cisterns began to lumber up from the south-west, as they drove by Devil's Bridge over the rolling road in the teeth of the wind. Morning touched the clouds with fleeting fires, and a thousand rivulets, that ran over the heather and drowned the sheep tracks, flashed back out of the sodden gloom. Beside every upstanding stone there lay a pool, and each grass hollow and old-time excavation was full of crystal clear water, with imprisoned air glimmering on the grass blades beneath. The risen sun fitfully swept the Moor between storms, and even the fiercest, blackest torrent bursting out of the sky seemed to be fringed with September blue—that ineffable, rain-washed azure proper to the fall of the year. Now it ran along the hill-tops, to be reflected on the wet granite and in the pools and streams; now it broke from the very midst of the huddled cumuli—its lustre veiled by the curtains of the rain.

After her unhappy marriage to Charles Pascoe, Anstice is permitted to see her cousin James from time to time; and on one occasion they walk together across the Mire and visit Childe's Tomb and Fox Tor Farm:

The occasion was sunless and cold, with a hint of snow in the air. But the Moor was dry, and they wandered through Fox Tor Mire, over dead grasses and under a grey sky, through which the place of the low sun was marked by gentle brightness on the clouds.

They descended to Childe's Tomb, an ancient memorial in the waste, where tradition told that a hunter of old time had been overtaken by tempest and perished with his steed. A modern cross had taken the place of the original stone, destroyed before the monuments of the Moor were cherished; and here, upon steps that supported the sacred symbol, they sat together in the sobriety of the great heath, with no sound but the streamlet at hand and the sighing of the wind in the rushes . . . They proceeded to the ruins of Fox Tor Farm, and sat down once more where a wall sheltered them from the north . . . They set out again presently by Swincombe River, climbed up to Great Sherberton Farm, crossed Dart, and came out upon the main road. The west brightened with fleeting waves of rosy cloud as they passed the lodge of Prince Hall; then light quickly died.

Prince Hall Lodge, it may be recalled, was portrayed in *The River* as the reputed home of Merryweather Chugg, the water bailiff. From Prince Hall, Anstice and James continue to Two Bridges, where they meet with Barry Worth and Marian Dennis and all take tea together at Marian's home at New London, just outside Princetown, before returning to White Works.

111

Miser's Money ends, as it begins, with a picture of Fox Tor Mire. When Barry Worth's plans have all come to fruition—in a manner satisfactory to all parties concerned —and all the inhabitants have moved away from the settlement, James Worth and his little adopted daughter Anstice return from Drewsteignton for a brief visit to the deserted hamlet; and the book concludes with a summer portrait of that remote spot:

The bloom of a delicate east wind was on the hills—a warm, grey haze afar off, that deepened as it approached, and under the sunshine turned the cloud shadows to gentian blue, where they roamed the wilderness. It was mid-June and Fox Tor Mire, brushed with quickening green, rolled out within its ambit of hills. New life of herbage smothered the grey sere of the past, and in the valleys lush grasses beckoned the flocks and herds again. The Mire was darkened by impermanent shadows from above and by the lasting stretches of heather that sprawled upon it, as yet untouched by blossom. From the bogs and reed-beds sparkled a cold, silver flash and fret of seeding cotton grasses. Peat cuttings yawned black in the fens, with scads piled to dry beside them, and cattle roamed even to the ridge of Cater's Beam, where it swung glimmering vast along the sky-line in a mantle of heat. Horned sheep with black faces and heavy fleeces panted and cried to be shorn; the dun and black Scots cattle herded apart; upon the green downs stood many a mare in the sunshine, with a little foal stretched sleeping in the grass at her feet.

On the western-facing hill rose the fragments of Fox Tor Farm —a cluster of grey with broken walls jutting into nothingness round about; while, a mile distant, ascended the more enduring twin masses of Fox Tor itself beneath the Beam.

Round Strane Steps the whitethorn and alder bloomed again and threw blossom over the green bushes. A feather of smoke ascended from the kitchen chimney and a new tenant sat at meat within; but Nathan Mortimer's little farm in the old mine workings was empty, and the Black Houses stood lifeless, save for cattle that clustered red in the shade of the northern wall. Their gardens were green with weeds; no fowls strutted at their barred thresholds; no dog barked; no linen flapped on the drying line; no short blind, with a geranium blinking behind it, hid the parlour windows. Only the heath larks twinkled aloft and the carrion crows croaked on their highways over the heights. The great, patient, unchanging Mire held sunshine to the brim and, for once, seemed to relax its eternal gravity and smile under the most peaceful conditions it could know.

Overlooking this familiar scene, on a bank where golden tormentil and lotus, starry white bedstraw and blue milkwort wove their radiance into the grasses, there sat a man and a child. Before them opened the little valley of White Works; behind them the leat threw a shining loop, as it made a concave dip into the hill-side.

Note. Latterly the Black Houses have been tenanted again; while the projected scheme for the construction of the much-discussed Swincombe reservoir— should it ever be implemented—would undoubtedly alter in some measure the hitherto unchanging landscape of Fox Tor Mire; the lonely theatre of *Miser's Money.*

Crossing's Guide: Princetown and Two Bridges District. Excursions 2, 3

O.S. Sheets: SX 66, SX 67

7

The Virgin in Judgment

For the setting of *The Virgin in Judgment* the scene moves westward of Fox Tor Mire, across some three miles of undulating moorland, to the little village of Sheepstor, lying in the shadow of the great bulk of Sheep's Tor. The book opens with a graphic description of Ringmoor Down, ascending to the south east of the village; a description reminiscent of Thomas Hardy's portrayal of 'Egdon Heath':

Night stirred behind the eastern hills, and a desert place burnt with fading splendour in the hour before sunset. The rolling miles of Ringmoor Down lay clad at this season in a wan integument of dead grass. Colourless as water, it reflected the tone of dawn or evening, sky or cloud; now sulked; now shone; now marked the passage of the wind with waves of light.

Ringmoor extends near the west quarter of Dartmoor Forest like an ocean of alternate trough and mound, built by the breath of storms. This region, indeed, shares something with the restless resting-places of the sea; and one may figure it as finally frozen into its present austerity by action of western winds that aforetime laboured without ceasing here on the bosom of a plastic earth . . .

The expanse is magnificently naked, yet sufficing; it is absolutely featureless, but never poverty-stricken. To the confines of a river it extends, and ceases there; yet that sudden wild uplifting of broken hills beyond strikes not so deeply into human sense as Ringmoor's vast monochrome fading slowly at the edge of night; fading without one stock or stone or man or beast to break the tenor of its way.

A favourable vantage point to survey the theatre of *The Virgin in Judgment* may be found on the western slope of

Ringmoor Down, about a quarter of a mile north of Ringmoor Cottage. At our feet lies Sheepstor, its handful of cottages clustered about the church tower. West of the village appears the tree-girt reservoir of Burrator, a feature which arrived in the landscape at a date later than the assumed period of the book. Beyond rise Yennadon Down, Sharp Tor and Lether Tor, and the distant bow of North Hessary, surmounted by a lofty television mast. Above the village ascends the leonine shape of Sheep's Tor, whose vast outline hides more northerly features. To the east, the gradually-rising sweep of Ringmoor Down conceals Ditsworthy Warren and the heights of Shell Top and Pen Beacon beyond; but to the south and south-west appear respectively the spread of Plymouth Sound, and the distant Cornish moors dominated by the recognizable outlines of Kilmar Tor and Brown Willy.

Ditsworthy Warren, a lonely spot on the upper reaches of the River Plym, is the reputed home of Elias Bowden, the warrener, and his large family:

A river destined to name the greatest port in the west country, makes humble advent at Plym Head near the Beam of Cater in mid-Dartmoor. Westward under the Harter Tors and south by the Abbot's Way to Plym Steps the streamlet flows; then she gathers volume and melody to enter a land of vanished men. By the lodges of the old stone people and amid monuments lifted in a neolithic age; beside the graves of heroes and under the Hill of Giants, Plym passes and threads the rocky wilderness with silver. And then, suddenly, a modern dwelling lifts beside her—a building of stern aspect and most lonely site. Round about for miles the warrens of Ditsworthy extend, and countless thousands of the coney folk flourish . . .

Inflexible Ringmoor approaches Ditsworthy on one side; while beyond it roll the warrens. Shell Top and Pen Beacon are the highest adjacent peaks of the Moor; and through the midst runs Plym with the solitary, stern Warren House lifted upon its northern bank.

Descending into the village from our viewpoint on Ringmoor Down, we shall find it remarkably unchanged over the intervening years since the book was written—or, indeed, since the imagined period of the story (*circa* 1848):

Sheepstor lies beneath the granite hill that names it like a lamb between a lion's paws. Chance never played artist to better purpose, for of the grey roofs and whitewashed walls that make this little village, there is scarcely one to be wished away. Cots and farm-buildings, byres and ricks cluster round about the church; a few conifers thrust dark spire and branch between the houses, and fields slope upward behind the hamlet to the shaggy fringes of the tor. A medley of autumnal orange and copper and brown now splashed the hills everywhere round about; and great beeches, that hemmed in the churchyard and bull-ring, echoed the splendour of the time and spread one pall of radiant foliage on all the graves together. Behind the church, knee-deep in thick-set spinneys, ascended the giant bulk of Sheep's Tor, shouldering enormous from leagues of red brake-fern, like a grey dragon that lifts suddenly from its lair; but the saddle of the hill fell westerly in a more gentle slope, and sunset painted wonderful pictures there; while beyond, breaking very blue through the haze of distance, Lether Tor and Sharp Tor's misty heights enclosed the horizon.

A brook ran through the village and in a noon hour of late November this stream made all the music to be heard; for no sound rose but that of the murmuring water, and not any sight of conscious life was to be noted. Clear sunshine after rain beat upon the great hill; its ruddy pelt glowed like fire under the blue sky, and beneath the mass a church tower, whose ancient crockets burnt with red-gold lichens, sprang stiffly up. Sheepstor village might now be seen through a lattice of naked boughs, fair of form in their mingled reticulations and pale as silvery gauze against the sunlight. Their fretwork was touched to flame where yellow or scarlet leaves still clung and spattered the branches.

A cottage near the lich-gate of the churchyard is described as the home of Bartley Crocker, his mother and a maiden aunt; whilst Bartholomew Stanbury, his wife

116

Eden Phillpotts (1950)

On Bonehill Rocks: looking across the Vale of Widecombe

Widecombe and Hameldown from near Blackslade

Constance, and their two children Bart and Margaret, are portrayed as inhabiting the farm of Combeshead. The ruins of that farmstead may be found in Deancombe (Dennycoombe) under Combeshead Tor, easterly of Sheep's Tor:

Like a picture set between two great masses of fruiting white-thorn, Dennycoombe spread eastward into Dartmoor and climbed upward through glory of sinking light upon autumnal colour. To the west, Sheep's Tor's larch-clad shoulder sloped in pale gold mottled with green, while northerly Down Tor broke the withered fern. Between them lay a valley of lemon light washed with blue hazes and stained by great darkness where the shadows fell. Many a little dingle opened on either hand of the glen; and here twinkled water, where a brook leapt downward.

Coombeshead Farm, the home of the Stanburys, stood at the apex of this gorge and lay under Coombeshead Tor. Still higher against the sky rolled Eylesbarrow, its enormous and simple outline broken only by the fangs of an old ruin; while flying clouds, that shone in opposition to the sunset, crowned all with welter of mingled light and gloom. The modest farmhouse clung like a grey nest into the tawny harmonies of the hill, and above it rose blue smoke.

High on the southern slope of Sheep's Tor may be found the Pixies' House (or as Crossing calls it, the Pixies' Cave); the scene of a stormy encounter between Rhoda Bowden and Bartley Crocker, on an equally stormy day:

In the very bosom of the great south-facing rocky slope of Sheep's Tor, where the lichen-coated slabs and boulders are flung together in magnificent confusion, there may be found one narrow cleft, above which a mass of granite has been split perpendicularly. Chaos of stone spilled here lies all about, and numberless small crannies and chambers abound; but the rift alone marks any possible place of concealment for creature larger than dog or fox; and beneath it, invisible and unguessed, lies the Pixies' House, one of the local sanctities and a haunt of the little people . . .

The day was one of elemental unrest and the clouds unrolled great planes of shifting gloom and splendour, of accidents of vapour that concealed and of light that illumined. But at mid-day a mighty shadow ascended against the wind and thunder rumbled along the edges of the Moor. The storm-centre spun about a mile off, then it drove in darkness over Sheep's Tor . . .

The storm shouted to the hills and cried savagely against the granite precipices; it leapt over the open heaths and roared into the coombes and valleys. The waste was all a dancing whiteness of hail, jewelled ever and anon by the lightning . . .

Now bright weather-gleams of blue and silver opened their eyes to windward; the storm had gathered up its skirts of rack and flame into the central waste; a thousand gurgling rivulets leapt over the grass; the hail melted; the ponies turned their heads to wind again and went on grazing, while their wet sides steamed.

The scene of the prize-fight arranged by 'Frosty-face' Fogo between David Bowden and Bartley Crocker is the ancient Bull-Ring of Sheepstor, situated to southward of the church:

The Bull-Ring of Sheepstor is a grassy field of near an acre in extent, surrounded west and east with beech trees, hemmed by a road and a little river southward, and flanked by the churchyard wall on the north. Here bull-baiting, cock-fighting, cock-shying, and other rough sports of our great-grandfathers were enjoyed . . .

Dennycoombe Wood is the venue of the tryst between David Bowden and Margaret Stanbury, when she agrees to marry him. David proposes to provide a home far from other dwellings; a ruin at Black Tor Fall, on the upper reaches of Meavy, could be restored and made a comfortable home, and there he could breed ponies and sheep:

On a day in summer, David Bowden wandered up the higher valleys of Meavy and stopped in a little dingle where the new-born river tumbled ten feet over a great apron of granite into a pool beneath. In four separate threads the stream spouted over this mossy ledge, and then joined her foaming forces below. Grey-green sallows thronged the top of this natural weir and the wind flashed a twinkle of silver into their foliage as the leaves leapt and turned. Low hills sloped to the spot and made a nest of it. Black

Tor and Harter ascended at hand, and on the horizon northerly Princetown's stern church tower rose against the sky. Beside the pool, wherein Meavy gathered again her scattered tresses, an old ruin stood; and round about the dwelling-places of primeval man glimmered grey upon the heath. David Bowden had chosen this spot for his home, and his reason was the shattered miner's cottage of Tudor date that rose there. Four-square, crowned with heather and fretted with pennyworts and grasses, stone-crop, grey lichens, and sky-blue jasione, the old house stood. Broken walls eight feet high surrounded it; an oven still gaped in one angle, and the wide chimney-shaft now made a green twilight of dewy ferns and mosses.

In due course, David and Margaret are married in Sheepstor Church, and take up their abode in the imagined reconstruction of the old mining house. Rhoda Bowden, David's sister, later joins them at Meavy Cot—so named from Margaret's choice.

Crazywell Pool, lying on great moorland slopes north-east of Sheepstor is the setting, in high summer, of a meeting between Margaret Bowden, Bartley Crocker and Rhoda Bowden:

Nature, passing nigh Cramber Tor, where old-time miners delved for tin, has found a great pit, filled the same with sweet water, and transformed all into a thing of beauty. Like a cup in the waste lies Crazywell; and, at this summer season, a rare pattern of mingled gold and amethyst glorified the goblet. Autumn furze and the splendour of the heath surrounded it; the margins of the tarn were like chased silver, where little sheep-tracks, white under dust of granite, threaded the acclivities round about and disappeared in the gravel beaches beneath . . .

Peace, here brooding after noon, was suddenly wakened by the stampede of half-a-dozen bullocks, goaded by gadflies. Down they came from above with thundering hoofs and tails erect. They rushed to cool their smarting flanks, sent ripples glittering out into the lake, and presently stood motionless, knee-deep, with their chestnut coats mirrored in the water . . .

A spirit neither malignant nor benign, but wondrously in-formed, dwelt here—a sentient thing, a nether gnome, from whom was not hidden the future of men—a being who once a year could cry aloud with human voice and tell the names of those whose race was run. Many dreaded the sortilege of the unknown thing that haunted Crazywell; but since its power was restricted to Christmas Eve, little sense of horror or mystery hung over the pool.

From time to time meetings, innocent enough, occur between Margaret Bowden and Bartley Crocker. One such, on Lether Tor, depicts a characteristic Dartmoor day of mingled gloom and light:

A great uncertainty prevailed above Margaret Bowden, where she sat on the lofty side of Lether Tor before noon and waited to meet Bartley. The aerial doubt was reflected on earth in shadows and darkness shot with fitful light; an increasing opacity threatened rain; yet, where the vapours crowded most gloomily and massed their hooded cowls, light and wind would break their conclaves and scatter them upon the humid bosom of the Moor. Through this welter, sunshafts fell and flashed over the grey and russet of the wilderness . . .

Now the ragged crest of Sheep's Tor was glorified with a nimbus of light that revolved in a broad, wet fan, and then shut up again, as the clouds thrust between sun and earth.

Crazywell Pool figures again in very different circumstances on Christmas Eve, when it is the scene of Billy Screech's absurd plan to frighten Jane West and Bart Stanbury by impersonating the voice of the supernatural creature supposed to inhabit the pool:

Presently, ascending above Kingsett Farm, he reached Crazywell where it stared up out of the waste, like a blind eye in a black socket. Silence and desolation haunted the pool . . . But little wind blew; no cloud stirred in the grey vault of heaven, but beneath at earth level, fog crept leisurely along and hung motionless in patches . . .

But the day grew more dark and more still. A lifeless, listless gloom haunted the spot, a blank despondency that reached even Billy's nerves, dashed his spirit, and made him long heartily to be away. Then came the crawling tentacles of the fog, and they stole over the brim of Crazywell and thrust here and there, like some blind, live creature feeling for food. They poured down into the hollow presently and crept over the water at the bottom. Half an hour passed and the vapour increased in density. It hung drops of moisture on the thorns of the furze and spread a glimmering dew over Billy's hairy face and ragged eyebrows . . .

The pool is also the setting for the culminating tragedy of Margaret Bowden's suicide, while of unsound mind following the mistaken accusation of infidelity made by David's sister, Rhoda.

The *Virgin in Judgment* ends as it began, on the immensities of Ringmoor Down, when Rhoda Bowden, driven from Meavy Cot by David, makes her slow and desolate way to her parents' home at Ditsworthy Warren:

Upon Ringmoor she came at last, and even here no air was stirring. The mighty spaces of the waste were faintly lighted within a little radius of the wanderer, but beyond, the naked earth rolled away into utter darkness at every side. The sky, while luminous in contrast with the world beneath it, was entirely overcast. A complete and featureless cloud without rift or rent to break its midnight monotony spread upon the firmament. Only at the horizon might one perceive the difference between the earth and sky, and the illumination spread by the one and swallowed by the other . . .

She breasted the last slope which separated her from her home; then among the burrows of the warren she threaded her way until, black against the night, towered Ditsworthy.

Crossing's Guide: Princetown and Two Bridges District. Excursion 2.
Yelverton District. Excursions 38, 39

O.S. Sheets: SX 56, SX 57

8
The Three Brothers

The little village of Shaugh Prior, some three miles south
of Sheepstor across Wigford Down, forms the setting for
The Three Brothers. From Shaugh Moor, east of the village,
the Trowlesworthy Tors rise against the sky; and from the
summit of Great Trowlesworthy Tor we gain a first
impression of the scene:

From Great Trowlesworthy's crown of rosy granite the world
extended to the Moor edge, and thence, by mighty passages of earth
and sky, to the horizons of the sea. A clear May noon illuminated
the waste, and Dartmoor, soaking her fill of sunshine, ran over with it.

One white road ran due north-east and south-west across the
desert, and round about it, like the tents of the Anakim, rose huge,
snowy hillocks and ridges silver-bright in the sun. Here the
venerable granites of Dartmoor suffer a change, and out of their
perishing constituents emerges kaolin, or china clay.

A river met this naked road, and at their junction the grey
bridge of Cadworthy saddled Plym. Beyond, like the hogged back
of a brown bear, Wigford Down rolled above the gorges of
Dewerstone, and, further yet, retreated fields and forests, great
uplifted plains, and sudden elevations, that glimmered along their
crests with the tender green of trees.

The atmosphere was opalescent, milky, sweet, as though
earth's sap, leaping to the last tree-top and bursting bud, exuded
upon air the incense and savour of life. Running water and lifting
lark made the music of this hour . . . high on Trowlesworthy,
where the rushes chatter and where, to their eternal treble, the
wind strikes deep organ notes from the forehead of the tor. The
sun shone over the flattened dead rushes round about this place,
and turned them into pale gold.

Descending the tor and approaching the village by way of Trowlesworthy Warren and Cadover (Cadworthy) Bridge, we are enabled to examine it in greater detail:

The hamlet of Shaugh Prior, a gift to the monks of Plympton in times past, stands beneath Shaugh Moor at the edge of a mighty declivity. The Church of St Edward lifts its battlemented tower and crocketed pinnacles above a world of waste and fallow. It is perched upon a ridge and stands, supported by trees and a few cottages, in a position of great prominence.

Round about the church dark sycamores shine in spring, and at autumn drop their patched and mottled foliage upon the dead. Broad-bosomed fields ascend to the south; easterly a high road climbs to the Moor, and immediately north of Shaugh the slopes of High Down lead by North Wood to Cadworthy Farm and Cadworthy Bridge beyond it . . .

A school, a rectory, the White Thorn inn, and a dozen dwellings constitute Shaugh Prior, though the parish extends far beyond these boundaries; and on this spring day one thrush, warbling from a lilac bush at a cottage door, made music loud enough to fill the hamlet.

The three brothers, Vivian, Nathan and Humphrey Baskerville, each different in character, play their various parts in the life of the village. Vivian and his family dwell at Cadworthy Farm, about a mile from Shaugh on the left of the road to Cadover Bridge: Nathan is the innkeeper of the White Thorn, a hostelry standing nearly opposite the church on the road descending steeply to Shaugh Bridge in Bickleigh Vale; whilst the widowed Humphrey lives with his son Mark and his housekeeper Mrs Hacker at Hawk House. This may be taken to be Collard Tor Cottage, standing in its enclosures under the tor of that name, a mile south-east of Shaugh Prior on the road to Cornwood. Undershaw (Nethershaw) Farm, situated in the valley west of the village, is the imagined home of Mrs Lintern and her family.

125

Hawk House and its environs are vividly pictured:

When man builds a house on Dartmoor he plants trees to protect it. Sometimes they perish; sometimes they endure to shield his dwelling from the riotous and seldom-sleeping winds. Round the abode of Humphrey Baskerville stood beech and pine. A solid old house lurked beneath, like a bear in its holt. A few apple trees were in the garden, and currant and gooseberry bushes prospered indifferent well beneath them. Rhubarb and a row of elders also flourished here. The latter were permitted to exist for their fruit, and of the berries Mrs. Susan Hacker, Humphrey's widowed housekeeper, made medicinal preparations.

Hawk House lay under a tor, and behind it the land towered to a stony waste that culminated in wild masses of piled granite, where the blackthorn grew and the vixen brought her cubs. From this spot one might take a bird's-eye survey of Humphrey Baskerville's domain.

Humphrey himself now sat on a favourite stone aloft and surveyed his possessions and the scene around them. It was his custom in fair weather to spend many hours sequestered upon the tor. He marked the passage of time by the coming of migrant birds and by other natural signs and tokens. Beneath Hawk House there subtended a great furze-clad space flanked with woods. The Rut, as it was called, fell away to farms and fertile fields, and terminated in a glen through which the little Torry river passed upon her way to Plym. Cann Wood fringed the neighbouring heights, and far away to the south Laira's lake extended and Plymouth appeared—faint, grey, glittering under a gauze of smoke.

Vivian's son, Rupert, calls on his uncle Humphrey; they walk over Shaugh Moor and ascend Hawk Tor:

They stood on Hawk Tor, and beneath them stretched, first, the carpet of the heath. Then the ground fell into a valley, where water meadows spread about a stream, and beyond, by woods and homesteads, the earth ascended again to Shaugh Prior. The village, perched upon the apex of the hill, twinkled like a jewel. Glitter of whitewash and rosy-wash shone under the grey roofs; sunlight and foliage sparkled and intermingled round the church tower; light roamed upon the hills, revealing and obscuring detail in its passage. To the far west, above deep valleys, the world appeared again; but now it had receded and faded and merged in tender blue to the horizon. Earth spread before the men in three huge and simple planes: of heath and stone sloping from north to south; of hillside and village and hamlet perched upon their proper crest; of the dreaming distances swept with the haze of summer and rising to sky-line.

Rupert Baskerville and his cousin Mark, with Milly Luscombe and Cora Lintern, spend a day's holiday on the high Moor:

At high summer two men and two maids kept public holiday and wove romance under the great crown of Pen Beacon. It was a day of lowering clouds and illumination breaking through them. Fans of light fell between the piled-up cumuli, and the earth was mottled with immense, alternate patches of shadow and sunshine. Thick and visible strata of air hung heavy between earth and sky at this early hour. They presaged doubt, and foretold a condition that might presently diffuse and lift into unclouded glory of August light, or darken to thunderstorms . . .

Eastward under Pen Beacon, lay an ancient lodge of the neolithic people. The circles of scattered granite shone grey, set in foliage and fruit of the bilberry, with lichens on the stone and mosses woven into the grass about them. Gold autumn furzes flashed along the waste, and the pink ling broke into her first tremble of colourless light that precedes the blush of fullness. The party of four sat in a hut circle and spoke little while they ate and drank . . .

Drifting apart by half a mile or so, the young couples left the Beacon, climbed Penshiel, and thence passed over the waste to where the red tor rose above Milly Luscombe's home, where they were to drink tea presently.

The wild land of the Rut, sloping down from Hawk House to the valley beneath, is the scene of the tryst between Mark Baskerville and Cora Lintern when she heartlessly breaks their association; and in the desolation of that experience Mark eventually hangs himself in the belfry of Shaugh Church, after ringing his own passing bell. Reference to that incident is made in *The Thief of Virtue*, when the news of the tragedy is brought to Postbridge by Philip Ouldsbroom.

The death of Vivian Baskerville provides the clue as to the date of the events in the story; for when upon his deathbed he dictates an inscription for his tombstone, the year is given as 1889.

Blackaton (or Roman) Cross is the setting for a meeting between Rupert Baskerville and his pleasure-loving brother Ned:

Upon the highway between Cadworthy and the border village of Cornwood there stands an ancient granite cross, and to north and south the white road sweeps by it; easterly tower Penshiel and Pen Beacon, and westerly rolls Shaugh Moor.

Here, upon a day one year after the death of Vivian Baskerville, there met two of his sons. Ned Baskerville was riding home from Cornwood, and his brother Rupert, knowing that he must come this way, sat by St. Rumon's Cross, smoked his pipe and waited . . .

Ned galloped off, and his brother, having sat a little longer by St. Rumon's Cross, rose and struck over Shaugh Moor in the direction of Humphrey Baskerville's dwelling.

Humphrey Baskerville visits the lonely ruin of Hen Tor House, which from time to time he had considered rebuilding as a hermit's retreat:

Inner darkness turned Baskerville to the Moor again, and he rode—where often he had already ridden, to inspect the ruin of an old dwelling upon the side of a great hill above the waters of Plym. Brilliant summer smiled upon this pilgrimage, and as he went he fell in with a friend, where Jack Head tramped the high road upon his way to Trowlesworthy. Jack now dwelt at Shaugh, but was head man of Saul Luscombe's farm and rabbit warren . . .

Trowlesworthy was reached and Jack went his way. Then Humphrey proceeded by the river, and presently ascended a rough slope to his destination. The ruin that alternately drew and repelled him lay below; but for the moment he did not seek it. He climbed to the high ground, dismounted, turned his pony loose, and took his pipe out of his pocket.

The great cone of granite known as Hen Tor lies high upon the eastern bank of Plym, between that streamlet and a bog-foundered tableland beyond. From its crown the visitor marked Cornwall's coastline far-spreading into the west, and Whitsand Bay reflecting silver morning light along the darker boundaries of earth.

North Wood, above the River Plym, is the chosen rendezvous for a meeting between the supposed widow Priscilla Lintern, of Undershaw, and the innkeeper Nathan Baskerville, the secret father of her children; when the reason for their not marrying is revealed to the reader:

The setting sun burnt upon Dewerstone's shoulder and beat in a sea of light against the western face of North Wood, until the windworn forest edge, taking colour on trunk and bough, glowed heartily . . .

The sun began to sink where Cornwall, like a purple cloud, rose far off against the sky; yet still the undulations of the land, mingling with glory, melted into each other under the sunset, and still North Wood shone above the shadows. But a deep darkness began to stretch upwards into it, where the Dewerstone's immense shade was projected across the valley. At length only the corner of the forest flashed a final fire; then that too vanished, and the benighted trees sighed and massed themselves into amorphous dimness under the twilight.

Following upon the death of Nathan Baskerville, his solicitor wishes to discuss affairs with Humphrey Baskerville; and Humphrey rides over to Cornwood to keep that appointment:

There chanced an hour when he rode upon his pony under the high ground above Cornwood . . . He passed across the shoulder of Pen Beacon, through a wild world of dun-coloured hills, streaked with flitting radiance, and clouded in billowy moisture driven before the wind. Stone and steep and sodden waste stared blindly at the pressure and flinched not, but, in the sky, the breath of it herded the clouds into flocks, that sped and spread and gathered again too swiftly for the telling. They broke in billows of sudden light; they massed into darkness and hid the earth beneath them; then again they parted, and, like a ragged flag above a broken army, the clean blue unfurled.

Over this majestic desolation suddenly there shot forth a great company of rooks, and the wind drove them before it—whirling and wheeling and tumbling in giddy dives, only to mount again. Then the instinct unfathomed that makes vast companies of living creatures wheel and warp together in mysterious and perfect unison inspired them. They descended swiftly to the level of the ground, and, flying low, plodded back together whence they had come. A yard or two above earth's surface they flapped along and cheated the wind. At a hedge they rose, and Humphrey marked how they worked in the teeth of the gale. He was near enough to see their grey bills, their anxious, glittering eyes, and their hurtling feathers blown awry as they breasted the hedge, fought over and dipped again.

Taking leave of the Moor, the rider descended and arrived at the lawyer's house upon the appointed hour.

At the close of the book, when he has done so much for his dead brothers' families, and has settled all Nathan's outstanding debts, Humphrey's stern nature has arrived at 'a peace so exalted and a content so steady that he rested his spirit upon it in faith and sought no further'. At Hawk House on Christmas Eve he is overcome with emotion when the carol singers from Shaugh Church unexpectedly arrive to sing for him:

The gibbous moon sailed through a sky of thin cloud, and light fell dimly upon the open spaces, but sparkled in the darkness of evergreen things about the garden. Earth rolled night-hidden to the southern hills, and its breast was touched with sparks of flame, where glimmered those few habitations visible from this place. A lattice of naked boughs meshed the moonlight under the slope of the hill, and from beneath their shadows ascended a moving thread of men and boys. They broke the stillness with speech and laughter, and their red lantern-light struck to right and left and killed the wan moonshine as they came . . .

130

Acute emotion marked his countenance; yet this painful tension passed when out of the night there rolled the melodious thunder of an ancient tune.

'Singing for me!' he murmured many times while the old song throbbed.

Crossing's Guide: Plympton and Shaugh District. Excursions 36, 37

O.S. Sheet: SX 56

9
The Mother

The small settlement of Merivale, where the Tavistock to Ashburton road crosses the River Walkham (or Walla) westward of Princetown, is the centre of activity of *The Mother*. The widowed Avisa Pomeroy, her son Ives, and her daughter Lizzie inhabit Vixen Tor Farm; Matthew Northmore occupies 'Stone Park' (Shillapark) Farm; and Ruth Rendle lives with her cousins, the brothers Peter and Joel Toop, joint licencees of the little inn called 'The Jolly Huntsmen' (The Dartmoor Inn). Early in the book we are given an impression of the Pomeroy's home lying immediately under the southern scarp of Vixen Tor:

Like a child in its mother's arms the little homestead of the Pomeroys reposed on the southward slope of the Vixen and cuddled there beneath the immense rock-masses of that tor. No nobler pile of granite shall be found upon Dartmoor. It towers gradually to its crown by rampart and bastion; a happy relation of parts has chanced to weld the three main divisions into one perfect whole, and Vixen rises, the very impersonation of strength, solidity and settled purpose, to be a landmark for time, the haunt of nocturnal birds, an emblem of mystery and of power . . . None now ever scrambled up its ascents or stood upon its summit but Ives Pomeroy . . . Beneath him lay the farm and its immediate cultivated lands. A few small fields subtended the kitchen garden. Then plantations of larch and pine sank to the water. Walla ran near enough to be heard at all times, and her murmur came to Ives through the thinning gold of the larches. About the dwelling of the Pomeroys stood a fir or two, and, behind it, the Moor stretched in a rugged coomb upward.

The scene then extends to a vivid portrayal of the immediate environs of Merivale:

After Walla has fallen from her fountains near the cradle of her greater sister, Tavy, in midmost Moor, she winds south-west and passes downward under Mis Tor into the wooded glens beneath the Vixen. But, before she leaves the waste, a bridge of grey stone spans her growing stream, and road and river meet at right angles. Down the great slope eastward this highway falls, then upward climbs again under the triple crown of the Staple Tors; and just beyond the bridge, extended straggling by the path, like a row of tired folk tramping home after a revel, shall be seen the few cottages of Merivale. Northward, separated from the village by moorland, and its own surrounding fields, the farm of Stone Park stands naked, treeless and solitary; southward, where Walla flows from the upland austerities into a gentler domain of forest and arable land, there extends regions of cultivation with their dwellings in the midst.

All round about upon this day, the stone monarchs of the land thrust sombre heads upward into a stormy sky. Beyond Great Mis Tor something of the central desolation might be seen swept with fog-banks; and the river, in spate from heavy rain, cried aloud through the valley.

Low, grey and black, with whitewashed faces and tar-pitched roofs, Merivale stood and faced the south. No special feature marked this uneven row of habitations threaded up the hill, save where, in the midst, from a square building of two stories, a sign-board hung and swung backwards and forwards at the thrust of the wind . . . proclaiming that the brothers Toop were licensed to sell tobacco, snuff and spirits.

To the south-east of Merivale, King Tor crests the slope rising from the left bank of the River Walkham; and here Jill Wickett and Samuel Bolt are discovered ascending towards the summit of the tor:

One evening in early spring, Jill Wickett and Samuel Bolt climbed up the hill east of Walla valley, and ascended those wide and shaggy slopes of wilderness that rise upward to King Tor. Near this elevation men have scratched in Dartmoor's bosom for stone, and great quarries still yield their wealth of granite; while upon the commons beneath appear many evidences of a neolithic people who haunted these uplands and sequestered deserts when the world was younger. Cairns, parallelitha, ruined lodges and other aboriginal monuments lay round about; and from King Tor's summit also appeared the winding waters of Walla, dancing over the Moor, sinking to the low lands, and glimmering through the first verdure of spring woods. In the valley, larches spired with the light behind them, and Vixen Tor rose gloomy against the grass slopes at its feet. Jill's eyes rested on the farm beneath the Vixen; then they turned to her lover's cottage standing beside the road that ran, like a white thread, through Merivale. Anon a flash of water again attracted her attention to the home of the Pomeroys, where sinking sunshine caught a streamlet and set it glittering. Far distant, under the increasing glory of the west, Cornwall lay like a cloud, and her hills and vales, mingling with the magic of the air, rolled unsubstantial as the pageant of sunset above them.

The little village of Sampford Spiney stands above the right bank of the River Walkham, some miles downstream from Merivale:

The hamlet of Merivale boasted no place of worship, but Sampford Spiney's crocketed church-towers were visible in the distance, and when the rainy wind blew, thin bell-music filtered up Walla valley on the seventh day, and certain of the folk would answer that summons . . . Against the tower of the unnamed church, bursting beech-buds spattered the newborn green; round about were lifted the boles of many trees; and spring moved amid the sleeping-places beneath. Primroses peeped from the mounds where children had planted them, and the wood-sorrel drooped its frail, lovely bells above much dust of vanished men. Here the folk slept; the wind murmured; the seasons marked their passage in lush growth of dock and darnel at the time of the scythe; in falling rain and falling leaves; in starlight and frost and the silences of winter nights. Grey through the thickening trees, the heights of Pu Tor towered northerly, and round about the land fell by fields and homesteads to the river.

134

The track to Powder Mills under Longaford Tor. (*overleaf*) Littaford, Longaford and Higher White Tors from Cherrybrook Newtake

It is of interest to record that for Eden Phillpotts Pu Tor had a particular and personal significance.

The Walkham is crossed by Ward Bridge in the valley below Sampford Spiney. Ives Pomeroy accompanies his family to church on Easter Day, but suddenly decides against attending the service:

Ives hung over Ward Bridge, lighted his pipe, and smoked in gloom. Before him Walla's waters foamed under a haze of grey twigs and drooping branches. Spring had fondled the trees and they were full of the mellow light of opening buds. The river ran clear and flashed a salute to each moss-clad stone upon her way. She twinkled into foam at many falls; she loitered in backwaters and little bays; she smoothed her face to stillness that young stars and buds and delicious things bursting their sheaths, might bend and see their own loveliness. The oaks were giving out an amber light under the sunshine; the alders opened tiny trim fans of green; the great woodrush and water parsnip sprawled with their feet in the river; and kingcups, cuckoo-flowers, and the foliage of the iris brightened the water-meadows. Aloft, along deep hillsides under Vixen Tor, countless pavilions of the larch were glittering in their first rapture of young green . . . And beneath them ran the river and spread fields that echoed with the music of lambs.

As Merivale Hill is ascended towards Princetown, the imagined home of Matthew Northmore, 'Stone Park' (Shillapark), can be seen, half a mile to the north:

Walla rises in midmost Moor near Tavy Head by Cut Hill. It is a region very remote, and she has travelled many miles before any sign of civilisation can be seen upon her banks; then, in scattered colonies, the ruined homes of vanished men appear beside her, and lower still, under the eastward sweep of Great Staple Tor, stands a human dwelling of to-day. Stone Park, the farm of Matthew Northmore, was surrounded by grassland reclaimed from the waste; but at this season the cattle were afield until winter; the hay meadows were shorn; there was little work upon the land.

137

Across the open moor upstream of Shillapark, the walker will in about 1½ miles reach Langstone Moor, spread beneath the commanding heights of Great Mis Tor:

Langstone Moor stretches to the north-west of Great Mis Tor, and lies thick set with traces of these vanished people. Beside Walla occur many of their ruined homes; elsewhere stands a menhir, or 'long stone', which names this waste and betokens the spot where a stone hero is sleeping; while between that tomb and the village, dominating heath, morass and ambient hills with its own mysterious significance, shall be seen a cirque of sixteen unhewn boulders.

The granite masses loom suddenly, like magic creatures, upon the vision of the wanderer; they come as some sleight and unreal trick of the desert; they lift themselves out of nothing. At one moment the enduring and featureless fabric of the Moor surrounds a chance spectator; in the next he stands startled before the silent company of the Lone Stones . . .

Viewed on a day of late August against the purple background of Great Mis Tor, the Lone Stones glimmered under sunshine and lacked much of that mystic and foreboding air that oftentimes hung over them at hours of fleeting mist, in morning and evening twilights, or during the darkness of night and storm. Scarcely a cloud lower than the dreaming cirri of the firmament dimmed the September blue; the air danced along the immense planes of the Moor; cattle roamed far off, yet their frequent presence within the circle was manifest, for upon more than one of the old stones might be seen flecks of red, black and dun hair from the wandering herds that here sometimes gathered to ruminate and rub their hides against the granite. The circle continued its vigil of ages, subject only to Time's tireless hand.

The home of the old poacher, Moleskin, cannot be identified with certainty, as we are not given its precise location. Nevertheless, a small cottage close to the track across the Moor from Rundlestone in the direction of Great Mis Tor answers the following description reasonably well:

Moleskin's house, which stood midway between Princetown and Merivale, was set into the side of a hill a quarter of a mile from the road, and more resembled the habitation of a cave-dweller than the home of a civilised being. It looked like some gigantic and suspicious live creature with its head thrust through a hole, yet ready to dive back into the earth at a moment's warning. Two small windows glimmered under a straw roof, and upon the thatch heavy stones were laid to keep the winter storms from blowing all away.

From the River Walkham great slopes ascend north-east to the lofty crags of Great Mis Tor; and the immense view from the crest dwarfs all lower eminences in that great scene:

From the rocky breast of Great Mis Tor on a day in spring, those many miles that separated this little mountain from the sea stretched but as a span. Crushed by perspective, whole parishes huddled together like the sections of a child's puzzle map . . . Only the horizons of the sea were huge, where the little scroll of the earth ended and the waters rolled onward to the edge of the world. They and the actual Moor itself, that stretched in waves of peat and flung up pinnacles of granite instead of foam, were obviously immense; but the inhabited regions between them appeared reduced almost to nothing by the sleights of space. Rare beauty reigned upon earth. The cloud shadows that swept it with wandering islands of purple, brightened the glitter of the sunshine by contrast with their gloom; and between these fleeting shades the light fell in a reign of splendour—fell and found villages and church towers, that flashed like signals to the beholder, before they vanished again in shadow . . .

The more immediate scene embraced Dartmoor's own ridges, water-worn valleys and natural fortifications. To the west towered the trinity of the Staple Tors, and beyond them rose Cox and Roose. Shrunk from this elevation to a mere blot in the valley at stream side, the Vixen squatted, and behind it Pu erected a ragged crown. The east was hidden, and the whole mass of Great Mis itself was softened somewhat by a heath fire that leisurely gnawed the wilderness with red teeth and lifted before its progress a vapour of azure and transparent smoke. This veil swept gently over the summit of the hills, over the buttresses and rocky heights, the avalanches of scattered stone, the single pinnacles and the grassy slopes and coombes between.

The Moor around Merivale is the scene of a tremendous thunderstorm, on a day when Ruth Rendle has set out for Princetown, but after meeting with Matthew Northmore, she changes her mind and returns to the hamlet:

The day was Sunday and drowsy peace held Merivale after the hour of midday dinner . . . Thunder clouds hung heavy over the central Moor . . . As yet the approach of the gathering storm was not perceptible. It hung in a curtain of gloom low to the north, and the Moor, as far as Great Mis Tor and beyond it, basked in sunshine and shimmered with heat . . .

All around her road was darkness: above, around, beneath; and it seemed to Ruth that this gloomy descent amid gathering storm offered a very true picture of her young life's passage. But then, against the savage purple of unshed torrents, and even as the first thunder growled from the horizon, sudden light burnt along the summits of Great Mis and the tor stood out like a mountain of red gold against the pall of the sky behind it. The setting sun had pierced the broken vapours of the west, and for a few moments wrought this wonder upon earth. The immense hill flamed, and every detail seemed to glow through ruddy fire; every track and great stone and solitary wind-beaten tree appeared stark and shining in that flood of light against the tenebrous sky. Then the moment of transfiguration passed and the mighty hill drew down the darkness of heaven and wrapped itself therein. Lightning already licked its granite bosom as Ruth reached the bridge and felt a moment's thankfulness, despite sorrows of spirit, that her Sunday finery had escaped the deluge. As she entered 'The Jolly Huntsmen' a thunder peal seemed to shake the earth. Glorious, ragged rifts of lightning rent the sky with fire; streamed from tor to tor; leapt across the rivers; dropped a brand where the Lone Stones struck up blue and wan in the heart of the storm, and slew certain terrified beasts that huddled together there. They tottered, turned up their eyes to heaven and so fell and died. Walla already began to wake, to rise, and murmur with great rain messages from the midmost Moor. Anon her volume came down and her valleys echoed with huge riot. The river lifted a sound as of myriads that made mighty exodus to the bellow of trumpets and the thunder of drums.

Ruth Rendle and Ives Pomeroy tramp together and reach the ragged crown of Great Mis Tor, from where they gaze over the innermost recesses of Dartmoor:

A high wind laden with occasional showers flogged the Moor, hummed against the granite and set the dying herbage shivering with waves of colourless light. Upon the sallow spaces of the hills cloud shadows rolled heavily; aloft, in a wild grey herd, the clouds stampeded over the blue. Here stragglers broke away and fled alone; here, afar, the masses darkened and slant rain fell from them, brightening the gloom of one mountain and dimming the light of another. The brief colour-song of the ling had ceased; but there was rich harmony of chocolate and amber in the bogs, seeding rushes and dark peat-cuttings.

Pomeroy sat himself with his face to the utmost desolation. He turned from the fertile low lands and let the wind buffet his left cheek, so that his eyes might reflect only the north and north-east of the wilderness. Ruth did likewise, and together they gazed very far off into the passes of Tavy and upon the dim, huge crowns of Great Links. Nigh Hare Tor, Ruddyford Farm and its little grove lay like another cloud shadow; great sunlit and storm-foundered slopes fell brokenly to the rivers; High Willhayes was not seen; but easterly the head of Fur Tor blotted the grey sky; and Devil's Tor's squat front was also visible, where it led to the wild ways of Dart.

On the early morning of his wedding day, Ives Pomeroy meets Moleskin, who gives him a gift for Ruth:

Ives went out of doors, sank to Walla, crossed the stream and ascended on the other side. The sun had not risen and only the earliest birds were waking. A thrush made sleepy music from a silver birch that stood on the edge of the grey light. The glens were full of dew and the sky was almost clear.

Hither came Moleskin to meet Ives. The old man brought a little bunch of primroses culled from some secret spot familiar to him . . . Moleskin knew their haunts and the hidden places of their earliest budding . . .

As the men vanished, each upon his path, there wakened a great light out of the east, and the birds sang together.

Crossing's Guide: Princetown and Two Bridges District. Excursions 1, 6. Tavistock District. Excursions 7, 8. Yelverton District. Excursion 40

O.S. Sheet: SX 57

10

The Whirlwind

For the setting of *The Whirlwind* it is necessary to move north to the border village of Lydford (in which parish the whole of the Forest of Dartmoor—as distinct from the border commons—is situated) and to the great ridges of land rising easterly which form the western bastions of the Moor. Our introduction to the scene is a picture of the chief character, Daniel Brendon, as he crosses White Hill on his way to his new place of work, 'Ruddyford' (Redford) Farm:

A high wind raged along the sky and roared over the grave-crowned bosom of White Hill on northern Dartmoor; and before it, like an autumn leaf, one solitary man appeared to be blown . . . Grey cairns of the stone heroes of old lie together on the crest of White Hill, and the man now climbed one of these heaps of granite, and stood there, and gazed upon an immense vision outspread easterly against oncoming night. Two ranges of jagged tors swept across the skyline, and rose, grey and shadowy, against the purple of the air. Already their pinnacles were dissolved in gloom, and from Great Links, the warden of the range, right and left to lower elevations, the fog banks rolled and crept along under the naked shoulders of the hills. Over this huge amphitheatre the man's eyes passed; then, where Ger Tor lifts its crags above Tavy, another spirit was manifest, and evidence of humanity became apparent upon the fringes of the Moor. Here trivial detail threaded the confines of inviolate space; walls stretched hither and thither; a scatter of white dots showed where sheep roamed; and, at valley-bottom, a mile under the barrows of White Hill, folded in peace, with its crofts and arable land round about it, lay a

143

homestead. Rounded clumps of beech and sycamore concealed the dwelling; the farm itself stood at the apex of a triangle, whose base widened out into fertile regions southerly . . . The contrast between such ambient desolation and this sequestered abode of human life impressed itself upon the spectator's slow mind. Again he ranged the ring of hills with his eyes; then lowered them to Ruddyford Farm . . . Like a map rolled out before his eyes, lay the man's new home and extended the theatre of his future days.

Ruddyford was driven like a wedge into the stony wilderness beneath Dartmoor's north-western ramparts. White Hill sheltered it from the west; the flank of Ger Tor sloped easterly; to the south flowed Tavy through fertile tilth, grey hamlets, and green woods.

Shortly after his arrival at Ruddyford, Brendon is sent by his employer, Hilary Woodrow, on an errand to the lonely and abandoned peat works on Amicombe Hill:

Now Brendon climbed aloft to the lonely bosom of Amicombe Hill. He breasted the eastern shoulder of Great Links, and then stood a moment, startled by the strangeness of the scene before him. This field of industry had already passed into the catalogue of man's failures upon Dartmoor, and ruin marked the spot. Round about, as though torn by giant ploughs, the shaggy slope of the hill was seamed and ripped with long lines of darkness. A broken wall or two rose here and there, and, radiating amid the desolation of bog and mire, old tramways ran red. In the midst of these morasses stood the peat-works, like a mass of simmering, molten metal poured out upon the Moor and left to rust there. Low stone buildings with rotten roofs, gleaming corrugated iron still white, black walls, broken chimneys, and scattered debris of stone and steel huddled here in mournful decay. Everywhere cracked wheels, broken trolleys, twisted tram-lines, and dilapidated plant sank into wreck and rot amid the growing things. Like a sea the waste billowed round about and began to swallow and smother this futile enterprise.

The guardian of this industrial wilderness is Gregory Friend, a man of fanatic spirit and unconquerable hope regarding the eventual success of the ill-fated project. He lives with his daughter, Sarah Jane, in a cottage on Amicombe Hill, referred to as 'Dunnagoat Cottage'. This may be taken as the ruined Bleak House, standing above the Rattlebrook under the twin outcrops of Higher Dunnagoat and Lower Dunnagoat, to the south-east of Great Links Tor:

They tramped over coarse fen, spattered with ling and the ragged white tufts of the cottongrass. Through the midst ran a pathway on which the gravel of granite glittered. Pools extended round about, and beneath them the infant Rattlebrook, new-come from her cradle under Hunter Tor, purred southward to Tavy.

The men followed this stream, and so approached a solitary grey cottage that stood nakedly in the very heart of the wilderness. Stark space surrounded it. At first sight it looked no more than a boulder, larger than common, that had been hurled thither from the neighbouring hill at some seismic convulsion of olden days. But, unlike the stones around it, this lump of lifted granite was hollow, had windows pierced in its lowly chambers, and a hearth upon its floor. It seemed a thing lifted by some sleight of power unknown, for it rose here utterly unexpected and, as it appeared, without purpose. Heather-clad ridges of peat ran to the very threshold; rough natural clitters of rock tumbled to its walls; doors and windows opened upon primal chaos, rolling and rising, sinking and falling in leagues on every side.

The centre of activity of this area is the village of Lydford, and here we meet several of the characters of the story: Philip Weekes, the huckster, and his wife Hephzibah; their son, Jarratt, the keeper of the remains of Lydford Castle; Adam Churchward, the schoolmaster; Noah Pearn, the landlord of the Castle Inn; Nathaniel Spry, the postmaster; and other local worthies:

The late Norman castle of Lydford belonged to the twelfth century. It was a true 'keep' and a stout border fortress. Within its walls were held the Courts, beneath its floor were hidden the dungeons, of the Stanneries . . .

In the midst extends a square of grass; aloft, a spectator may climb to the decayed stump of the ruin, and survey Lydford's present humility; her church, dwarfed largely by the bulk of the

145

castle; her single row of little dwellings; the dimpled land of orchards and meadows round about her; and the wide amphitheatre of Dartmoor towering semi-circular to the east.

Many of the cottages had small gardens before them . . . and on either side smiled red phloxes, bell-flowers, tiger-lilies with scarlet, black-spattered chalices, and pansies of many shades . . . The Castle Inn stood almost under the castle walls; and beyond it rose a bower of ancient trees, through which appeared the crocketed turrets of St Petrock's.

Daniel Brendon climbs the Moor to keep a Sunday appointment with Gregory Friend, and discovers an attraction in Gregory's daughter, Sarah Jane:

He stood where the little Rattle leapt to Tavy, flung a last loop of light, and, laughing to the end of her short life, poured her crystal into a greater sister's bosom. Sinuously, by many falls, they glided together under the crags and battlements of the Cleeve; and the September sun beat straight into that nest of rivers, to touch each lesser rill that threaded glittering downward and hung like a silver rope over shelf of stone, or in some channel cut by ancient floods . . .

Daniel seated himself on rocks overlooking the Cleeve. His massive body felt the sun's heat strike through it; and now he stared unblinkingly upward, and now scanned the glen upon his right. That way, round, featureless hills climbed one behind the other, until they rose to a distant gap upon the northern horizon, where stood Dunnagoat Cottage against the sky. Low tors broke out of the hills about it, and upon their summits, like graven images, the cattle stood in motionless groups, according to their wont on days of great heat . . .

He crossed Wattern Oke, then looked down where Tavy winds beneath the stony side of Fur Tor. A bright blue spot appeared motionless at the brink of the river. Daniel . . . hastened forward and, in a quarter of an hour, stood beside her.

Their friendship continues to ripen into courtship:

Daniel Brendon asked Sarah Jane to marry him on an afternoon in November, when the wind blew like a giant from the west, and the life of the Moor slept.

146

They sat in a nook of Great Links Tor, looked at the world outspread beneath them, and listened to the hiss of the wind as it flogged heath and stone and chattering rushes. A million tiny clouds dappled the sky with pure pearl, and far beneath this apparently motionless cloth of silver was woven another cloud-pattern of darker tone where tattered vapour fled easterly across heaven before the roaring breeze.

Saturday night at the Castle Inn is a regular occasion for the meeting of familiars; such an occasion calls forth a graphic picture of a Dartmoor fog:

After heavy rain the evening cleared awhile and the sky showed palest blue, touched with little clouds that carried the sunset fire. But banks of mist already began to roll up with night, and their vans, as they billowed along the south, were touched with rose. Darkness swiftly followed; the world faded away under a cold fog that increased in density until all things were hidden and smothered by it. Outside the Castle Inn it hung like wool, and across it, from the windows of the bar, streamed out radiance of genial light. But this illumination was choked within a dozen yards of its starting-point; and, if a door was opened, the fog crept in with the visitor.

Daniel Brendon, now married to Sarah Jane, and becoming involved in matters which inevitably draw to a tragic conclusion, engages Jarratt Weekes in a violent quarrel on his way to Bridestowe; but first he witnesses a spectacle of rare beauty:

It was necessary that morning that he should go into Bridgetstowe, and through a wet autumnal Moor he walked, passed under Doe Tor, and presently reached the little Lyd, where she foamed in freshet from the high lands.

The springs had burst, and the wilderness was traversed with a thousand glittering rillets. In the deep coombs and wherever a green dimple broke the stony slopes of the hills, water now leapt and glittered. Traced to their sources, the springs might be found beginning in little bubbling cauldrons, from which, through a mist of dancing sand, they rose out of the secret heart of the granite. Then, by winding ways, they fell, and the green grass marked their unfamiliar passing with beads of imprisoned light on every blade.

John Prout, headman at Ruddyford, having learnt in dramatic fashion of the secret association of Sarah Jane with his master, Hilary Woodrow, meets her outside Woodrow's dwelling in Lydford and walks with her over the Moor to Ruddyford:

Through the wild weather they passed, presently breasted White Hill, and bent to the tremendous stroke of the wind. Fierce, thin rain drove across the semi-darkness, and where a rack of cloud was torn wildly into tatters, the hunter's moon seemed to plough and plunge upon her way through the stormy seas of the sky . . . Then a wonderful spectacle appeared above them in the firmament.

From the depth of the northern heavens there sprang an immense halo of colourless light, where the moon shone upon un-numbered particles of flying rain. Wan, yet luminous, flung with one perfect sweep upon the storm, it endured—the only peaceful thing in that wild world of tumultuous cloud and clamouring wind. The arch of the lunar rainbow threw its solemn and radiant span across the whole earth from west to east. It framed all Dartmoor, and one shining foot seemed to sink upon the Severn Sea, while the other marked the places of the dawn.

Brendon and Jarratt Weekes meet again, when further misunderstandings ensue:

Beneath December sunlight Dartmoor stretched in sleep—a sleep that lay hidden under death. But mortality so exhibited revealed nothing unseemly or sad, for much beauty belonged to it. On the shoulders of the Moor drowsed pallid sunshine, though little warmth was yielded thereby. Dartmoor soaked up this illumination like a sponge, and did not waken at its tepid touch. The wilderness slept at noon; and in its sleep it frowned. Over all spread the mighty, mottled patchwork of the hour—the immeasurable, ancient, outworn habit flung down by Nature when she disrobed for sleep.

Then the west darkened and the pale gold of the sky became blurred by veils of rain. They swept up slowly and cast gloom over the light. The Moor colours all changed beneath their shadow and ran together. Caught in the heavy rain, a man who walked upon the side of Great Links ran for the summit, and dived into a familiar cavern, where rocks fell together and made shelter. To his surprise the first wayfarer found a second already taking refuge against this sudden storm; and thus met Jarratt Weekes and Daniel Brendon on a day near Christmas.

The story rolls on to its inexorable conclusion with Woodrow's illness and death, and Sarah Jane's dramatic self-destruction at the old peat-works on Amicombe Hill: and Brendon and his little son Gregory enter on a new life of service to the community under the banner of the Salvation Army. Our last glimpse of him is on a night of mid-December when, as captain of the Lydford branch, he is preparing an address on a text of Job:

Behind the mass of Lydford Castle a moon, just short of full, was sinking amid vast clouds. Some were very dark and some were luminous; some, while circled with flame, yet moved in masses unutterably black. The firmament seemed troubled by this conflagration. The setting moon, surrendering her silver, took upon her bosom the tinctures of earth; and the stormy clouds burnt with her stained radiance. Above them the light exhaled and shot upward into heaven, where stars shone through the vaporous floor of the sky. Orion wheeled his far-flung glories westward and followed the red moon.

The wonder of this silent and nocturnal pageant endured awhile; then it slowly died away. The planet flashed a farewell ruby above the edge of the world, and dreamless darkness brooded upon earth for a little space before the dawn.

Crossing's Guide: Tavistock District. Excursion 9. Lydford District. Excursions 11, 12

O.S. Sheet: SX 58

11

The Portreeve

The village of Bridestowe, three miles north of Lydford, is
the main setting of *The Portreeve*. During the course of the
narrative, the scene moves to Okehampton, later returning
to Bridestowe.

The book opens with a description of Bridestowe; a
quiet enough village now that the trunk road from London
to Cornwall, which formerly traversed the main street,
bypasses it on the north:

Beneath Dartmoor's northern wing, removed from the central
wilderness by some miles of forest, fallow and fertile land, a little
church-town sunned itself and basked under the rare weather . . .
Small gardens spread before the cots of Bridgetstowe, and its roofs
were of weathered slate. The dwellings extended in rows slantwise,
and woodstacks, barns and trees broke up the lines of them. Iron-
blue roads dropped into the village from the north and west and
south. In the central spaces extended a sort of rialto, or resort,
before the door of the 'Royal Oak'; and over against this rallying-
point, separated by a low wall from the stir and tumult of existence,
there lay the sleeping-places of the dead. The men and women of
Bridgetstowe plunge into life's very heart within twenty yards of
the dust that bore them . . . The churchyard lies, like a green
jewel, in shining setting of sun-baked house-roofs; and tower and
trees spring together therefrom.

The home of the principal character, Dod Wolferstan, is
depicted:

Beside the road that enters this village from the neighbouring
market-town of Okehampton, a dark-browed cottage shall still be
seen. Its strip of garden on this summer day was aflame with

150

crimson phloxes, and along with them strong clumps of Michael-mas daisies were preparing future bloom. Over the wicket gate a mountain rowan had been trained upon an arch, like a wild thing tamed and taught to do a stupid trick. Already its fruit reddened to scarlet.

Wolferstan, a hard-working man combining a variety of small trades and crafts, also holds an office of dignity— that of Portreeve of Bridgetstowe, 'a title thought to lend lustre to the hamlet, albeit the real duties proper to that position had long been abstracted and bestowed elsewhere'. He is courting Ilet Yelland, who lives with an aunt at the neighbouring village of Sourton. Ilet's cousin, Abel Pierce, is also in love with her:

Abel Pierce and his mother dwelt in a cottage beside West Okement, where that river winds beneath the northern ramparts of Dartmoor. A rivulet called Fishcombe Head Water here joins the parent stream, and at the junction stood Pierce's most lonely home under Homerton Hill. Enormous undulations of the land billowed down to the valley and then rolled up again on the other side. They merged their foothills at this snug and sheltered dingle and hemmed in silence, save for the endless music of the river . . .

Behind the house a deep dingle sloped upward between the hills of Homerton and Longstone to the boggy apron of Black Tor; and through its midst Fishcombe Head Water tumbled and clattered by granite and heather . . . Westerly of the cot sprang up South Down—a mighty hill where the seasons worked their patterns as on a loom. Tangled brakes of hawthorn and furze climbed upward to the fringe of forests, and, between them, naked clitters of blue stone shone or sulked according to the sky . . . These stones faced the east, so that morning touched them as the sun heaved above Yes Tor and woke their responsive neutral tints to reflection of rose or silver on fair mornings, or the leaden grey of rain when day broke darkly.

All that now remains of the little cottage at Fishcombe Head now lies submerged beneath Meldon reservoir.

We are introduced to Abner Barkell and his son, Richard, who visit Fishcombe Cot:

They dwelt a mile distant in Meldon valley near the railway bridge. Mr. Barkell's labours had ceased, and he passed through the latter phases of his existence under the shadow of the mighty steel structure he had assisted to build. It dominated his life, and that fragment of the world's energy represented by his working days, was now to some extent embalmed amid the numberless rivets of Meldon Viaduct. He had laboured at its construction and, since its completion, had been employed to assist in repairing the giant when need arose. He knew the bridge as a watchmaker knows a watch or an engineer his engine. It was his life, as art is the life of an artist, as the oak is the life of her proper hamadryad. Abner's son was also employed by the South Western Railway, and pursued his business of signalman in a box beyond the viaduct, where the railroad splits and a branch winds north-west to Cornwall.

Meldon Viaduct still stands, a mighty edifice spanning the deep gorge of the West Okement River; but the London and South Western (later Southern) Railway main line to Plymouth via Tavistock, and the branch line into Cornwall, are now closed and the track lifted.

Ilet Yelland starts one morning for the Moor to pick whortleberries on the shaggy slope of Black Tor:

The day smiled clear and cool, touched with hazes of east wind, that tempered the sunlight but cast no shadow. This aerial condition brought the huge composition of nature together, in a translucent and lilac light that leavened, without altering, the proper colours here harmoniously mingled. The brooding eyes of the woman saw Oke plunge through a glen beneath and part into twin cascades that foamed away to right and left of an island. Set in a ring of broken and dancing water, this islet shone . . .

A faint and faded radiance still spread upon the western hills, where the ling now died; and above them, in shapes uncouth and monstrous, here huddled close, here scattered wide, like a herd of feeding dinosaurs or dragons from the earth's morning, there towered the hooded battlements and masses of Shilstone Tor.

152

With tumultuous outlines it broke the sky, and behind it, higher still, in shape of greater simplicity, the bosom of Corn Ridge flung its huge curve. Wrapped in milky lustre as of pearl, it ascended and sank from south to north, and only one dim detail crowned the summit, where stood the tumulus of a stone man's grave.

Bowden Farm is the home of Wolferstan's one-time employer, Alexander Horn, and his wife and daughter Primrose. The latter is destined to play a significant part in the narrative:

The farm of Bowden was situated on lofty ground near the Moor edge; and South Down, the hill that rose before Pierce's cottage by Oke, formed its northern boundary. Beyond certain woods that crowned this height, the farmhouse itself stood and looked due west over Tamar to the high lands of Cornwall.

There can be little doubt that Higher Bowden Farm is the imagined home of the Horns; though if that be the case, South Down forms the southern, rather than the northern, boundary of the farm.

Primrose Horn has certain dark schemes in mind, and asks the labourer, Abel Pierce, to meet her at Lints Tor:

To the tryst she came riding, and from the low hill of Lints surveyed a scene of huge and simple planes subtending the river at her feet and rising round about her. Oke wound hither and thither—a glittering thread from its confines in Cranmere. It passed under Fordsland Ledge upon the one hand and the boggy desolation of Amicombe Hill upon the other. Mighty ravines haunted by shadows and falling waters faced northerly, and to the south the slopes of High Willhayes made a theatre for the display of complete cloud shadows. Their masses marked the ridges and threw hillocks and stones into relief; their outlines ever changing, ever moving, transformed the silver of waters into lead, now imposed a tone of pure purple upon the jade-green of the waste. Scotch cattle—black and dun—roamed in scattered herds along; and upon a knap that rose between her standpoint and the rocks of Dinger Tor, Primrose marked men with a horse and cart standing beside them.

Drama is played on the slopes of the Moor, where Ilet is to meet Wolferstan on Yes Tor; but he does not keep the appointment, for Primrose Horn, with the aid of Abel Pierce, stages a reckless accident with the purpose of involving Wolferstan and drawing his attentions to herself:

From the summit of Yes Tor the stir of the sky was visible, and clouds that huddled their purple over the southern horizon, though huge in magnitude, yet filled but a small part of the immensity of the air. From their bosoms rain slanted sharply and made a haze of light against darkness; but the storm was many miles distant; it travelled slowly; the moil and mass of it thinned to the south-west, then burnt away into flame and azure about the naked, noonday sun . . . In primal stringency and rigour rose the tableland—lone mother of rivers and cradle of silence. Its granite planes and shattered declivities were dark; its scarps and crags lowered savage about the tamed world at their feet. The squat skull of High Willhayes, Kneeset's rounded cone, the rock masses of Great Links, like a cloud against the clouds—these towered to south and west; and round about interminable ridges and undulations swept shadowy upward to the central Moor.

Ilet, now married to her cousin, Abel Pierce and expecting a child, finds her highest happiness alone on the Moor:

Slowly and steadily she pressed upward, and a whim took her to the very crown of Devon. On the squat, rock mass of High Willhayes she stood poised with a fluttering robe—the woman by many feet nearest the sky in all the West Country . . .

The colour of the heather made darkness of morass and fen deeper by contrast, and the brightness thereof was a foil that enriched the chocolate-coloured earth, the seeding rushes, the glimmering bog, and the lichened stone. A far-flung foam of flowers fledged and feathered the great rocks; it climbed the boulders, sparkled from their clefts and cavities, and softened their outlines; it irradiated whole hillsides; illumined the ridges; shone against the darkness of cloud-shadows and, when itself enveloped by them, lent an inner tenderness of light to their passing purple. With scattered tufts, like jewels, it adorned the marsh edge and black peat cutting, in league on league, now massed, now scattered, it gladdened the great wastes, uttered the highest colour-song that Dartmoor knows, and made the hour a joy.

Wolferstan undertakes a photographic commission in the inmost recesses of the Moor:

Wolferstan . . . tramped steadily from the central waste homeward. That day he had finished his photographic commission with the regret proper to completion of a pleasant task. He had just taken certain pictures of the shaggy, desert scenes round Cranmere Pool. Heavy rain had partially filled the ancient cradle of rivers and lent a little of its old-time beauty to that austere desolation. Under conditions of sunshine and blue sky, Dod worked successfully; then, a little after noon, he ate his bread and cheese, smoked his pipe and rested for a while before setting off on his homeward journey. At grey dawn he had started, and watched the nightly mists steal away at the advent of the sun . . .

He was now on the flank of High Willhayes, far under Fordsland Ledge; and next he sank into the defile between that hill and the precipices west of Oke. He intended to follow the river by Black Tor Copse onward until it flowed beneath South Down.

Among the oaks of Black Tor Copse Wolferstan meets Ilet Pierce and her child. Ilet is now a widow, for her husband has been killed in a quarrying accident. Dod asks her to marry him, and she accepts his proposal:

Black Tor Copse spreads straggling under the granite masses above. It is a stony grove set in a wilderness, flanked by the steep of a mountain on one side, fringed by the silver of Oke upon the other. The song of this river met the lisp of the leaves in ceaseless strophe and antistrophe through summer months. Now the wind woke the foliage and diminished the voice of the water; now the tinkle and whisper of glittering falls dominated any listening ear with their music. Sometimes the trees slept and not a leaf stirred; sometimes their arboreal slumbers would suddenly be broken by a mighty clatter, when blue-winged wood-doves clashed away from hiding places under the low boughs. Or at twilight a fox might bark and break the primal peace of this most ancient wood. These and countless lesser things knew the place for home; but conscious creatures rarely haunted it.

155

Wolferstan and Ilet marry; and they decide to move to Okehampton:

With mingled emotions Wolferstan resigned his office of Portreeve and left Bridgetstowe, that he might enter upon the larger life that Okehampton offered.

His house was high up on the hill that climbs to Dartmoor from the little market town below. Behind it ran the road to the artillery camp; before it spread the expanses of North Devon crowned with cloud. Glorious skies sank to that low horizon, and all the magic of dawns and sunsets might from this lofty region be observed by those who had leisure or love to watch the pictures of the air; but for Wolferstan most of his time was spent among men, or upon the acres that he had acquired by Oke river, in the valley near the ancient ruins of Okehampton Castle.

Wolferstan goes cub-hunting at Halstock Wood, near Okehampton:

To-day he arrived a little late and hounds were just going to cover. They found quickly and soon their fox took them into the fresh glory of sunrise on the Moor . . . Where the little Blackavon falls into Oke the fox turned right handed, passed behind Harter Farm, then, still keeping to the right, followed Blackavon's windings under Curters Clitters, and so held straight on, over the heavy ground to the east of Dinger Tor. The pace was very fast, and presently the huntsman, two hundred yards behind hounds, and half a dozen riders, a hundred yards or more behind him, were separated from the rest of the straggling field by a quarter of a mile . . . Then hounds turned left handed, crossed a wall and got into the heavy morasses under Okement Hill. No horses could live with them here; the field gained a little ground on the leaders; but the hunt disappeared . . . They kept on over Okement Hill and then hounds were sighted racing towards Taw Head.

During the hunt, Wolferstan sustains a fall, but suffers no injury. This incident provides an opportunity for Primrose, now married to Orlando Slanning, a wealthy miller, to strike him a severe blow by passing on erroneous bad news to Ilet, with devasting results.

156

Tragic events continue to accumulate. Wolferstan and Ilet move back to Bridestowe, and a climax is reached when Wolferstan enters the contest for the vacant office of Portreeve. Although he is elected, through a terrible misunderstanding, he attacks and gravely injures Primrose's husband. In a demented condition he hurries away to seek out Primrose, the cause of his accumulated troubles; but he meets his death in Slanning's mill, when Primrose, to save herself, starts the machinery working.

The final chapter relates the placid reflections of Abner Barkell and his ancient friend Ned Perryman, walking home from worship on a day in early January:

A dry, bright day reigned over the naked earth; easterly, clean-cut and stern of aspect, the changeless hills rose into a pale blue sky.

Crossing's Guide: Okehampton District. Excursions 14, 15

O.S. Sheets: SX 58, SX 59, SX 69

12
The Secret Woman

For the setting of *The Secret Woman* we move to the little village of Belstone, set high on the side of a ravine cleaving the northern escarpment of Dartmoor and commanding a vast expanse of farming country extending towards distant Exmoor:

Near the hamlet of Belstone, where Cosdon Beacon's enormous shoulder heaves along the skyline of eastern Dartmoor, and the jagged manes of Belstone tors lie north and south, the little Oke departs from her cradle of granite, gathers Blackavon brook to swell her volume, dips under Halstock Hill and takes farewell of childhood.

On a day in spring, while the Moor still slept and no touch of young green broke its monochrome, the glen of Oke was alive with bird music and agleam with flowers . . . Far away, towards the Severn Sea, great rains were falling and the air was washed with sheets of cloud, that deepened almost to night where Exmoor, like a purple wale, spread luridly along and mingled her high places with the storm. From the south one roaming pencil of light passed ten miles off, and fallow land shone out, as though a ruby had been flung down there amid the welter of grey rain and flying cloud. Then the ray was swallowed by darkness, and that red earth vanished.

The mellow light of the oak-buds bursting, the blaze of the spring gorse, the immense and storm-foundered distance, and the tenebrous sky, full of wild clouds hurrying and the curtains of the rain, combined to make a mighty theatre for the exhibition of two young human figures.

Here, in Halstock woods, Jesse Redvers asks Salome Westaway to marry him; but she defers a definite reply, and they cross the river and ascend the hill to Salome's home, where she lives with her father, Joseph Westaway, the flockmaster, and her sister Barbara:

The mean dwelling-house of Watchett Hill faced north. Plain, tar-pitched and slated, it huddled on the great slope—a blot against the gleaming furzes that rippled to its side. Before the entrance a cabbage plot extended; the cow-yard and outbuildings lay in the rear, while the farmlands rose above them in a wide and gentle slope to the crown of the hill.

The farmhouse, still to be found on the western gorse-clad slope of Watchet Hill, is now deserted and ruinous, and few signs of cultivation remain. A recent visit, however, disclosed that the passing years have altered its setting but little: Halstock Hill, 'Harter' Farm and the East Okement valley are visible from the farm; the knocker is still on the front door; but the wooden soldiers, targets from Dartmoor's artillery ranges, which are described as forming the east and south borders of the farm's adjacencies, are no longer to be seen.

From the summit of Watchet Hill, a graphic picture is drawn of the environs of Belstone and the great expanse visible to the north:

Watchett Hill rose above Joseph Westaway's farm, and viewed from its rounded summit, Belstone village appeared in a snug and clustered congeries of little dwellings that faced all ways and exhibited every beauty of whitewash and rosy-wash, old thatch and venerable slate. Its roofs were crusted with moss cushions and stonecrops, or lichens of orange and grey. Blue smoke drifted along and mellowed every line. A squat church tower in the midst seemed dwarfed by eternal wind, even as the grove of sycamores round about it. In winter this ancient fane appeared through a tracery of many boughs; in summer it vanished behind the green . . .

A great common, reflecting the sky in two pools that spread upon its midst, extended beneath the village; and from here the land stretched away north-easterly to the distant storm in three principal ridges marked off from each other. The first was fretted with detail of husbandry, where lay a mighty patchwork of fallow, green meadow and upspringing grain, with hedgerows between and scattered farms and homesteads. The second and wider sweep was robed in forests, commons, chases and a thousand fields all fading together under the rainy weather. To Hatherleigh it extended on the one hand; on the other it vanished behind the ramparts of the Moor. Lastly, against the tumultuous sky, there swelled darkling the edge of the earth.

A scene so vast spreads round this vantage ground, that the varied weather of all Western England can be marked from it. To-day, while Dartmoor is curtained in flying mist, one may note sunshine to the north and grey weather brooding upon Cornwall; to-morrow, lapped in summer, you shall gaze far off into distant tempests and observe each particular storm sweep over half a county, as it passes to the Channel, retreats inland, or fades upon the bosom of the Atlantic.

Anthony Redvers, his wife Ann and his sons Jesse and Michael inhabit 'Harter' (East Okement Farm) on the eastern slopes of Harter Hill, within the artillery ranges on northern Dartmoor:

Seen from afar, the home of Anthony Redvers and his family represented three points of colour clustered closely together in the midst of the surrounding waste. One spot was blue, one was red, the third glittered like silver if the sun touched it; and by night, when all else at Harter was swallowed in darkness, the moonlight sometimes rested here and made an earth-born star.

These patches of colour lay in the heart of the hills above Oke river. Westward the peaks and points of Rough Tor, Mil Tor and Yes Tor rose raggedly behind each other to the highest ground in Devon; and in the immediate west a ridge of lofty land sheltered the farm from sleepless winds. Infinite loneliness marked this homestead; according to the instinct of the beholder, he rejoiced at the spectacle of such isolation, or lamented over it as a scene forlorn.

Upon near approach, the blue spot resolved itself into slate tiles above a sturdy dwelling-house, whose narrow windows, like

anxious eyes, frowned upon the east; the red spot was a tiled barn
of ample proportions and modern erection; while the other side
of the yard appeared the pale and glittering point, now enlarged
to a sheet of corrugated iron upon a stable . . . Walls of dry-built
stone surrounded Harter, and its outlying lands rose in a fork
between the Blackavon brook and the Oke, where these streamlets
ran together at the ford of Culliver's Steps. Beneath the Belstone
Tors a rough track ran to Harter.

On a June night on Halstock Hill, Ann Redvers discovers
that she is not the only woman in her husband's life:

Upon the bosom of Halstock Hill the approach of darkness was a
thing magnificent, and dawn, a spectacle less solemn but not less
splendid. Round about the broom patch extended eminences,
far-flung slopes and tremendous declivities. Furze and bilberry,
heath and the great brake-fern clothed this hill; and through their
interwoven textures the granite broke in peaks, flattened slabs
and shattered moraines, all mellowed to beauty by lichens and
stonecrops and small, bright-eyed flowers that found root-hold in
the riven stones . . . An owl passed by from Halstock Wood; a
night-jar made the gathering gloom throb with his strange and
solitary note. From far below, Oke river cried in a voice unlike her
daily music.

Ann turned to the East where the Belstones stretched ragged to
their skyline. They rose to peaks and turrets; they fell in wide
concavities between their various tors. The brightness of the sky
increased above them, until suddenly a million simultaneous
points of light greeted the moon as she swam gently out from
behind the uplifted earth and every dewdrop glittered welcome.

On the morning of the day when Ann Redvers challenges
her husband with his secret, she walks alone on the Moor:

She climbed through the wild weather where ridge rolled up
above ridge, and where divers hues of storm soaked the high land
in planes of grey and black and purple. Tremendous forces were
moving; the wind raved, and round about Ann, where she sat
under the shelter of great boulders upon Rough Tor, the Moor
whispered with water and every pool and puddle ran in miniature
waves. A deep organ sound ascended from the harps of the granite,

and an under moan answered the wind where it lashed the heath and bending reed-bed. The music rose and fell as the wind panted, and, in the silences, came the call of the rivers between the cry of the stones.

Anthony admits his guilt to Ann, but through tragic misunderstanding due to the noise and violence of the storm, no reconciliation follows; and as he leans over the farm well to draw water, she strikes him. The fall into the well kills him, and the deed is witnessed by their two sons, Jesse and Michael. They agree to say nothing; and Anthony's death is taken to be the result of an accident.

In the first faint light of morning, Ann sees the dawn from her casement window:

Definition of dawn, sharp and pure, lightened the foreground, and there, as though Night's self had wept at that forlorn threshold, the dew glittered like a frost of silver upon the grass. Each adjacent stock and stone stood keenly forth under the light, but all the earth beyond was buried in a slate-coloured mist, that floated heavily in layers along and covered the Moor like a grey and still and waveless sea. Above it rose the broken peaks of the land all islanded, and upon the distant horizon this great vapour grew darker of hue and spread purple under the feet of the morning. Eastern skies that stretched above the cloud-bank were of deep, ineffable orange, and aloft they faded gradually into the green-gold of a chrysoprase; while westward night sank peacefully away. Aldebaran died in the dawn; Vega and Altair vanished from the kindling zenith. She watched the sun rise and saw it touch the exhalations of the earth. Then the valley mists, yielding their hearts to him, blushed, diminished and dislimned. They sank from their nightly hugeness and, waning to flakes and rosy wisps around the rose-touched granite, departed into the untarnished blue.

Jesse Redvers, oppressed with the truth concerning his father's death, again asks Salome to marry him and is met by a refusal. In the little omnibus plying between Belstone and Chagford, he overhears a conversation on rationalism; and he instinctively climbs to high ground in an attempt to sort out new ideas and old opinions:

He turned his face to the Moor; then he passed westerly by a valley and anon climbed Steeperton's lofty mitre above the marshes of Taw . . . Changeful weather held the moment, and the south gradually darkened, but the sky still continued bright, while great cloud movements developed slowly . . . Floods of sunshine still fell over the valleys, but where Yes Tor and his twin towered against the west, their heather's royal purple partook of gloom, soaked up the gathering darkness like a sponge, and spilt it upon the lesser hills and coombs beneath. Water crawled leaden there until sunshine broke through and touched it to gold . . .

So silent Jesse sat that heath-larks fluttered to his feet. His eyes removed from their small bodies narrowed again to focus distance, then fell on Taw river where she glittered, an infant stream, from her cradle in Cranmere. And still the sun reigned over the north, burst the cloud-meshes, and scattered glory into the amphitheatre of a mighty vale, where it spread, all decked for the pomp of the time, between Cosdon and the jagged Belstones. Here Nature, working in loneliness upon the loom of morass and winding river, water-worn gravel reaches, heather ridges, vast banks of furze and slopes of dying fern, had fashioned a triumph for the victory of Autumn. Blended, inwrought and inwoven; leavened with the light that burns on the brink of rain; like a jade cup brimming with jewels; rich in all imaginable harmonies of primary colour; stately in primitive strength of huge and simple forms, there spread forth the marshes of Taw. Here the mists generate, and the great cloud shadows sail; here is a trysting-place for rainbows and the rain; and here lie regions wide enough to display the whole pageant of the seasons, to exhibit the ephemeral procession of all the hours.

Ann Redvers returns home after an errand of goodwill to some gypsies whose caravans are in a sandpit on the east side of Cosdon Beacon:

A rainbow hung in the stormy air of spring. The time was afternoon; the bow stretched enormous, and framed Cosdon Beacon's bosom within its span of purple and emerald, gold and ruby. Upon a background of dark cloud it burnt like a column of jewels and simulated solidity; but where the earth stood behind, the transparency of this liquid light was manifest, and the hills and

163

valleys shone transformed through it. Heath and wild water-courses, bogs deep-fringed with the ashy death of last year's reeds, tattered thorns, lonely pathways and concourse of great stones— all showed lustrous behind the rainbow's misty veil. Ponies galloped beneath it, and cattle were also transfixed by the magic of the light. A heron rose at stream-side, and his wing gleamed for a moment. Then he passed from the radiant arc and vanished. The rainbow endured for a long while, and before the last ghostly shadow of it had faded, a woman emerged out of the sobriety of the hill and descended into the valley beneath. Here rolled Taw at the foot of Cosdon, and the voyager crossed carefully; then set her face to the last slopes of the Belstone hills and proceeded towards Harter Farm.

Salome Westaway yields to Jesse Redver's repeated offers of marriage, albeit with reservations of which Jesse knows nothing:

There came a Sunday when the green slopes about Belstone village were musical with the cry of young life, when the lambs played and bleated, when the cuckoo called from many a misty glade and the church bells crowned the melody of the morning with wind-borne cadences. They throbbed and lulled, broke out harmoniously together, set the sweet air stirring, then sank as the organ woke beneath them. A murmur of prayer and song hung round the church and filtered beyond the gravestones. Now music rolled again, now a single old voice threaded the silence with lesson and sermon. Anon the folk returned to their homes. They issued in an irregular and many-coloured stream from the porch, and the bravery of the women contrasted with the shiny blackness of the men. Then the tide of them broke and thinned away down this alley and that; the noise of them faded until their homes had received them all and the village lay deserted and silent. Familiar figures moved upward together towards Watchett Hill. Joseph Westaway and Ann Redvers walked in front and discussed the engagement between their houses.

Joseph Westaway has for a long time been engaged in a losing struggle at Watchet Hill. Now the time has come for them to leave the farm for a small cottage at Church Hill

Cross, on the road to Sampford Courtenay. He discusses the matter with his daughter Barbara in the little garden of the farm:

Presently he came, lighted his pipe and sat down not far from an old straw bee-butt on the sunny side of the house. Bees were going and coming in hundreds swiftly, and their little bodies wove a pattern on the blue air—a flashing network that rose from the hive into the blue sky. The returning host settled slowly and some, heavily burdened, missed the alighting board and rolled in the grass beneath it. There they crawled and rested a little, then mounted and entered the hive. But those that streamed out from it, shot straight into the air and went about their business as swiftly as though propelled by some invisible force far stronger than any stroke of insect wings.

Nothing definite having developed regarding the engagement between Salome and Jesse, they meet on Halstock Hill. Here, Jesse, for complicated motives, reveals his mother's secret to Salome, and cannot understand her reaction. Salome decides to see Ann Redvers at 'Harter', and in a dramatic scene confesses the truth concerning herself and Ann's dead husband. Michael, becoming aware that Ann's secret is now known to Salome (though ignorant of Salome's own confession), walks part of the way home with her, and makes her swear never to reveal what she has learnt about his mother:

They stood beside the 'Nine Stones'—a concourse of granite boulders set in a circle on the Moor by men of old. At this ancient monument Michael parted from her. Neither spoke again, and Salome went forward alone. Turning once to rest upon the hill, she looked back and saw him there—a shadow waiting in the way.

On her homeward journey, Salome meets Jesse and warns him that Michael awaits him at the 'Nine Stones' to deal with him for having revealed their mother's secret. Jesse avoids his brother, and destroys himself in the quarry on Halstock Hill. Ann Redvers, with Michael's consent,

165

gives herself up to the authorities, and after serving a long prison sentence, returns with Michael for a last visit to Belstone. Salome's secret remains safe in Ann's keeping:

Early on a Christmas morning, while yet it was moonlight and Cosdon's head towered darkly under the stars, there came slow feet to the lych-gate of Belstone Church, and an old man and a sleepy boy proceeded to the vestry door. Rime of frost lay heavy on the earth; the moon shone brightly; Taw river murmured in the valley and glittered over its frosty falls . . .

Presently the sexton took his lantern and entered the bell-chamber, where five ropes depended. He put his foot in the hold and began to ring the tenor bell . . . the sleepy-eyed boy stole out with a taper and lighted two candles upon the Lord's table . . .

The moon was dying and the stars dimmed their light. Not a cloud obscured the ineffable blue of the zenith, and morning moved behind the Moor . . .

Ann joined her son and before Salome realised that she was alone, their figures had vanished into the lustre of light now growing around her. It spread like some luminous exhalation born of earth rather than sky; it was neither fog nor mist, but the incarnate morning stealing over a frozen world . . .

Dayspring broke upon the world and the whole earth shone. Between the morning shadows of the hills there leapt a glory that spread like fire over the frost; each granite turret of the land was touched to gold, and from the East streamed upward a roseal splendour that mantled and flushed the visible universe. Then the sun ascended and all high heaven kindling, flamed with the majesty of the dawn.

Crossing's Guide: Okehampton District. Excursions 16, 17

O.S. Sheets: SX 59, SX 68, SX 69

13
The Beacon

The opening chapter of *The Beacon* introduces the reader to the massif of Cosdon Beacon, the corner-stone of north-eastern Dartmoor:

Springing directly from the marches, with never a foothill to break her northern steeps, Cosdon, that great frontier height of Dartmoor, almost assumes the contour of a mountain. High Willes and Yes Tor, Fur Tor and Great Mis soar nearer to the blue . . . while other hills and uplifted wastes of the tableland are only a little lower than they; but Cosdon Beacon's arc, seen featureless against the southern sky, arrests and challenges among the needles and turrets of the tors by reason of its distinction and its might . . .

A river skirts the western faces of Cosdon; while to the south she breaks into lesser hills and flows out by the undulations of Metheral, Hound Tor, and Kennon upon midmost Moor. Eastward her approaches to the land of farms and fallow are also gradual, for there lie the great swamp of Raybarrow and the commons of Throwleigh and Tawton; but northerly she leaps sheer aloft, flings off a forest like a garment and towers to her high places . . .

Yet Cosdon's immensity is apparent rather than real; for Nature has built her, rounded her and ordered her uprising with such cunning architecture that the hill's dimensions, in their perfection of proportion and balance, imply an amplitude that they do not possess. The mount attains to a sublimity and asserts a vastness beyond man's senses to refute, though within the measuring rod's power to deny . . .

Elisabeth Densham, a barmaid in a London hotel, is travelling to work in Devonshire. She looks out of the train at Yeoford, and gains her first distant glimpse of Cosdon Beacon:

She was upon the way and sat at the window of a third-class carriage on the South-Western Railway. The train had carried her from Waterloo, and would presently bring her to Okehampton . . .

And now Elisabeth was come to the good red earth and gazed on it with wonder. Then Exeter appeared and disappeared. She reached Yeoford and guessed that her journey must be nearly ended . . .

Here were elms upon broad meadows, and then woods and the glint of kerning corn, that challenged the sunlight and rippled to the wind upon a gentle hill. Beyond, a heat-haze danced and the country rolled away into close perspective dimmed by distance and drenched in the splendour from the sky; while at the horizon a small shadow, like a blue mole-hill, rose—a mere hillock under the brightness of golden cumuli that towered their mighty heads beneath the throne of the sun.

Elisabeth is met at Okehampton by Ned Startup, driver to the Oxenham Arms in the little hamlet of South Zeal, where she is to work as barmaid:

The thatched roofs of Zeal fall in steps from west to east, where the village lies upon a hill. First comes a row of white-washed cots, with white-washed walls between their gardens; then a little inn appears and other dwellings under tar-pitched roofs . . . He drove slowly down through the village to where stood the Oxenham Arms, the stateliest and most ancient abode of the hamlet . . .

In the midst of Zeal rose a graceful cross above four crooked steps. It lifted with a long stalk and short arms, and the road divided here to right and left, leaving the cross and an open space and a little chapel together in the midst. A shining clock beamed from the chapel, and the hands moved over golden figures; while above, two exposed bells hung together in a tiny turret, and at times twittered thinly like birds, to call the people to prayer.

The village was quite soaked in sunshine. Zeal basked happy as a lizard beneath Cosdon's uplifted heights. It lay like a nest in the hollow of a desert place, and the sun burnt into it and lighted the cottage faces and blazed in the little flower-gardens by the way and cast deep purple shadows between the cots to make cool places for the children to play in and the dogs to rest . . .

The master of the Oxenham Arms, Tom Underhill, is married to Minnie Burgoyne at the church at South Tawton, a mile north of Zeal:

Beyond the blacksmith's shop and the inn of the Seven Stars there stands at South Tawton a great elm. Beside its foot are bedded a drinking-fountain and a pillar-box; behind it rise steps to the lich-gate of St. Andrew's a fine old perpendicular fane with tower embattled and pinnacled, and a heavy, south-facing porch.

After the wedding, Elisabeth walks back to the Oxenham Arms with Nelly Jope, the shoemaker's daughter. She looks up to Cosdon:

The hill towered under noon-tide light, but the light was broken by clouds. Rain swept over the Beacon, and its curtains of grey, tagged with glittering silver, extended for a few moments into the valley. The Beacon sank behind this brief storm; light and colour died out of it, until its higher and lower ridges rolled huge and dim and removed, like a cloud upon a cloud. But the rain quickly passed, the vapours thinned and feathered away, and the sun shone again.

Elisabeth meets many of the local characters portrayed, including Charles Trevail, the nephew of Abraham Pike, the lessee of the South Tawton quarry. Trevail is the tenant of 'North Combe' Farm, which may be identified as Spitlar Farm, lying north-east of the quarry on the road to Spitlar Cross:

North Combe Farm was happily planted in the hollow of the land beneath Tawton. It stood half a mile beyond Pike's quarry, and the blue-stone face of the dwelling-house contrasted pleasantly with the grey and mossy thatches that covered it.

Trevail becomes interested in Elisabeth, and one Sunday they walk to Cosdon Beacon:

They passed through the valley behind the inn; then they crossed the main road and began to climb. The Sunday afternoon shone fair and, since it was the season of harvest, out of the immense tessellation spread beneath them through the undulating leagues of Devon, there gleamed intermittently the glory of corn. It lay in little squares and wedges upon the face of the earth; and where distance reigned, and forest and farm lands blended and melted together in a blue haze, the harvest still flashed, like far-off signals, or burnt in patches of gold where a sunbeam touched it and picked it out of the welter . . .

At a height of about a thousand feet Charles Trevail called the first halt and made Lizzie rest awhile above Horder's Wood. The bosky valley of Taw wound away immediately before them, and South Tawton's tower peeped above its grove; while far beneath, upon their right hand, like a brown and blue snake, wound Zeal's solitary and straight street across the meadows of hill and vale.

Elisabeth beheld all and found herself moved to a wonder beyond words. Such far horizons were a new vision to her. The man talked and showed her where rolled the Severn Sea, where Exmoor stretched grey against the north, and where his own farm might be seen at their feet beyond the quarry . . .

They climbed on, and when they had ascended some hundred yards higher up Cosdon's side, the village beneath was hidden from them; the forest trees disappeared and the upper loneliness of the Beacon began to encompass them and make itself felt . . .

At the summit of the Beacon was rough, broken ground over which a fierce west wind roared mightily, while the crystal air throbbed at heath level along the lifting planes of the hill. Earth hereabouts was torn and deeply scarred. A torrent had scratched Cosdon to her granite bones and left a deep wound in the black peat; a wilderness of stone scattered the waste and great patches of sward stretched upon it. Here were rhomboidal scars where man had stripped the pelt off the hill and carried it away. Heath and furze made a spasmodic splendour, but the summit, where the beacon pile of grey granite crowned all, was desolate with mire and sedge and morass . . .

They sat sheltered from the wind by a great ring of piled stones at the summit. He pointed out Chagford and Moreton, Hameldown and Hey Tor far away to the south, the valley of Teign and the mouth of Teign open to the misty sea.

The great quarry of South Tawton plays a prominent part in the narrative:

Beyond the village of South Tawton is a natural fault or fissure in the country-side. Here are things useful to man, and for generations he has gathered from this place blue limestone for his needs. The earlier workings round about have passed back into Nature's hand, and at the entrance to the great quarry, rented from the manor lord by Abraham Pike, lofty, artificial slopes arose, and a deep tarn spread amid them. The little hills and the great pit were alike human work, but now larch and oak clothed the one and water filled the other.

On an autumn day the hollow beneath these well-fledged elevations was shining like a cat's-eye stone set in rich borders of emerald and jade . . . Dragon flies glittered with green and topaz fire upon the weeds at the brink and hawked overhead with crisp rustle of flashing gauzes; a moorhen clucked danger to her chicks, and the tiny black creatures seemed to run along the face of the water to safety in their mother's secluded haunt.

Elisabeth is invited by Reynold Dunning, the master of Clannaboro', to take tea with him and his housekeeper, Mrs Vallance:

His farm was a long, low building, two hundred years old. Its chimneys of granite and brick rose out of a deep, silver-brown thatch mottled with moss. A few elms sprang beside it, and in the garden that opened before the front was a single great fir, with a flat head. A laurustinus and a rhododendron grew beside the door, and over the white-washed face of the homestead a mighty cydonia flourished and spattered half the house front with crimson in the spring time. The porch was deep and the door massive. The rooms were low but large, and there were many of them unoccupied. Byres and cattle houses of modern build, mostly roofed with iron, clustered a little apart from the dwelling, while before it spread a wedge-shaped expanse of turf. At the end of the garden a rill from the adjacent Moor fed a pond. Behind Clannaboro' towered the Beacon, and before it the hill sank into a bottom of forest that rose again to green fields beyond. Then ascended a further slope, whose wooded ridges were surmounted by the church tower of Throwleigh.

171

On a wild December day, Elisabeth climbs Cosdon:

Chance visitors had found the winter waste desolate and for-
bidding. In its stern, brumal coat Cosdon rolled all dun and drab,
lit only by the ash-coloured pallor of dead heath-bells and livid
grass. Waterlogged, lifeless, dark, the hill ascended under a low
sun that now seemed to creep in the actual arc of the Beacon—to
follow its rise, hang at noon above its loftiest barrows and then
slide westerly by its descent into night again. To-day the air was
full of moisture and the top of the hill burnt in a radiant, silvery
mist of cool fire. Lances and shafts of light broke briefly along the
crest of the hill. But the fog shredded away before Elisabeth
reached it, and the splendour of that afternoon was not with
Cosdon, but with the world spread out underneath.

A magnificent and dusky earth met her gaze. It was swept with
grey rainstorms and lighted by windows in the high clouds,
through which fell broad fans of pale sunshine, chilled by the
sodden heaviness of the air. The light roamed from west to east
over the surface of the land and rolled onwards, like a flood rather
than a fire, through the midst of the prevalent gloom. Earth
heaved to her knaps and knolls, fell again to her coombs and
valleys and deep, river-haunted denes; but a great darkness and
heavy pressure of atmosphere was upon her. Her forests were
painted in colours of purple; her fallows and fields in umber and
lead. All were washed together and harmonised by passages of
gloom, where uplifted Exmoor mingled afar off with the clouds of
a storm. The thick air released the light reluctantly, and Cosdon
presently stood almost pallid, by contrast with a sinister blackness
to windward. So dark were the approaching clouds that the
wayfarer, while she rejoiced at the tremendous sight spread out
above and beneath her, yet turned her back to the coming storm
and made haste to descend where shelter might be found. Now the
Moor rolled darkly to her feet, unlighted save for the wan flicker
of granite dust upon the pathway.

Charles Trevail invites Elisabeth to go for another walk
with him. The day is threatening, but she is for 'Cosdon or
nothing'. On the hill a beautiful and transient spectacle
occurs:

172

A flash of sunlight breaking out of the storm-clouds along the hill's shoulder touched a dozen sheep that fed together some distance beneath the summit of the Beacon. They had the light behind them and, until this transformation, were dark as the waste on which they grazed; but a sudden thread of gold now flashed each woolly back and outlined each horned head, so that every creature moved about in an aureole of pure sunshine. The flock had been almost invisible in the gloom of the heath until this ray revealed them; now, outlined in delicate fire, they lent a great beauty to the stormy hill-side and softened the threatening desolation with their brightness.

On a later walk over Cosdon, Trevail and Elisabeth declare their love for each other; and in due course they marry, and settle down at 'North Combe', where, 'from her bed Lizzie's wakening eyes could see Cosdon rising into the morning sky'. Trevail likes better the valley regions, and sometimes they stroll beside the river Taw, where it winds amid the meadows:

Taw Green was a favourite haunt of the farmer's. Here the river meandered, purring and peaceful, among flat meadows and beneath many trees. It came at length to a bridge of one span. A little gravel beach spread to the brink under it; alders thronged the bank and trailed their lower branches in the water; and the stream, taking a sudden turn and running deeply in a channel, widened again, spread out her shining tresses over a comb of stones and then stole silently away into the green shadows of great oaks.

To-day the sun shone brightly upon the stream after noon; a trout rose under the bridge, where was darkness that fell like a velvet pall across the water between two expanses of sparkling light. Overhead trembled reflected illumination from the river. It flashed up under the bridge and found little stalactites that made pearly pendants about the keystone of the arch . . .

Now they could see Cosdon's mighty mound rising above the river valley and the woodlands that girdled it. The Beacon had entered upon one of its moments of colour. At the crown of the hill light shone, and where its southern shoulder fell, smoke of fire spread in a transparent blue veil and ascended rosily in the glow that came over the edge of the hill.

173

Elisabeth Trevail visits Clannaboro' to collect holly for winter decorations at 'North Combe':

In the deep woods under Clannaboro', twilight of evening already hastened at three o'clock on a late December day. The sun was sinking behind Cosdon and under the trees the lemon light of it touched dead brake fern to splendour, glittered over the hollies, flashed upon their crimson harvest and found the hazels also, where they straggled, naked save for the little tight catkins awaiting spring. This beauty spread beneath a network of ash-coloured oaks that lifted trunks, mossy and ivy-clad. Here and there leaves still clung to them and made fire through the grey forest; here and there a blue fir lifted its distinctive colour amid the duns and drabs of the hibernal wood. Aloft a fresh wind sighed; a pigeon sometimes clattered away, like a noisy arrow; and small birds flittered with subdued twittering from tree to tree. They were long-tailed tits and moved in a little company together. Above all, through sun-touched reticulations of the boughs, there shone out pale December blue, flecked here and there with feathers of cloud touched to rose by the last light of day.

Reynold Dunning, who has long shown an interest in Elisabeth, remains friendly with her and believes that a time will come when Trevail and his wife will part. Dunning and Elisabeth meet on Cosdon:

On Cosdon's eastern flank, between the summit and South Tawton Common flung out below, there runs a triple row of stones. The shattered monument extends from east to west and its fragments are thrust at all angles from the supporting earth. Seen now, in a spring gloaming, they appeared to totter up the hill, like an army of weary grey trolls, that crept through the fading light to their home in the mountain's heart.

Elisabeth, believing that her husband will remain permanently under his uncle's severe domination, decides to leave him for Dunning; but on the evening in which she arrives at Clannaboro', Dunning is murdered by Pike, who is enraged at having been worsted over the renewal of the lease of the quarry. Circumstantial evidence leads to the arrest of Charles Trevail; but Pike eventually confesses to the deed, though before he is apprehended, he drowns himself in the depths of the lake in the quarry.

After his release, in spite of Trevail's desire to see his wife again, Elisabeth avoids him, and, as the narrative closes, she returns to London; but the reader is left with a strong impression that she will eventually rejoin her husband, though away from Cosdon and Dartmoor:

Elisabeth Trevail sat in a train that hastened from Okehampton to London . . . The day was dark and rain swept the window of the carriage. As the train approached Yeoford she rose . . . lowered the glass and leant out . . . Her eyes were fixed at edge of earth, where a slate-grey mound, washed by leagues of wet air, rose— small and dim—beyond the hills and dales. It persisted in her sight for a moment; then ribbons of steam swept past the train and the vision vanished.

Note. The railway line from Okehampton to Yeoford, once part of the main line of the London and South Western (later Southern) Railway from Plymouth and North Cornwall to London, is now closed to passenger traffic.

Crossing's Guide: Okehampton District. Shorter Excursions 43, 46. Cosdon

O.S. Sheet: SX 69

14
Sons of the Morning

For the setting of *Sons of the Morning* we move to the north-eastern slopes of Dartmoor where, under the high ridges of the Moor, subtend the maze of hilly lanes surrounding the village of Gidleigh (or Godleigh)—the 'Little Silver' of the book—above the valley of the North Teign River:

Woodland roads wound at hand, and in a noontide hour of late July these paths were barred and flooded with golden sunlight; were flanked by trunks of gnarled oak and wrinkled ash; were bridged with the far-flung limbs of the former, whereon trailed and intertwined festoons of ivy and wreaths of polypody fern that mingled with tree mosses. Through this spacious temple, seen under avenues of many a pillar, sparkled falling water where the sisters Teign, their separate journeys done, murmured together and blended their crystal at an ancient bridge. Henceforth these two streams sweep under hanging woods of larch and pine, by meadows, orchards, homesteads, through the purple throat of oak and fir-crowned Fingle, and so onwards, by way of open vales, to their sad-coloured, heron-haunted estuary.

Here walks Honor Endicott with Christopher Yeoland. Honor is being courted by Christopher, the last of the line inhabiting the ancient manor of Godleigh:

Godleigh, or Godbold's Leigh, as it was first called after its earliest Norman owner, may be identified among the Domesday manors of Devon . . . Now hill and valley immediately around Godleigh, together with those tracts upon which stood the village and church of Little Silver, with sundry outlying farms, were all that survived of the former domain . . . The present old fifteenth-century house, built on foundations far more ancient, peeped,

176

with grey mullioned windows and twisted chimneys, from forest of pine on a noble hill under the eastern ramparts of Dartmoor. Granite crowned this elevation, and Teign turned about, like a silver ribbon, far beneath it.

Honor Endicott, an orphan, and also of ancient Devon stock, is the owner of 'Bear Down' (Berrydown) Farm, a large property on the fringe of the Moor, where she lives with her blind uncle Mark Endicott and sundry farm workers:

Bear Down lay in the centre of hay lands immediately beneath the Moor. Above it stretched the heather-clad undulations of Scor Hill, and beneath subtended forest-hidden slopes. The farm itself was approached through a little avenue of sycamores, whose foliage, though it fell and turned to sere, black-spotted death sadly early in most autumns, yet made dimpled play of cool shadow through summer days on the great whitewashed barn beneath it. Then, through a grass-grown yard and the foundation of vanished buildings, one reached a duck-pond set in rhododendrons, and a little garden. The house itself was a patchwork of several generations, and its main fabric stood in shape of a carpenter's mitre, whose inner faces fronted east and south . . . Behind the farmhouse were huddled a dairy, outbuildings and various erections, that made fair medley of rusty red tile, warm brown wood-stack, and silver thatch.

Myles Stapledon, Honor's cousin, a farmer with capital to invest, comes to stay for a period at Bear Down. Together they set out for an excursion upon the high Moor:

They stood upon Scor Hill and surveyed their subsequent way, where it passed on before. Beneath swelled and subtended a mighty valley in the lap of stone-crowned hills—a rare expanse of multitudinous browns. Through every tone of auburn and russet, sepia and cinnamon, tan and dark chocolate of the peat cuttings, these colour harmonies spread and undulated in many planes. From the warmth and richness of velvet under sunshine they passed into the chill of far-flung cloud-shadows, that painted the Moor with slow-moving sobriety and robbed her bosom of its

177

jewels, her streamlets of their silver. Teign wound below, entered the valley far away under little cliffs of yellow gravel, then, by sinuous courses, through a mosaic of dusky peat, ripe rushes, and green banks overlaid with heather, passed where steep medley and tanglement of motionless boulders awakened its volume to a wilder music . . . Beyond, towards the heart of the Moor, there arose Sittaford's crown; to the west ranged Watern's castles; and northerly an enormous shoulder of Cosdon climbed heaven until the opaline hazes of that noontide hour softened its heroic outlines and something dimmed the mighty shadows cast upon its slopes. Light winds fanned the mane of Honor's pony and brought with them the woolly jangle of a sheep-bell, the bellow of distant kine, the little, long-drawn, lonely tinkle of a golden bird upon a golden furze.

Honor, Christopher and Myles walk together on the Moor at sundown:

They walked together at sunset on the high lands of Godleigh . . . all round about a glory of purple heather fledged the granite, the evening scent of the bracken rose, flames of sunset fire touched stones and tree-tops, and burnt into the huge side of distant Cosdon Beacon until that mountain was turned into a mist of gold . . .

The rosy sky was paling, and already a little galaxy of lights afar off marked the village of Chagford, where it stood upon its own proper elevation under the Moor. Thus placed, in opposition to the vanished sun, detail appeared most clearly along the eastern hills and valleys. Cot, hamlet, white winding road stood forth upon the expanse, and there ascended a vast and misty shield of pearl into the fading sky. Through parallel bands of grey, like a faint ghost, it stole upwards into a rosy after-glow. Then the clouds faded, and died, and wakened again at the touch of the moon, as she arose with heightened glory and diminished girth.

Honor and Christopher ride together over the Moor, upon the heathery wastes where northern Teign and Wallabrook wind underneath Scor Hill:

Over against the sunset, creeping magically as she is wont to creep, from the bosom of the Moor and the dark ways of unseen

178

water, arose the Mist Mother. She appeared suddenly against the blue above, spread forth diaphanous draperies, twined her pearly arms among the stocks and stones and old wind-bent bushes of the waste. Catching a radiance from the westering sun, she draped the grey heads of granite tors in cowls of gold; she rose and fell; she appeared and vanished; she stole forward suddenly; she wreathed curly tendrils of vapour over sedge and stone, green quaking bog, still waters, and the peat cuttings that burnt red-hot under the level rays of the sun. Great solitary flakes of the mist, shining with ineffable lustre of light, lessened the sobriety of the heath; and upon their dazzling hearts, where they suddenly merged and spread in opposition to the sun on the slope of western-facing hills, there trembled out a spectral misty circle—a huge halo of colour-less light drawn upon the glimmering moisture. Within it, a whitethorn stood bathed in a fiery glow without candescence; and from beneath the tree some wild creature—hare or fox— moved away silently and vanished under the curtain, while a curlew cried overhead invisible. The riders reined up and watched the luminous frolics of the Mist, where she played thus naked, like an innocent savage thing, before them.

Through various circumstances the engagement between Honor and Christopher is broken off, and he departs for Australia. Honor and Myles Stapledon experience snow on Scor Hill:

There came a day when Honor and Myles rode out upon a dry and frozen Moor under the north wind . . . Presently, upon their homeward way from Watern's granite castles, they stopped to breathe their horses, where a ring of horrent stones sprouted abrupt, uneven, irregular, out of the waste, and lay there, the mark of remote human activity. All the valley presented a stern spectacle unsoftened by any haze, untouched by any genial note of colour. The Moor's great, iron-grey bosom panted for coming snow; and Teign, crying among her manifold stairways, streaked the gorges with ghostly foam-light, where naked sallows and silver birches tossed lean arms along the river. Only the water offered action and sound in the rocky channels; all else, to the horizon of ashy hills under a snow-laden sky, waited and watched the north. Two horses stood steaming in Scor Hill Circle—that ancient hypaethral place of the Damnonians—while their riders surveyed the scene . . .

Snow began to fall in earnest, and fluttered, tumbled, sidled, scurried over the Moor. The wind caught it and swept it horizontally in tattered curtains; the desolation grew from grey into white, from a spotted aspect, still lined and seamed with darkness, into prevailing pallor. The tors vanished; the distance was huddled from sight; and they hastily trotted down the hill homeward . . .

Early darkness closed down upon the land before tremendous snow. Within the farm candles guttered, carpets billowed, cold draughts thrust chill fingers down stone passages, and intermittent gusts of wind struck upon the casement, like reverberations of a distant gun.

Certain labouring men from Bear Down ascend Scor Hill at dawn to see the sun dance on Easter morn—'a spectacle familiar and famous in ancient days but unheeded and little remembered at the period of these events':

The party moved onward to the crown of the hill. Through pearly dews they went, and passed forward where the soft, green mantle of on-coming spring hung like a veil on hedgerows and over wild waste places. A world stretched before them lighted by the cold purity of spotless dawn, and the day-spring, be-gemmed with primrose stars, was heralded by thrushes in many a dingle, by the lark on high. As yet earth lay in the light that is neither sunshine nor shadow, but out of the waxing blue above, from whence, like a shower, fell his tinkling rhapsody, one singing bird could see the sun, and himself shone like a little star.

To the upland heath and granite plodded these repositories of obsolescent folk-lore . . . Over against the watchers, lifted above a grey glimmer of ruined Damnonian hut villages and primaeval pounds, there towered the granite mass of Kes Tor, and from the distant horizon arose the sun. He bulked enormous, through the violet hazes of nightly mist that now dwindled and sank along the crowns of the hills; then the effulgent circle of him, ascending, flashed forth clean fire that flamed along unnumbered crests and pinnacles of far-flung granite, that reddened to the peaty heart each marsh and mire, each ridge and plane of the many-tinted garment that endued the Moor.

Silently the labourers watched sunrise; then was manifested that heliacal phenomenon they had come to see. A play of light, proper to the sun at ascension, ran and raced twinkling round his disc; and like an empyreal wheel, the blazing star appeared to revolve and spin upon its upward way . . . They waited and watched until the glowing glory defied their vision; then all started to return homewards.

Stapledon, who has invested in the enterprise of Bear Down, takes up residence in the sexton's cottage at Little Silver. News arrives from Australia of Christopher Yeoland's death, and his body (as is supposed) is laid to rest in the family vault at Little Silver. A visit of the sexton, Noah Brimblecombe to the Yeoland's vault provides an opportunity for a pleasant picture of Gidleigh:

Little Silver is a hamlet of almost beggarly simplicity. In the midst stands a trinity of three great buildings beneath the bosom of a hill; certain ruined barns, with a few thatched cots and a pound, embrace the remainder of the village; while a duck-pond outside the churchyard gate, orchard lands sloping to the valleys beneath, a little winding road and a stone wall, beside which grow yellow bullace plums, complete the picture. Variety in form and wide divergence in point of age characterise the central features of this spot. Paramount, by virtue of years and pristine significance, stand the ruins of Little Silver Castle; the church comes next—an erection of the customary moorland pattern, with a ring of small, sweet-toned bells, and a crocketted tower, something too tall for its breadth; while, between these two, there stands an old-time manor-house—empty as the ruined castle at the date of this narrative; but more recently repaired for habitation.

Honor goes fly-fishing along the river Teign; she meets Myles Stapledon, and they walk together over the Moor:

They were passing over the face of Scor Hill . . . where stood that ancient monument of the past named Scor Hill Circle . . . Now it basked under sunlight, and spring had touched both the splinters

181

of granite and the lonely theatre in which they stood . . . Upon a fallen stone in the midst, where young heather sprouted in tufts and cushions Honor sat down awhile . . . The giant block of the circle stood on the north of its circumference, and upon more than one of the unshaped masses were spots rubbed clean by beasts and holding amid their incrustations red hairs of cattle, or flecks of wool from the fleeces of the flocks. Even now a heifer grazed upon the grass within the circle; its herd roamed below; round about the valley rose old familiar tors; while sleepy summer haze stole hither and thither upon the crowns of Watern and Steeperton, and dimmed the huge bulk of Cosdon Beacon where it swelled towards the north.

Honor and Myles are married in Little Silver church; and the following year a great and sudden shock to Honor causes her expected child to be still-born. Christopher Yeoland reappears in Little Silver, the circumstances surrounding his supposed death being fully explained.

Early on a Sunday morning, Myles decides to take a lone tramp on the Moor with his dog, a great red setter, though thunder has threatened since dawn:

To the north remote banks of low cloud, with edges serrate and coppery, sulked above the distant sea, and all manner of cloud shapes—cumulus, stratus, and lurid nimbus—were flung and piled together, indicating unusual turmoil aloft . . . The farmer, with his thoughts busier than his eyes, strode swiftly onward, for he pictured himself as coming to great definite resolutions at some spot hid in the heart of the heather, bosomed deep upon the inner loneliness, beyond the sight of cattle and the sound of bell-wether. He desired to reach a region familiar to him, lying afar off to the south of Cranmere, that central matrix of rivers. Here the very note of a bird was rare and signs of animate life but seldom seen. The pad-marks of some mountain fox upon the mire, or a skeleton of beast, clean-picked, alone spoke of living and dead creatures; sometimes a raven croaked and brooded here; sometimes, from a great altitude above the waste, fell cry of wild fowl that hastened to some sequestered estuary or fruitful valley of waters afar off . . .

182

Over Scor Hill he passed, among the old stones that encompassed each supreme experience of his life with their rugged circle; then, his leathern leggings dusted to yellow by the ripe pollen of the ling, he walked onward over a splendour of luminous pink, crossed northern Teign under Watern, proceeded to Sittaford Tor, and, steadily tramping westward, left man and all traces of man behind him. The unmarked road was familiar, and every gaunt hill-crest about him stood for a steadfast friend. He crossed the infant Dart; he ploughed on over the heavy peat hags, seamed and scarred, torn and riddled by torrents; he leapt from tussock to ridge, and made his way through gigantic ling, that rose high above his knees. Cranmere he discarded, and now his intention was to reach the loneliest and sternest of all these stern and lonely elevations. He beheld the acclivities of Great and Little Kneeset and other mountain anchorites of the inner Moor; he passed the huge mass of Cut Hill by the ancient way cleft into it, and from thence saw Fur Tor's ragged cone ahead, grassy and granite-crowned . . .

A sudden gloom descended upon the traveller from Cranmere, and under its oncoming the Moor heads seemed massed closer together . . . A part of the sky's self they seemed—a nearer billow of cloud burst from the rest, toppled together like leaden waves on the brink of breaking, then suddenly frozen along the close horizon —petrified in horror at tremendous storm shapes now crowding above them . . . Over this region, now to a timid heart grown tenebrous and appalling in its aspect, pale lightning glared and, still remote, came the growl and jolt of thunders reverberating above distant granite. As yet no rain broke from the upper gloom, and the Moor retained its aspect of sentient and vigilant suspense . . .

Stapledon now perceived from the congested accumulations of the sky that a tempest of rare severity must soon have him at the heart's core of it. He increased his pace therefore, and broke into a run. To turn was futile and he hurried forward upon Fur Tor, wherein some niche or rocky crevice might offer shelter. Such a spot he knew to the lee of the great hill; and now he stumbled forward, while the black edge of the thunderstorm billowed and tumbled to the zenith, and swallowed up the daylight as it came . . . The vanguard of the wind buffeted him; the riot above his head deafened him; the levin dazed his senses; then by good chance that spot he sought was reached, and he crept into a stony hollow opening upon the south-east—a natural cave among the clatters of the tor, where two masses of stone stood three yards apart, and a block falling upon them from above made a pent-house nearly weather-proof.

The great storm rages for many hours, and as twilight falls, Stapledon considers his isolated situation:

Fur Tor stands near the heart of the Devonshire moorland. It is a place not easy to reach at all times, and impossible to depart from under the conditions now obtaining. Water-springs unknown had burst their founts, and the central sponges were overflowing in deep murmurs from the hills . . . His mind drew pictures of the nearest human habitations around him and the means by which they might be reached. Five miles away, by the western fork of Dart, was 'Brown's house'—a ruined abode of one who had loved the Moor as well as Myles and built his dwelling upon it. Only shattered stones stood there now; but further south, by Wistman's wood of dwarf and ancient oaks, a warrener dwelt in a cabin on the hillside. Yet a network of young rivers and a cordon of live bogs extended between that haven and Myles. Tavy's stream encircled him with its infant arms and wound between him and safety beyond the forest boundaries. Approach to Mary Tavy or Prince-town was also impracticable, and, after very brief deliberations, the wanderer decided that nothing could be done until the morning . . .

Soon the man piled stones before the entrance of his hiding-place, filled a draughty gap with fern and heather, and made himself as comfortable as the circumstances allowed. Great content was in his heart, and when, near midnight, the clouds passed, the moon rose and painted with silver the waters spread below, with frosted silver the fog that rolled above them, he deeply felt the silence and peace, their contrast with the frenzy of the past storm; he roamed in thought through the unutterable silence of that moonlit loneliness; and presently he slept.

The following morning Myles sets out upon his difficult and arduous homeward journey, and reaches Watern Tor

184

where he rests on the northern side of the crags; but in endeavouring to rescue a mortally injured sheep on Watern's abrupt western-facing cliffs, he slips and falls to his death.

After her husband's death, Honor leaves home for a long period, and eventually, whilst abroad, she marries Christopher Yeoland. Following upon their return to Devon, Honor experiences great sadness on overhearing the musing aloud of her blind uncle, Mark Endicott, who believes, quite mistakenly, that Myles Stapledon had taken his own life for his wife's sake—an erroneous belief, which, however, cannot be disproved.

The book closes as Honor and Christopher stand upon Scor Hill above the Moor:

Far below them, in fulvous light of a wild sunset, the circle of Scor Hill appeared. Concerning the memories its granite girded, Christopher knew little; but, at sight of Watern's crest, now dark against the flaming sky, he remembered that there lay the scene of Stapledon's end, and regretted that he had come within sight of it that night. To him the distant mountain was a theatre of tragedy; to Honor, an altar of sacrifice.

Without words they waited and gazed upon the sky to witness after-glow succeed sunset. Over the Moor a vast and radiant mist burnt under the sun and faded to purple where it stretched beneath the shadows of the hills; and the earth, taking this great light to her bosom, veiled herself within it. All detail vanished, all fret of incident disappeared, while the inherent spirit of the place stood visible, where loneliness and vastness stretched to the sunset and heaved up their huge boundaries clad only in a mystery of ruddy haze. Particulars departed from the wilderness, save where, through alternate masses of gloom and transparent vapour, carrying their harmonies of orange and tawny light to culmination and crown of fire, there twinkled a burn—twinkled and tumbled and flashed, under mellow drapery of air and cloud, beneath flaming depths of the sunset, and through the heart of the earth-born mist, like a thread of golden beads. Here colour made a sudden music, sang, and then sank back into silence.

For heavy clouds already reared up out of the West to meet the sun; and amid far-flung banners and pennons and lances of glory he descended into darkness. Then the aspect of earth and heaven changed magically; day waned and grew dense, while a great gloom swept over the heath and rose to the zenith under a cowl of rain. Dim radii still turned upon the clouds where light fought through them; but their wan illumination was sucked away and they died before their shafts had roamed full course. The cry of the river rose and fell, the rain began to whisper, and all things merged with unaccustomed speed into formless chaos of twilight.

Crossing's Guide: Chagford District. Excursion 19. Shorter Excursions 49—55. Lydford District. Excursion 11. Routes to Cranmere

O.S. Sheets: SX 68, SX 78, SX 58

15
Children of the Mist

Children of the Mist has for its setting the little town of Chagford nestling amid the lush countryside that presses upon Dartmoor's eastern flanks. In this book, the first of the Dartmoor Cycle novels, Eden Phillpotts has yet to develop to the full his talent for the imaginative descriptive paragraph so evident from *Sons of the Morning* onward. Description is here in plenty; but so much more is it integrated and intertwined with the narrative and action of the story, that comprehensive portraits of scenes with the power to conjure up the authentic ethos of Dartmoor are fewer to discover.

Nevertheless, this compelling tale of Miller Lyddon, his daughter Phoebe and Billy Blee; of tempestuous young Will Blanchard and his sister Chris; of Clement Hicks and the brothers Grimbal; and of a host of minor worthies is a colourful picture of Devon village life during the latter years of the nineteenth century.

At the outset of the story, Phoebe Lyddon is discovered awaiting her sweetheart, Will Blanchard, at the Pixies' Parlour, a heap of rocks in one of the fields of Combe Farm overlooking Teign river:

From a position upon swelling hillsides above the valley of a river, she scanned a spacious scene . . . Beneath and beyond, separated from her standpoint by grass lands and a hedge of hazel, tangled thickets of blackthorn, of bracken, and of briar sank to the valley bottom. Therein wound tinkling Teign through the gorges of Fingle to the sea; and above it, where the land climbed upward on the other side spread the Park of Whiddon, with expanses of sweet stone-scattered herbage, with tracts of deep fern, coverts of oak, and occasional habitations for the deer.

This spectacle, through a grey veil of fine rain, Phoebe noted at mid-afternoon of a day in early August; and as she watched, there widened a rift under the sun's hidden throne, and a mighty, fan-shaped pencil of brightness straggled downwards, proceeded in solemn sweep across the valley, and lighted the depths of the gorge beyond with a radiance of misty silver . . .

She stood out of the weather, where sundry giant rocks to the number of five arose in a fantastic pile. Nature's primal architects were responsible for the Pixies' Parlour . . . outposts of the eternal granite, though themselves widely removed from the central wastes of the Moor. This particular and gigantic monument of the past stands with its feet in land long cultivated. Plough and harrow yearly skirt the Pixies' Parlour; it rises to-day above yellow corn, to-morrow amid ripening roots; it crowns the succeeding generations of man's industry and watches a ceaseless cycle of human toil.

We are given a first glimpse of their adjacent homes:

Together the young couple marched down over the meadows, gained the side of the river, and followed its windings to the west. Through a dip in the woods presently peeped the ancient stannary town of Chagford, from the summit of its own little eminence on the eastern confines of Dartmoor. Both Will and Phoebe dwelt within the parish, but some distance from the place itself. She lived at Monk's Barton, a farm and mill beside the stream; he shared an adjacent cottage with his mother and sister. Only a bend of the river separated the dwellings of the lovers—where Rushford bridge spanned the Teign and beech and fir rose above it.

'Monk's Barton', the residence of Miller Lyddon, may be taken as Rushford Mill Farm, on the west bank of the Teign half a mile to the north of Chagford:

Monk's Barton stood, a picturesque agglomeration of buildings, beside the river. The mill-wheel, fed by a stream taken from the Teign some distance up the valley and here returned again to the parent water, thundered on its solemn round in an eternal twinkling twilight of dripping ferns and green mosses; while hard by the dwelling-house stood and offered small diamond panes and one dormer window to the south. Upon its whitewashed face three fruit-trees grew—a black plum, a cherry, a winter pear; and before the farmhouse stretched a yard sloping to the river ford, where a line of massive stepping-stones for foot passengers crossed the water . . . The mill and outbuildings, the homestead and wood-stacks embraced a whole gamut of fine colour, ranging from the tawny and crimson of fretted brick and tile, to varied greys of drying timber, from the cushions and pillows of moss and embroidery of house leeks and valerian, that had flourished for fifty years on a ruined shippon, to the silver gleam of old thatches and the shining gold of new. Nor was the white face of the dwelling-house amiss . . .

At the dwelling of Mrs Blanchard . . . already sunset fires had waned: but the high top of the fir that crowned Rushford Bridge still glowed with a great light on its red bark, and uprising Whiddon, where it lay afar off under the crown of Cranbrook, likewise shone out above the shadowed valley.

John and Martin Grimbal set off to fish in the Teign downstream towards Fingle Bridge:

A pearly clearness, caught from the clouds, characterised earth as well as air, and proved that every world picture depends for atmosphere and colour upon the sky picture extended above it. Again there was movement and some music, for the magic of the wind in a landscape's nearer planes is responsible for both. The wooded valley lay under a grey and breezy forenoon; swaying alders marked each intermittent gust with a silver ripple of upturned foliage, and still reaches of the river similarly answered the wind with hurrying flickers and furrows of dimpled light. Through its transparent flood, where the waters ran in shadows and escaped reflections, the river revealed a bed of ruddy brown and rich amber. This harmonious colouring proceeded from the pebbly bottom, where a medley of warm agate tones spread and shimmered, like some far-reaching mosaic beneath the crystal. Above Teign's shrunken current extended oak and ash . . . Upon one bank rose the confines of Whiddon; on the other, abrupt and interspersed with gulleys of shattered shale, ascended huge slopes whereon a whole summer of sunshine had scorched the heather to dry death. But fading purple still gleamed here and there in points and splashes, and the lesser furze, mingling therewith, scattered gold upon the tremendous acclivities even to the crown of fir-trees that towered remote and very blue upon the uplifted sky-line.

Will Blanchard marries Phoebe without her father's consent, though she continues to live at 'Monk's Barton'. Blanchard's uncle dies, leaving him a legacy; he considers leasing an empty farm high on the Moor, his home as a boy, known as 'Newtake'. This farm may be identified as Metherall, above the South Teign where it emerges from the modern Fernworthy reservoir:

Newtake stood, a squat and unlovely erection, under a tar-pitched roof of slate. Its stone walls were coated with a stucco composition, which included tallow as an ingredient and ensured remarkable warmth and dryness. Before its face there stretched a winding road of white flint, that climbed from the village, five miles distant, and soon vanished amid the undulations of the hills; while opposite, steep heathery slopes and grassy coombs ascended abruptly to masses of weathered granite; and at the rear a hillside, whereon Metherill's scattered hut circles made incursions even into the fields of the farm, fell to the banks of Southern Teign, where she babbled between banks of brake-fern and heather. Swelling and sinking solemnly along the sky, Dartmoor surrounded Newtake. At the entrance of the yard stood a broken five-barred gate between twin masses of granite; then appeared a ragged outbuilding or two, with roofs of lichen-covered slate; and upon one side, in a row, grew three sycamores, bent out of all uprightness by years of western winds, and coated as to their trunks with grey lichen. Behind a cow-yard of shattered stone pavement and cracked mud stood the farm itself, and around it extended the fields belonging thereto . . . Seen from the winding road, or from the bird's-eye elevation of the adjacent tor, Newtake, with its mean shippons and sties, outbuildings and little crofts, all huddled together, poverty-stricken, time-fretted, wind-worn and sad of colour, appeared a mere forlorn fragment of civilisation left derelict upon the savage bosom of an untameable land.

A favourite haunt of Clement Hicks, the bee-keeper, is a vantage-point on the side of Nattadown:

Above Chagford rise those lofty outposts of Dartmoor, named respectively Nattadown and Middledown. The first lies nearer to the village, and upon its side, beneath a fir wood which crowns one spur, spread steep wastes of fern and furze . . . The hill fell abruptly away, and near the bottom glimmered whitewashed cots along a winding road. Still lower down, extended marshy common land, laced with twinkling water-courses and dotted with geese; while beyond, in many a rise and fall and verdant undulation, the country rolled onwards through Teign valley and upwards towards the Moor. The expanse, seen from this lofty standpoint, extended like a mighty map, here revealing a patchwork of multicoloured fields, here exhibiting tracts of wild waste and wood, here beautifully indicating by a misty line, seen across ascending planes of forest, the course of the distant river, here revealing the glitter of remote waters damaskeened with gold. Little farms and outlying habitations were scattered upon the land; and beyond them, rising steadily to the sky-line, the regions of the Moor revealed their larger attributes, wider expanses, more savage and abrupt configurations of barren heath and weathered tor.

On a bright summer morning, with her father's reluctant agreement, Phoebe at last sets out to join her husband at Newtake:

Over against the farmhouse rose moorland crowned by stone, and from off their granite couches grey mists blushing to red now rose with lazy deliberation and vanished under the sun's kiss. A vast, sweet, diamond-twinkling freshness filled the Moor; blue shadows lay in the dewy coombs, and sun fires gleamed along the heather ridges. No ling bloom as yet had budded, but the flame of the whins splashed many undulations, and the tender foliage of the whortleberry, where it grew on exposed granite, shone scarlet and flashed jewel-bright in the rich texture of the waste.

Clement Hicks, who has confidential knowledge concerning Will Blanchard, sets out across the Moor to meet John Grimbal and reveal the secret; before his purpose is accomplished, however, sudden artillery action causes him to fall to his death from the edge of Oke Tor:

Patches of mist all full of silver light moved like lonely living things on the face of the high Moor. Here they dispersed and scattered, here they approached and mingled together, here they stretched forth pearly fingers above the shining granite, and changed their shapes at the whim of every passing breeze; but the tendency of each shining, protean mass was to rise to the sun, and presently each valley and coomb lay clear, while the cool vapours wound in luminous and downy undulations along the highest points of the land before vanishing into air.

A solitary figure passed over the great waste. He took his way northward and moved across Scorhill, leaving Wattern Tor to the left. Beneath its ragged ridges, in a vast granite amphitheatre, twinkled the cool birth-springs of the little Wallabrook, and the water here looked leaden under shade, here sparkled with silver at the margin of a cloud shadow, here shone golden bright amid the dancing heads of the cotton grass under unclouded sunlight. The mist wreaths had wholly departed before noon, and only a few vast mountains of summer gold moved lazily along the upper chambers of the air. A huge and solitary shadow overtook the man and spread itself directly about him, then swept onwards; infinite silence encompassed him . . .

From that distant sponge in the central waste, from Cranmere, mother of moorland rivers, the man presently noted wrinkles of pure gold trickling down a hillside two miles off. Here sunshine touched the river Taw, still an infant thing not far advanced on the journey from its fount; but the play of light upon the stream, invisible save for this finger of the sun, indicated to the solitary that he approached his destination. Presently he stood on the side of lofty Steeperton and surveyed that vast valley known as Taw Marsh, which lies between the western foothills of Cosdon Beacon and the Belstone Tors to the north. The ragged manes of the latter hills wind through the valley in one lengthy ridge, and extend to a tremendous castellated mass of stone, by name Oke Tor.

This erection, with its battlements and embrasures, outlying scarps and counterscarps, remarkably suggests the deliberate and calculated creation of man. It stands upon a little solitary hill at the head of Taw Marsh, and wins its name from the East Okement river which runs through the valley on its western flank . . . Below it on this July day the waste of bogland was puckered with brown tracts of naked soil, and seamed and scarred with peat-cuttings.

Here and there drying turves were propped in pairs and dotted the hillsides; emerald patches of moss jewelled the prevailing sobriety of the valley, a single curlew, with rising and falling crescendos of sound, flew here and there under needless anxiety, and far away on White Hill and the enormous breast of Cosdon glimmered grey stone ghosts from the past—track-lines and circles and pounds—the work of those children of the mist who laboured there when the world was younger, whose dust now lay under the newborn light of the budding heath. White specks dotted the undulations where flocks roamed free; in the marsh red cattle sought pasture, and now was heard the jingle-jangle of a sheep-bell, and now the cry of bellowing kine.

As winter approaches, adverse weather conditions bring anxieties to the inhabitants of Newtake Farm:

With the last week of the old year, winter swept westerly on hyperborean winds, and when these were passed a tremendous frost won upon the world. Day followed day of weak, clear sunshine and low temperature. The sun, upon his shortest journeys, showed a fiery face as he sulked along the stony ridges of the Moor, and gazed over the ice-chained wilderness, the frozen waters, and the dark mosses that never froze, but lowered black, like wounds on a white skin. Dartmoor slept insensible under granite and ice; no sheep bell made music; no flocks wandered at will; only the wind moaned in the dead bells of the heather; only the foxes slunk round cot and farm; only the shaggy ponies stamped and snorted under the lee of the tors and thrust their smoking muzzles into sheltered clefts and crannies for the withered green stuff that kept life in them. Snow presently softened the outlines of the hills, set silver caps on the granite, and brought the distant horizon nearer to the eye under crystal clear atmosphere . . . The high Moors were a throne for death. Cold below freezing-point endured throughout the hours of light and grew into a giant when the sun and his winter glory had huddled below the hills . . . Only the hut circles, grey glimmering through the snow on Metherill, laughed at those cruel nights.

After many exigencies and bitter experiences, happiness comes at last both to Will Blanchard and to his sister Chris;

and the narrative closes on the night of Queen Victoria's Jubilee:

Upon the shaggy fastnesses of Devon's central waste, within the bounds, metes, and precincts of Dartmoor Forest, there shone a whole constellation of little suns, and a wanderer in air might have counted a hundred without difficulty, whilst for the beholders perched upon Yes Tor, High Willhays, or the bosom of Cosdon during the fairness and clearness of that memorable night, fully threescore beacons flamed. All those granite giants within the field of man's activities, all the monsters whose enormous shades fell at dawn or evening time upon the hamlets and villages of the Moor, now carried on their lofty crowns the flames of rejoicing. Bonfires of varying size, according to the energy and importance of the communities responsible for them, dotted the circumference of the lonely region in a vast, irregular figure, but thinned and ceased towards the unpeopled heart of the waste. On Wattern, at Cranmere, upon Fur Tor and under the hoary, haunted woods of Wistman, no glad beacons blazed or voices rang. There Nature, ignorant of epochs and heeding neither olympiad nor lustrum, cycle nor century, ruled alone . . . Seed and stone, blade and berry, hot blood and cold, did her bidding and slept or stirred at her ordinance. A nightjar harshly whirred beneath her footstool; wan tongues of flame rose and fell upon her quaking altars; a mountain fox, pattering quick-footed to the rabbit warren, caught light from those exhalations in his round, green eyes and barked.

Crossing's Guide: Chagford District. Excursions 19, 20. Shorter Excursions 57, 65—69

O.S. Sheets: SX68, SX78

16

The Forest on the Hill

The Forest on the Hill—or *The Forest*, as the title appears in the 'Widecombe' definitive edition of 1927—is a portrait of the large wooded estate of Yarner (now a National Nature Reserve), north of the road from Bovey Tracey to Wide-combe, under the eastern slopes of Haytor Down. In Yarner Wood and its environs is imagined the story of Timothy Snow, underkeeper at Yarner; Lot Snow, his uncle; Drusilla Whyddon; John Redstone, master of Dury, near Postbridge and one-time second keeper at Yarner; Willes Leaman of Middlecot and his daughter Audrey; and various other characters.

The action of the narrative is almost entirely confined to Yarner Wood and the neighbouring village of Ilsington, and the various descriptive passages relate mainly to the appearance of the great woodlands under the influence of the varying seasons.

At the outset, we are introduced to Yarner at the turn of the year:

Where certain high-climbing hills take leave of the lowlands, there spread, beneath the eastern frontiers of Dartmoor, extended ranges of forests; and amid these far-flung groves, lifted mightily upon the bosom of her proper mount, crested with the rugged wilder-ness and bound on north and south by little valleys, where streamlets draw a silver thread through the fringes of her robe, lies Yarner—a fair kingdom peopled by many myriads of the unconscious.

Approached at the epact of a vanished year, and viewed from the naked hill-tops before entering her precincts, she shone at

early morning under hibernal colours brightly, and the low sun
not only gilded the drab and iron-grey contours of her woods, but
wakened also a warmth of wine-colour therein, where spread the
growth of young birches in a straggling stain amid the sobriety of
adult trees. The physical proportions of Yarner were clearly
manifested under these conditions; the great main mass bosomed
upon one rounded hill in close-fitting garment of wintry ash and
silver, warmed to russet and chilled to lead; then on the right hand
and on the left the land, falling nobly, descended into deep
ravines, beyond which the earth climbed again. The northern
heights, making abrupt ascent, threw off the last straggling arms
of birches and swept upward to the stark Moor; but where
southern hills arose beyond the valley there mingled pine and fir,
in dim green and blue, that melted together under the dayspring.
Descending then upon Yarner, after long declivities of heath and
eagle fern, with sentinel spinneys standing like islands in a sere sea
of the fallen brake, there appeared a broken hedge of earth and
sprang a giant company of oaks, whose arms touched here, laced
there, and so made a cincture of many boughs for the margin of
the wood.

The ancient home of Lot Snow is found in the little
village of Ilsington, somewhat over a mile to southward of
Yarner:

The hamlet of Ilsington . . . lies, a straggling litter of cottages,
amid the southern foothills of Dartmoor. In the midst, springing
up above its neighbour roofs of thatch and slate, rises a church
tower, and houses press to the confines of the burying-ground.
Beside the entrance, so near, indeed, that it supported one side
of the lichgate, stood the home of Lot Snow. It faced the highway,
and to the rear the graves crowded so closely that from one low
window a man might thrust out his hand and touch a tomb . . .
The house was thatched, and the low eaves projected above the
upper window. Ivy mantled it; a few cottage flowers grew before
the door; the granite lintels and posts of the gate were whitewashed, that they might be seen on dark nights.

Timothy Snow, the new under-keeper to Yarner, lives
with his mother. 'Their home lay beneath the woods, in a

valley where a stream was caught and spread into a stew-pond.' Drusilla Whyddon lives with her aunt in 'a little house that stood beneath the Moor and above the woods. A road cut the hill horizontally here, and the house hid beside it in a copse of beech.' Timothy encounters Drusilla on the Moor above Yarner, nigh to Hay Tor:

There had fallen a great snow, and all the earth was white. Now, instead of the customary pelt of sad colours close woven, spread forth upon its hills and valleys, the forest appeared as a thin and tattered veil drawn raggedly over the white ground beneath. Once more reality shattered appearance, and the thing, so dense and solid yesterday, to-day was marked by its true tenuity and nakedness. It had seemed to conceal the ground from which it sprang; but the earth was now whitened into stark visibility, and upon it the forest spread—a mere, purple, transparent stain.

From north to south there lumbered heavy cloud-banks along the horizon, and the wind that drove them struck bitterly upon all flesh. The upper sky was clear, while earth still lay in deep shadow, over which mist wreaths curled and crawled with long white fingers, and all the lower world of woods and valleys was hidden beneath layers of flat, far-spreading cloud. But across the top of these vaporous seas rolled ripples of pure gold where the sun broke in upon them and set their crests aflame. The cloud-banks were edged and fluted with morning fire; and ever and anon, from among the surges of their waves where they beat together, there rose up little knaps and knolls of clustered trees, or barren ridges, where earth spired darkly upon the sunshine in islands ascending from a sea of pearl.

Above Yarner the Moor had vanished under the snow. Its planes were smoothed, its heights were subdued, and from the summits of the hills glittered the granite—here in tongues of white fire, where the snow was banked to the tor crowns; here intensely black, where the wind had swept them bare again. The magic of far-flung dazzling whiteness was over all things.

Under the waste, Ilsington church-tower lifted out of the fog, but beneath it the lower lands were all swept from sight; while above it the hills rose clearer and clearer, brighter and brighter by passages of white tilth and fallow netted with dark hedges, until the wilderness, soaring to the horizon, swept in planes of snow and broke in pinnacles of stone upon the blue of the winter sky.

Here, returning from business beyond Widecombe, tramped Timothy, the keeper. He had climbed from his home at dusk of dawn and was now passing back to it, under Hey Tor Rock, across the waste. The ponies were scraping with their fore-feet round the furze clumps to get a bite of moss and dead grass; their thick winter coats shone chestnut, tawny, black, and made contrast with the tremendous light of the snow in sunshine; their breath burst in little jets of steam from their nostrils.

Audrey Leaman is discovered by Timothy Snow gathering primroses in Yarner:

At the entrance to the woods a lake of primroses shone and rippled and foamed away faintly into the shadowy dingles round about. Through the mesh of the birches, where it spread in a close network of brown and dun, now hovered a delicate mist of green— the first radiant spring light of the year. Even in shadow this verdancy was brilliant enough, but where sunshine touched the wood it ran flame bright, fluttered like a torn veil, through the burnished splendours of the birch stems and made the way dazzling.

Very early on a July morning, Drusilla sets out to meet Timothy within Yarner:

The lark was overhead, and beneath the high lands, Yarner, like a grey blanket woven without pattern, covered the valley in one featureless and mighty sweep. Above it slate-coloured ridges of cloud hung in masses parallel with the horizon, and higher yet glittered Venus, like a bead of gold upon the pale amber of the sky . . .

Colour crept over the dewy hills and dusky woods. Within Yarner mysterious patches of gloom still lurked under the arms of the forest; but the heads of the trees were brushed with a tremor of light, for a morning wind played upon the hillside and set all things in glimmering motion. The awful purity of the hour persisted for some time; then the false dawn thrilled with its first flush, and cloudlets of grey, that sprang and grew out of the wind's eye, took a sudden roseate warmth on their slate-coloured breasts. The radiance spread and flowed over the sky to the zenith. It permeated the transparent blue, as a tincture irradiates pure water; and through the rosy light Venus still shone.

A chance encounter on a moorland road provides a vivid little pastoral picture:

John Redstone met Audrey Leaman on the high road under Rippon Tor, above Ilsington village. He rode on a horse behind a great flock of sheep newly shorn, and in the sunshine they shone silver-bright through the dust of their passing. They bleated with varying notes, and louder than their noise broke the explosive bark of a big black and white sheep-dog who circled about behind them . . . He whistled his dog, gathered his flock and went his way, and she proceeded on her journey to Widecombe.

Yarner appears in high summer:

Now did Yarner spread, equipped and uncurled, to her last expression of splendour. She was fully decked, and offered a wondrous canvas for the painting of light and darkness, twilight and dawn. Her barriers and planes of foliage allured the sun and moon; at her covert edges the leafy shields of the woods were grown almost impenetrable where they fell and feathered with many a pensile bough to shroud the regions within. Light homed still under the trees, as it had done in spring and winter; its lances and banners still penetrated, and forced a rain of August gold into the secret places. The forest was pervious to light and rain; the fern glades basked and exuded a hot savour, and the thing so solid and lumpish looked down upon from above, was in truth full of sunshine and motion and music.

The forest proceeded with its cycle of phenomena in punctual succession and ordered plan. Everything was happening as it had happened before and would happen again. Those inevitable mischances and mishaps on which were founded other prosperities and successes filled the wood. The great ants lifted their mounds, and their larvæ were food for birds; the tattered foliage and stripped bough told of full-fed grubs; the ichneumon, poised like a gold bead in a sunbeam, meant death to the caterpillar's resurrection; the briar's incised foliage told of a carpenter bee's snug home;

the scattered plumage of a redbreast revealed the feeding-place of a hawk; from unseen corpses death struck upon the nostrils; and everywhere, under the silent splendour of drowsy days and moonlit nights, the battle raged.

Yarner's mystery continued impenetrable; its beauty lay alone in the beholding eye; its very quality of impersonality belonged not to itself but the appraising mind.

Within the confines of Yarner may be discovered the ruins of an old copper mine:

On the eastern hills of Yarner, at the edge of fir plantations, and beneath a great heath that spread to the horizon above, there stood the ruined mine in a wood of silver birch. Fifty years before, copper had been sought and found here; but the enterprise languished; the mine was deserted . . .

The place stood on a slope, and beneath it fell ugly banks of ironstone, that half a century had failed to hide. These mounds persisted ungainly, and defied foothold to all green things. Round about fragments of wrought iron and rotten timber told of past industry; but the wood fast returned to earth, and the debris of red metal was rusted, twisted, fretted by the teeth of time. The spokes and splinters thrust out of the undergrowth and stone, like fossil skeletons partially denuded. At hand in the woods the main shaft had been sunk, but it was now choked up and not forty feet deep . . . The chimney still stood and towered over the birches. It sprang from a mass of masonry beneath, and stood above a deep pit, where floods had laid bare the foundations until it seemed that the huge mass of stone and brick must soon topple. Surrounding roofs, that had covered the machinery, were rotten, and had dropped in many places so that the grass-grown floors were littered with tiles and strewed with a rib-work of rafters. The chimney towered intact, but its red bricks were eaten away, and the wind had crowned it with dancing feathers of fern. Over the pit projected two great masses of mortared stone, like the fretted paws of a sphinx, and grass and dandelions covered each nook and cranny. Great cracked arches opened above, and fallen walls had left a splintered jag of steps, by which a climber might ascend to the secret chambers aloft. Here nestled wild birds, and the broken floors were littered with rubbish and filth of empty nests. The

200

birches had grown all round the ruin, and rowan and hazel found harbour in its walls.

The year moves on, and Yarner is now found under autumnal change:

The slopes of Yarner were hung as for a pageant, and the personal fashion and custom of manifold trees lent a pomp and diversity to the spectacle that a wood of one sole timber cannot know. Here larches were aflame, and their pavilions of lemon light gleamed against the russet and tawny of the woods; here the birches already towered silvery through the thinning flutter of their leaves; here an oak was green while his neighbour ash showed dreary grey creeping to blackness through her verdure. Fairest of all the stately things that ascended above the prevalent radiance now kindling over Yarner, did the beeches rise; for upon them autumn stole with delicious touch, to trace the anatomy of drooping boughs in flicker of flame; to light the shoulders of each gracious tree with gold, and feather their finials with red gold.

The hills spread melting and of a liquid lustre where ran together all tones of honey and amber; in sunshine they warmed to rose and orange; in shadow they dimmed and cooled to delicate chill fawn, or a brown and sepia; but ever across the darkest passages were flecked and spattered spots and little leafy galaxies of light upon the bough; while against even the shining places of far-flung fern or massy boughs aflame, there persisted the greater glitter of single, ineffable light points, flashing sun-bright upon the earth-bright heath or spinney edge. And though sad-coloured passages opened in the midst of these riotous splendours, where the rowan faded a misty grey, where the leaf of the lichen-clad thorns was sped, or the dogweed had sunk into a sulky purple; yet such sober things served but to heighten the general conflagration. At high noon, or in the blaze of great sunsets, a seeing eye ached before this bravery and sought the dim dingle, the shadow-haunted goyle, or the company of certain pines, that shone out with blue of azure set in the fiery garniture of the fall. Now Yarner ascended to the full passion of her colour glory, and as slowly sank therefrom.

At the close of the book, when the human story has

moved to its tragic conclusion, the seasons have turned full circle, and we leave Yarner under the sleep of winter:

A forest knows no universal slumber, for the sleep of the trees is the wakening of many lesser things. Though the grey trunk lifts upward into a suspended animation of branch and twig, yet its surface is mottled with much busy life. The mosses fruit and thrive; the lichens are plump, and stretch forth growing fingers to paint the bole and bough with wafers, discs, washes of ebony and ochre and silver grey. The underwoods sparkle with tufts and cushions of glimmering green, here dark, here emerald bright and shining. Much renewed minor life also wakens from the carpet of the fallen foliage.

The trees indeed sleep, but they also dream. In the heart of every leafless oak a dryad whispers that the days are fleeting; that the icy-footed winter hours are dancing with the snow-wreaths away in their chill processions; that the fountains of the sap will soon rise again to Spring's unsealing; that swiftly will the bud-sheath swell and pale and shimmer silky down, like a cast-off veil at the feet of the vernal beeches.

Crossing's Guide: Bovey Tracey District. Excursions 23, 25. Shorter Excursion 78

O.S. Sheet: SX 77

17
Orphan Dinah

For the setting of *Orphan Dinah* we move south-west from Yarner to the little village of Buckland-in-the-Moor, underneath the bold outline of Buckland Beacon. The narrative opens on the summit of Buckland Beacon, as Lawrence Maynard journeys to 'Falcon Farm' to commence work there as cowman:

The spectacle of free horizons from Buckland Beacon, at the southern rampart of Dartmoor, affords a vision orbicular and complete. Its gracious, yet austere, composition and its far-flung arena for the masques and interludes of the dancing hours render it a centre of ceaseless variation . . .

In this hour, after noon on a day of mid-September, the light was changing, not gradually at the sun's proper declension, but under the forces of a south-west wind bringing up vapour at twenty miles an hour from the distant sea.

From the rounded and weathered masses of the Beacon, the hill sloped abruptly and a receding foreground of dying fern and granite boulders broke on a gap of such extent that earth, reappearing far below, was already washed by the milky azure of the air, through which it glimmered, receded, and again rose to lofty hills beyond. The ground plan was a mighty cup, over which the valley undulated, rising here to knap and knoll, falling there into coombs and plains, sinking to its lowest depths immediately beneath the view-point, where wound the river Dart. Upon a distant and irregular line, now melting into the thick air, border heights and saliences sank and rose, repeating on a vaster scale the anatomy of the river basin . . .

Little by little, detail faded and the shadows of the clouds grew denser, the body of the clouds extended. Still they were edged with light, but the light died as they thickened and lumbered forward, spreading their pinions over the Vale. The air gradually grew opaque, and ridge after ridge, height after height, disappeared in it. They were washed away, until the fingers of the rain felt dumbly along the bosom of Buckland Beacon, dimmed the heath and furze to greyness, curled over the uplifted boulder, found and slaked the least wafer of gold or ebony lichen that clung thereto.

A young man, who had been standing motionless upon the Beacon, felt the cool brush of the rain upon his face, woke from his reverie, and prepared to descend where a building stood upon the hill below him half a mile distant.

'Falcon' (Beacon) Farm is represented as the home of Joseph Stockman, his daughter Susan and the new horseman Thomas Palk:

Beneath the Beacon, perched among open fields, that quilted the southern slope, there stood a stone house. Here was Falcon Farm, and over it the hawks that had given it a name would often poise and soar and utter their complaining cries. The cluster of buildings perched on the hillside consisted of a dwelling-house, with cartsheds, a cowhouse and stable, and a fine barn assembled round the farmyard. About them stretched square fields, off some of which a harvest of oats had just been shorn; while others were grass-green with the foliage of turnip. Beneath, between the farmhouse and the wooded road, extended meadows into which fern and heath were intruding ominously. A wedge of kitchen garden was scooped out of the hill beside the yard, and a dry-built wall fell from the shoulder of the Beacon above, broke at Falcon Farm, and with diverging arms separated its field and fallow from the surrounding wild.

Melinda Honeysett, her father Enoch Withycombe, and her brother Jerry live in a neat cottage in Buckland village:

Like beehives cluster the thatched roofs of Buckland, for the cottages are dwarfed by the lofty trees which soar above them. Oak and ash, pine and beech heave up hugely to their canopies upon the hill slope, and the grey roofs and whitewashed walls of the hamlet seem little more than a lodge of pygmies sequestered in the forest. The very undergrowth of laurel has assumed giant proportions and flings many a ponderous bough across the highway, where winds a road with mossy walls through the forest and the village.

The cottage coverings were old and sombre of tone; but on this September day sunshine soaked through the interlacing boughs and brought light to the low-browed windows, to the fuschias and purple daisies in the gardens. It flashed a ruby on the rays of Virginian creepers, that sometimes clothed a wall, and brightened the white faces of the little dwellings to pale gold.

Above stretched the woods, legion upon legion, their receding intricacies of branch and bough broken by many thousand trunks. Beneath, again the woods receded over steep acclivities to the river valley.

Though the houses were few and small, great distinction marked them. They held themselves as though conscious of their setting, and worthy of it. They fitted into the large and elaborate moulding of the hillside, and by their human significance completed a vision that had been less without them. There was a quality of massive permanence in the scene, imparted by the gigantic slope of the hill whereon it was set. Earth fell evenly, serenely from its crown on the naked Beacon above, down and down to the uttermost depths of the river valley and the cincture of silver Dart winding through the midst of it.

'Green Hayes', a farm at Lower Town, 'a hamlet sunk in the Vale to the west', is the home of Benjamin Bamsey, his wife and family, and his foster-daughter Dinah Waycott:

Green Hayes was 'a welcoming sort of place', as the owner always declared, though at first sight it did not seem so. The farmhouse was built of granite and faced with slate, which caused it to look sulky, but made it snug. A wide farmyard extended before the face of the dwelling, and pigeons and poultry lent liveliness and movement to it. A great barn, with a weathered roof of slate, extended on one side of the yard, and orchards and large kitchen gardens arose behind it.

Dinah Waycott is tokened to her foster-brother John Bamsey—water-bailiff on the river. They meet at Hazel Tor (Ausewell Rocks):

They met by appointment, strolled in the woods, then climbed through plantations of sweet-smelling spruce till they reached Hazel Tor, piled on a little spur of the hillside under Buckland Beacon. Here the granite heaved in immense boulders that broke the sweep of the hill and formed a resting-place for the eye between the summit of the Beacon and the surface of the river winding in the lap of the Vale beneath. The glories of the fall were at an end, on an afternoon when the wind was still and the sky grey and near, pressing down on the naked tree-tops.

On a winter's day, the bells of St Peter's ring for morning service:

The church of St. Peter's at Buckland-in-the-Moor has a fine wagon roof and a noble little oak screen. The windows are mostly of uncoloured glass, and the light of day illuminates the building frankly. It stands, with its burying-ground round about it, on a plateau uplifted among sycamore and pine. A few old tombs lie in the yard with others of recent date; but for the most part, on this January day, the frosty grass glittered over the mounds of unrecorded dead. The battlemented tower rose in the midst of meadows at a step in the great slope from the Beacon. Trees surrounded the gap, ascending above and falling below in their winter nakedness. It was a place of peace and distinction, marked by the quality of human care devoted to it.

The five bells rang through the frosty morning, and Melinda Honeysett, with her brother Jerry Withycombe, stood by the parapet of the burying-ground and looked across the valley, where Lower Town lay far beneath. It glimmered pale grey amid its dim orchards and ploughed lands, and beyond it Dartmoor flung out ragged ridges from south to north, clean and dark under the low sun.

Dinah decides that her tokening to John Bamsey has been a mistake: she tells him so, and they part company. Lawrence Maynard invites Dinah to take a Sunday walk as far as Hay Tor Rock:

The day came for Dinah's walk with Lawrence Maynard, and though the sky lowered at dawn, before noon the wind had travelled north of west and there was no longer any fear of rain.

They set out, climbed the Beacon, and advanced by those rolling stretches of heath and stone that extended to the north of it. They talked but little on their way, reached the White Gate, held to the winding road awhile, then returned to the moors, and presently stood looking down into the deserted quarries of Hey Tor . . .

They approached the granite bosses of the tor and stood presently beside it, where high on the cliff above them a face bulked enormous and stared into the eye of the westering sun . . . He looked up at the features above them, carved on the mass of the tor. Beyond swung out Rippon's granite crown against the sky, and nearer stretched miles of wild and ragged heath. The sun kneaded earth with its waning lustres until matter seemed imponderable and the wild land rolled in planes of immaterial radiance folding upon each other. The great passages of the hills and dales melted together and the stony foreground shone clear, where, through the hazes, a pool glinted among the lengthening shadows and reflected the sky. As the sun descended, tracts of misty purple spread in the hollows and flung smooth carpets for the feet of night.

Maynard is sent out by his master to search for granite:

Sent to find granite and bidden to choose a boulder that would split out, so that needful stone posts might be fashioned from it, Lawrence Maynard climbed the Beacon and loitered here and there, examining the great stones that heaved their backs or sides from the earth . . .

To-day a north wind shouted overhead, drove the scattered clouds before it and hummed in organ notes upon the mass of granite that capped the Beacon. Copper-red ribbons of beech fell broadly into the depths below—and, against their fire, the plantations of the pine wove darker patterns, where they descended over the shoulders of the hills, until the air and space wrought magic upon their distances and swept them together in one glowing integument for the lowlands. There it was as though a mighty tiger-skin had been flung down upon the undulating earth, so rich in orange-tawny and russet were the forest reaches, so black the slant shadows thrown by the low sun at spinney edge, along the boundary of hanging woods, or where open fields broke horizontally into the kingdom of the trees. There shone green meadows against the flame of the fall around them; and the ploughed fallows heightened colour by their contrast . . . Shadows flew to dim their splendour and then again reveal it; nor was the clarity of the air purchased without cost, for unseen moisture drenched it, and sometimes took shape of separate storms, sweeping in a low, grey huddle over the earth they hid. They drew their veils over half a league of the land at a time, then dislimned and vanished again. And far away, beyond the last peaks and saliences southward, stretched a horizon of dazzling and colourless light, where sea-girdled earth and Devon rolled dark against the liquid brilliance of the Channel lifted beyond it.

Lawrence meets Dinah in Ashburton; they take tea together, and he tells her his story and his real name—Gilbert Cartier. He is married, but for certain cogent reasons he had left his wife immediately after the marriage ceremony and had never seen or heard of her since.

Later, Lawrence plans to leave England for Australia; there he would take Dinah, and there, as 'Lawrence Maynard' he would marry her. Several men of Dinah's family become aware of their secret enterprise, and are concerned to upset the plan in the name of right.

Lawrence leaves 'Falcon Farm' and puts up for the night at Holne. He has arranged to meet Dinah early the following morning at 'Shepherd's Cross'; they will then walk to Brent, thence travelling to Plymouth, where they will embark. No reference is made by William Crossing to 'Shepherd's Cross', either in the *Guide to Dartmoor* or in the *Ancient Crosses of Dartmoor*. I am told, however, by John Reynolds that in the past Huntingdon Cross has sometimes been locally referred to as 'Shepherd's Cross':

The morning dawned fine and touched with frost. The wind blew gently from the east. There was no sting in it, but it created an inevitable haze, and distance quickly faded under its blue-grey mantle, while at hand all shone clear and bright in sunrise fires. The heavy dew of a cloudless night was not yet dried off the herbage, and the grass, nibbled to a close and springy velvet by sheep and rabbits, spread emerald-green between the masses of heather and furze, where the lover climbed Dene Moor. Still the Autumn heath shone with passages of colour; but into the rich pink of a month earlier had crept a russet warmth, where innumerable heather bells passed to death with a redness that drowned the purple . . . A few raddled sheep browsed their morning meal and made harmony with the bright colours of the dawn . . .

Swinging forward with an ash sapling in his right hand and a leathern portmanteau in his left, Lawrence presently saw his goal ahead. Sunshine played over the blue hazes and touched the grey summit of Shepherd's Cross, where the ancient stone stood erect and solitary on the heath.

Here is enacted the final drama; Lawrence is tied to the old cross by a group of men; Dinah arrives on the scene; the situation is at last resolved; and Dinah and Lawrence, leaving the assembled company, pass out of sight into a new life together.

Crossing's Guide: Ashburton District. Excursion 27. Shorter Excursion 92

O.S. Sheet: SX 77

18
Demeter's Daughter

For the scene of *Demeter's Daughter* we cross the river Dart
south of Buckland-in-the-Moor to the village of Holne,
standing on high ground under Holne Moor rising to the
west. The opening chapter provides a picture of the valley
through which the Dart makes its way towards the sea from
the meeting-place of the east and west branches of the river
at Dartmeet:

On the fringe of Holne Moor there is a valley that slopes upward,
mile upon mile, to the wilderness above it; but no harsh transition
marks their muster, for the fields ascend to the brake-clad bosom
of the Moor and a hedge of polled oak and hazel is all that
separates green corn and shining fern, where side by side they
flourish.

Here, on a summer noon, earth fell to the farm lands, where
verdure of roots broke the dark soil and shorn hay spread silvery
against the brightness of meadows. Then rose valley trees, with
rounded heads that basked in sunshine, and beneath them shone
many roofs of a little hamlet sprawling under its thatch and slate.
Deep coppices of pine and beech sometimes made patches of
darkness on the sun-soaked undulations of the land and broke the
interminable network of hedges; while higher yet, beneath a
southing sun, rolled the uneven contours of Holne Ridge, shattered
upon the skyline with masses of stone.

The valley opened mightily and stretched out forest-clad arms,
between which rolled Dart by Buckfast of the Monks under
Hembury Castle—places similarly weighted with a sense of Time's
stealthy and unhalting march ...

The mosaic of meadow, corn and naked earth, of forest and of
heath, grew closer in pattern and misty and dim behind the

flowing air. It faded upon the distance, touched with sparks of remote fire where roofing flashed from distant thorp, threaded with climbing and falling roads, crowned by knap and knoll, by spinneys and ragged woods. Brushed with aerial magic it melted away to the ends of the earth; it broke easterly where a river wound; and then it parted to a liquid horizon and showed the grey rim of the sea. Like a shadow the waters spread there between the lifting and the falling hill; and farther yet, from east to north, Dartmoor rolled out again, in many a frontier height by Rippon and Honey-bag, by mighty Hameldon and other saliencies.

We are introduced to Alison Cleave seated upon a ledge of rock on Combestone Tor:

A heavy mist enveloped Dartmoor, and from Combestone Tor the great earth ridges swept southerly away all smothered in vapour. Below the broken rock piles of the tor a steep hill fell sharply, and here nothing but a foxglove or two and a withered white-thorn rose stark against the dim wall of moving mist behind them. In varying densities it floated, and sometimes it was suddenly rent and parted like a ragged veil, to reveal the gorges of Dart beneath Combestone and the neighbouring hills beyond. The world visible at these moments was dimmed to delicate jade; it appeared and vanished at the freak of the mist; and now the crowns of Yar and Sharp and Bel limned ghostly out of the welter, and now again they vanished, while lower slopes were revealed. The wind dealt similarly with sound, for the cry of Dart rose up fitfully through it, and came and went, now clear, now hushed by the lull and lift of the breezes.

At one point, through a fissure in the grey curtain, fields broke the waste land, where man had snatched a coign for his crops upon a southern hill. Corn gleamed there—bright and moisture-laden through the mist—surrounded by eternal heath and stone.

Beside the tor, where stood its squat and weathered piles with fingers and filaments of vapour stealing among them, there browsed a sheep or two and a shaggy mare with a little mouse-coloured foal. The infant thing squeaked and galloped hither and thither, then it sucked and presently lay down to sleep. The grey air rang and rippled with lark music, and one might have heard four separate songs tinkling together up, up, up into the aerial places.

211

Alison Cleave lives with her husband Aaron—a lazy and vain man pursuing the trade of a thatcher—and their family in a lonely and ruinous cottage called Venford Brook Cot. Venford Brook descends northerly from Holne Moor, feeding Venford reservoir on its way to join the Dart, and the site of the little cottage on its bank may be imagined as adjacent to the reservoir or, indeed, beneath its waters. Alison meets her sons Giles, working at the long-deserted Hen Roost Mine, and Frank, a stone-breaker; and they travel home together:

They were travelling now over the heart of the Moor, and presently in a dip of the hills ahead there rose a grey cottage. It stood at a fold of two great undulations, and a stream, touched to twinkling flame by the sunset, broke out of the hollow and seemed to flash away from the very threshold of the dwelling. The abode was squat and mean, but its utter isolation imparted to it a certain dignity. On nearer approach the beauty of the spot became manifest, and the ruination of the home also appeared.

Stoke Farm, on the hillside above Holne Wood and the river Dart, is the home of Uriah Hamlyn:

It was a day of fierce summer heat, with transparent flickers of light at work on the high ridges. The purr of mowing machines came up from many a meadow, and here grass fell in lush banks, and here hay, flung out from the mows of yesterday, was being spread again for final drying, before carts came to carry it to the ricks...

Stoke spread its sloping acres above Dart, and from the entrance of the farm the great expanses of hanging woods, that fell to the many-folded ribbon of the silver water, spread in dim blue haze of heat. Buckland Beacon crowned the distant height, and Holne Chase, deep hidden in forest leagues of summer green, rolled to Dart's windings in the vale below.

A mile south-east of Stoke Farm appears the little village of Holne, the theatre of activity of the various characters of *Demeter's Daughter:*

Holne village nestles upon a great hill and faces the morning. Deep lanes drop from the hamlet northerly, and from the south ascend other roads, to meet in the midst where the squat church tower looms amid many trees and dwellings, like a grey hen among her brood. Beside the ivy-clad fane runs a row of snug, bright cottages with red chimneys and faces of blue slate hung with roses and woodbine. Their little gardens, at this season, were bright with hollyhocks, spiring red and yellow, with larkspurs and orange lilies, with snapdragons and sweet williams. Hard by stood the Church House Inn, with deep, welcoming porch, to shield from sun or shower . . . Northerly rose a little copse of pine and fir for winter sheltering of the village.

The Cleaves' second son, Frank, enlists in the army to fight in the South African War; he is killed in action, and Alison, now living with her family in Holne, has a strong desire to revisit the little ruin of Venford Brook Cot:

In the low light after noon the side of Holne Ridge shone dim green and mottled brown, all laced with glittering water. Heavy autumnal rains had fallen for a fortnight, and countless fountains from unseen springs spread out a network of silver on the hills. They writhed and turned and mingled and flowed to the forests beneath. Over the dark crown of the ridge rolled great broken clouds of pale gold darkening to grey beneath their billowy breasts, while above them in deep October blue there shone the naked sun. The air was full of the murmur of many waters, and the rain-foundered Moor spread sere and sober, save where sunlight found the red brake fern and brightly burned thereon. Light roamed between the clouds presently as they ascended and hid the sun. Then through their caverns and precipices there fell delicate fans and brilliant pencils of sunshine that misted on the hills like golden gauze, softened all natural colour to a dreamy, melting radiance, concealed the stark flash of the waterfalls and, magically lifting the whole mountain, seemed to carry it further away and drown it in the incandescent vapours poured from the sky. Then, still mounting, the cloud masses cleared the sun and carried their sleights with them, so that the Moor flashed forth again, many-coloured and vivid, to the edge of the fertile lands below it . . . The mosaic of the fields flowed out and descended over the foothills of the higher wilderness, and their many-coloured enamel, where partitions barred the land from south to north, was ribbed raggedly, not by the innumerable hedges themselves, for their tones melted into the patchwork, but by the heavy shadows of these hedges, which flung black serrated lines regularly across the brightness of the mass.

As Alison leaves the place, she meets with her dead son's lover, Drusilla White; they walk towards Hexworthy, and sit together on the rocks of Combestone Tor:

The thinnest veil of haze spread between Combestone and the distance set over against it, but this vapour in opposition to the sun was no more than a warm, transparent film permeating the crystal air. The hour sang the colour triumph of the fern—the fern that swept and garmented the hills, like a tattered cloak of all reds and browns and russets. In the midst ran Dart, and one might note her invisible channel marked out by the flaming flanks of Sharp Tor and Mel Tor, and by the little fields of Rowbrook lying tame on the breast of the tawny wilderness. Far, far beyond, under the pallid blue of the east, swelled Buckland Beacon, and lifted many a wooded knoll; and there also, drowned in long leagues of evening light, the unconquerable glory of the fern gleamed out again with radiance a little diminished, yet sweetly auburn through the setting sunshine. Remote Rippon basked unclouded still, but other tors were wrapt in shadow, and towered wine-dark above the nearer splendours of flame . . .

There fell a rain shower on the hither side of the hill, and a great, molten iris blazed out beneath and hung in a wide, low arc against the hill. The innermost violet streak found some belated heather and made a sudden jewel of ineffable glory.

On a much later occasion, and in greatly differing weather conditions, Alison again visits Venford Brook Cot:

Looking down from the high Moor, earth unrolled and disentangled from the sulky pallor of the morning. Low clouds moved slowly off, and beneath them the world was changed and reduced to a new pattern whereon everything had dwindled. The snow-clad crofts huddled together and appeared to have black lines ruled between them instead of hedges; the upland wastes were shrunk to mere white sheets flung smoothly upon their planes and crumpled where granite broke the hill-tops. The tors had apparently diminished, and their real elevations were reduced by the sleight of the snow. Upon the far-flung pallor naked thorns stood like black imps humped up and bowed against the wind, and each main stem, whereon stuck the snow, made a white backbone for the black skeleton of the tree . . .

But the sky of vapours huddled down again; grey clouds hid the high ground and crept over the snow; white clouds in woolly billows passed through the valleys; while separate driving, dancing storms of fine snow swept from air to earth and blotted out leagues of the Moor in their fleeting embraces.

Alison, taking small heed of these things, held on her way, and presently the shadow of her old home rose grey amid the candid spaces of the desert round about it. She had felt a vague desire to come again to Venford Brook Cot, look round the dead chambers and concern herself with the past. She reached the place presently, while snow was falling, and then she forgot the weather, and sat down in the alcove of the kitchen window and buried her spirit in the vanished days . . . She gazed out of the window and started, for a storm centred just now in the cradle of Venford Brook, and she could see nothing but a whirl of dark, falling snowflakes that fled horizontally past on the wings of the north wind.

The story moves on to its tragic ending: Alison Cleave meets her death as a result of her husband's drunken attempt to drive their horse and trap through a ford on the East Dart when the river is in flood; Aaron Cleave eventually marries Lavinia Hatch, who keeps the 'shop of all sorts' at Holne.

Crossing's Guide: Ashburton District. Shorter Excursions 96, 97. The Moors of Holne and Buckfastleigh

O.S. Sheets: SX 76, SX 77, SX 66, SX 67

19

Children of Men

For *Children of Men*, the last of the Dartmoor Cycle novels, the scene portrayed is the valley of the river Avon and the town of South Brent—the home of William Crossing's youth and earlier years of his married life.

The story, sombre yet full of interest, concerns Jacob Bullstone, his wife Margery and their children; Margery's parents, Judith and Barlow Huxam, who keep a drapery business and post office in Brent; Adam Winter of Shipley Farm; and sundry minor characters.

The book opens with a prologue, which includes an extended description of the locality. Jacob Bullstone's imagined home, 'The Red House' (Brent Moor House) is now a ruin; and when I walked up the Avon valley from Shipley Bridge to visit it one sunny October morning I found the destruction to be so complete that it was impossible to reconstruct the house in imagination:

On a day in high summer the valley was full of light, and Auna River, her moorland journey ended, bowed under a plantation of pine and fir, then sparkled forth, to learn what welcome awaited her in the lower lands. Above the stream, easterly, a green hill towered against the sky; stunted thorns broke the sweep of the eagle fern, grey rock clitters spread, and cloud shadows drifted . . .

The stone-built home of the Bullstones—a granite house, red-tiled, basked under the hot sun in a hollow notch of Black Tor, while the river ran at its feet and a grass lawn spread before the windows. Above, on the hillside, were scooped terraces, growing cabbage and turnip, and beyond sprang the trees to the hill-crest westerly. Laurel and rhododendron made the slope snug; the kennels extended behind the house, while Bullstone's property spread to the other side of the river also, and there an acre or two had been cleared in rich alluvial. The link between Red House and the outlying cultivation was a bridge of pine logs thrown across Auna, where her banks rose high.

Everything about the place was neat, trim and stern. The hedges were clipped, the ground clean . . . There were no flower beds, no attempt to decorate house, garden or river. Indeed Auna was chastened by stone-built banks, until she passed southerly away to the rocks and rapids and the deep mossy pools.

Margery and Jacob, engaged to be married, spend a long day together on the Moor:

There came an August morning when Margery and Jacob made holiday and left Red House after breakfast to climb a famous hill some miles distant. Bullstone designed to visit his two farms on the way.

The road ran west and brought them through ferny lanes, that twined like a necklace beneath the border heights of the Moor; while strung upon them at intervals stood farmhouses in coomb and hollow, where streams from aloft descended to the vale. Round each dwelling spread orchard and meadow and dark tilth; behind them heaved grey hills, now brushed with the light of the ling . . .

At Bullstone [Bullhornstone] the farmhouse stood back from the lane at the summit of a steep hill, and everything was well ordered. The whitewashed front of the house shone in bright sunlight, only broken by the open windows and a great climbing shrub of buddleia, whose purple tassels fell over the porch. The roof was a Delabole slate, and behind the farm a rising copse straggled up to frontier ridges of Ugborough Beacon . . .

Their way fell sharply beside an orchard beyond Bullstone and descended into a valley, where through the green and tangled bottom ran Glaze Brook. The road crossed this little water by a bridge of one arch, where, through a thicket of overgrown laurel, hazel and alder, peered the grey ruin of Owley Mill. But now its wheel had vanished, its roof was gone and only shattered walls remained. Beside the bridge stood a tall pear tree—a ghost of a tree draped in grey lichens that fluttered like an old woman's hair from every branch. Then they breasted the hill beyond and presently reached Owley. The farm showed fewer marks of prosperity than Bullstone. Green mosses throve on its ancient thatch . . .

217

They ascended to Ugborough's crown of cairns, and presently sat at the summit, with the sun and wind in their faces and their backs against the stones.

Beneath them extended the mighty prospect of the South Hams, a mosaic of hamlet, forest and field, that seemed to be basking in the sun and stretching itself like a living thing. The varied colours of fallow and pasture were washed in air, brought together and made harmonious. Earth rolled hugely out to the dim sky-line of the sea, and westerly the Channel bit into the land, while easterly Devon rose and swept the great waters out of sight behind her cliffs and ridges. Knap and knoll ascended to break the coverlet of the fields; here woods darkened the land, and cloud shadows, vaster than they, hid a parish in their passing and swept over the sun-soaked expanses, to quicken the landscape with play of light and shadow . . .

Presently they set their faces northward and tramped Ugborough Moor, where their goal, Three Barrows, towered ahead among lesser hills . . . They still held north over wild lands with the heights rolling about them; then they reached the ancient Abbot's Way, running east and west, and met Auna's stream near Huntingdon Cross, a granite memorial from olden time . . . The Warren House stood before them under a ragged sycamore, and its squat, white face peered out upon the wilderness from under a black, tar-pitched roof. The rabbit warrens spread on either hand and the dwelling lay in the protection of a tumulus that piled up to the northward . . .

Then a good thing happened, for in the shaking moss, where a spring was born and bubbled up out of the granite, Jacob marked a piece of bog heather, white as snow . . .

So they came home together beside the river.

Margery and Jacob, now married and with a young family, are beset by difficulty and misunderstanding. They walk together in a favourite spot:

Above the kennels, Auna River wound through a deep place, where the Moor descended to her margins and only a fisherman's path ran through the brake fern. Between the steep and verdant banks the waters came, and upon the hills round about flashed gems of golden green, where springs broke out of the granite and fell from mossy cradles to the valley. Here and there the water-side opened on green spaces cropped close by the rabbits, and at intervals a little beach of pebble and sand extended by the shallows of the stream. Now the river spread her arms to make an islet, where grey sallows grew and the woodrush; and sometimes she narrowed to a glimmering cleft, then by a waterfall leapt forward again into the light. A warm evening glow lay upon the eastern hill, and each isolated stone or tree burnt with sunset brightness; but the valley was in shadow, very cool after the heat of a late August day.

Many vicissitudes overtake Jacob Bullstone; his wife dies in distressing circumstances; his family have now grown up; and he determines to leave the Red House and take up residence at the lonely and now deserted Huntingdon Warren House with his daughter Auna, who is so like his dead wife, Margery. The book ends with Auna, who has been on a visit to a relative, meeting Jacob on the Moor, where he has been waiting for her, and walking home to Huntingdon together:

Far beneath him the sun fires lingered over the pavilions of a larch grove and warmed the young green to gold. The untiring cuckoo called awhile, then grew silent as twilight stole delicately over all things and detail died . . .

So they went up together, hand in hand, through the cool curtain of dusk; with fret of light and shadow all vanished for that day. They went up speaking very few words into the deepening gloom of night, while on the sky glimmered the stars again, and in the grass a glowworm. From his stony place among the fern, churn-owl throbbed a lullaby for the whole drowsy earth; and he touched their human hearts, old and young, with the mystery of his music—the mystery of all living songs that waken when the rest of the world is going to sleep. The two notes whirred on, rising and falling, fainting and trembling out again.

Then the white face of Huntingdon looked upon them.

Crossing's Guide: Brent and Ivybridge District. Excursions 29, 30. Shorter Excursions 106, 111, 112

O.S. Sheet: SX 66

20
Brunel's Tower

Although *Brunel's Tower* was included in the canon of the Dartmoor Cycle, it is actually one of a series of Eden Phillpotts's novels having a background of industrial activity, and has less association with Dartmoor than the other books of the Cycle. It is concerned with pottery and the pottery works imagined as being set up by George Easterbrook in the village of Kingskerswell, near Newton Abbot. The tower in question was a relic of Isambard Kingdom Brunel's short-lived experiment, in 1847, with atmospheric power as a means of propulsion on the South Devon Railway—later a part of the Great Western Railway system. The main venue of *Brunel's Tower*, therefore, does not fall within the scope of this survey; nevertheless, certain excursions are made on to the Moor, and these provide pictures of an area not otherwise covered by the Cycle.

Harvey Porter, a runaway lad who has become a useful member of Easterbrook's pottery works, visits the clay works in the valley of the river Erme with a competitor of Easterbrook, Wilberforce Todd, and his daughter Nellie:

Through the hamlet of Cornwood they drove, past a graceful cross that lifted beneath an oak; and then onward by hill and dale and farmstead, by water-meadows and streamlets, through woods and pastures, their road extended—so lonely, that it was grass-grown in places. The lanes—survivals of old pack-horse tracks—had burrowed deeply into the hills, and often the subjacent lands were far higher than the road. Deep set in green lay their route, under hedges of hazel and polled oak, while the sides of it glistened with the green of ferns and sparkled with many flowers . . . Mr. Todd

220

pointed out the saliences of the land. 'Yonder lie Shell Top and Pen Beacon', he said, pointing to the purple hills. 'That's Dartmoor above us, and the place is rich in potter's treasures' . . .

Beside Harford Bridge they sat awhile, where a feathery ash hung her foliage over the grey span and the stream purred and tumbled beneath—all black and silver among the moss-clad boulders. Ivy climbed the bridge and little ferns thronged the courses of the stones . . .

The stream fell beneath the bridge in two spouts of crystal, where a rock divided it. Then the foaming torrents mingled again at a pool with many a flash and ripple, grew peaceful once more, and slid away under oily dimples, to reflect the sky and the clouds, the banks and the rocks that rose beside the river. The young man and woman sat where music-making Erme swept to the wooded valley beneath, and watched a kingfisher flash down-stream . . .

They tramped the bank of the river northward, and presently climbed where a low tor stood on the western bank. Before them rolled the desert to the heights of Shell Top and Pen Beacon and the uplifted levels of Harford Moor. Here man had scratched the earth, and low white mounds began to lift—the beginning of a new enterprise. Its success remained in doubt; but far beneath it, where Erme wound away into the enfolding hills, and where the shoulders of the heights descended to her green margins, old clay-workings appeared, and lofty wheels and a great chimney-stack arose beside ancient rubble-mounds . . .

They looked aloft above the works to where feathers of steam billowed on Harford Moor, and a tiny engine, dwarfed to the size of a fly, crept over the waste and drew half a dozen little trucks behind it.

Harvey Porter, having left Easterbrooks and now working at Erme Clay-Pits, treats as a sanctuary Piles Wood, 'a grove of most venerable trees that thronged the eastern bank of Erme a mile above the clay-pit':

The trees in Piles Wood were dwarf, intimate things, and he felt as though he knew some of them personally. Their shoulders, draped in moss and fern, stood sometimes little higher than his own. There were comfortable, secret resting-places and sunny

221

stones among them. The knowledge of these he shared with the fox and the serpent. And for music, Erme purred at hand, or high above, on Harford Moor, the kine bellowed, and the sheep-bell uttered a muffled jangle.

Harvey sets off on a fishing expedition up the Erme:

He went his way soon after dawn, considered the weather, which was doubtful, and presently, while yet the dew was on the herbage and the cloudy sun low in the east, began his fishing . . .

He worked industriously down to Piles Wood again, and the sun, in doubt till now, burst forth brilliantly after noon, set the air quivering over the leagues of the Moor, and drove the cattle up on to the heights. They stood like graven beasts on lofty points outlined against the sky. Beneath, at water's edge, the heat grew intense, and the flies began to torment the fisherman. He wound up his line, therefore, and sought the wood where he had left his food and an old creel. Now, in a shady nook, with the lady-fern about him, and alone save for long-legged spiders that ran over his legs, and little flies that hung like golden beads in the sunlight overhead, he sat under the whisper of the oak-trees. To the south, a mile lower down the valley, he could see the blaze of the clay hillocks—very white under the summer sun.

A works outing from Easterbrooks visits Harford, and Porter meets some of his old colleagues as they inspect the clay works there: he then sets off over the Moor to meet his former employer at the clay-pit on Harford Moor. A thunderstorm ensues, and, on the little light railway connecting the pits with Harford, Porter saves Easterbrook from an approaching locomotive and trucks; he, however, is struck by the engine and loses his life:

The sky grew strange, and scarcely a grass-blade moved at earth-level, but overhead there was motion of vapour. From far up the valley, beneath the heavy darkness that shrouded it, came a strange sound—'the calling of the cleeves'. Porter knew that it foretold a change of weather. Before him whips of cloud, like quivering thongs, flew up over the head of the hill. The sun, now westering, grew sickly, choked with translucent and fulvous vapours. They robbed the earth beneath them of light and heat, and banished all detail from the distance. Forests and meadows, and the wide-wayed valleys to south and west, sulked in one great welter of purple. The clouds massed and herded as though at a muster; but the storm-centre was off the Moor, and tended to the south-east. Aloft, low ridges of grey mist hurried along the side of the hills, and the wind wakened again and whimpered fitfully. Between its silences, the river, far below him now, sang a new song and the cleeves still called. An air of watchfulness haunted the waste. The weather had wholly changed in an hour, as often it will in these high places, and before the young man could ascend another mile, the mist was upon him, brushing his hot cheek with its cool fingers. Far away a knotted ribbon of lightning fell upon the sooty distance . . . A nearer flash of lightning fell in a double streamer, diamond bright, ten miles away, and the thunder followed it more noisily than before . . .

Regardless of the dark garment of the thunderstorm that trailed swiftly across the sky from Ugborough Moor, Porter pushed forward up the hill, crossed a clay-drain wherein the liquid clay ran down from the moor to the valley beneath, and presently reached the railway which ran between Sharp Tor and Three Barrows—a height crowned with triple cairns. Here ran a length of double line where the trains passed each other, and a shed of corrugated iron stood beside the railway.

No sign of living marked the place. A few carrion crows croaked uneasily before the storm, and, under the gathering darkness the line, which ran on rubble from the clay-quarries aloft, stared stark, like a thread of wool drawn zig-zag through the gloom of the heath. Now the storm swept down from the north, and the lightning fell on Three Barrows . . .

The storm itself had passed and a cool, fresh wind arose from the east, while a sky of silvery cirri gave place to the blue again.

Crossing's Guide: Brent and Ivybridge District. Excursions 32, 33

O.S. Sheet: SX 66

NOTE ON REFERENCE LISTS

In place of the usual index, there follow two reference lists, which it is hoped the reader will find helpful: (a) a list of the topographical features and place-names appearing in the Dartmoor Cycle novels, together with their respective four-figure Ordnance Survey map references; (b) a dictionary of the characters appearing in the Dartmoor Cycle, grouped under book title, including brief descriptions and domiciles.

For the locations of domiciles, reference should be made to the list of topographical features and place-names.

Topographical features receiving only incidental mention have in some cases been omitted from the list.

List of Topographical Features and Place-Names

(WITH ORDNANCE SURVEY MAP REFERENCES)

WIDECOMBE FAIR

Widecombe	71/76	East Webburn River	72/77
St Pancras, Widecombe	71/76	Hameldown (Hameldon)	71/79
Old Inn, Widecombe	71/76	Grimspound	70/80
The Rugglestone	72/76	Honeybag Tor	72/78
Rugglestone Inn	72/76	Chinkwell Tor	72/78
Southcombe Farm	71/76	Bel Tor	72/77
Kingshead Farm	71/77	Bonehill Rocks	73/77
Coombe ('Woodhayes')	71/77	Bonehill Farm	72/77
Venton	72/76	Hemsworthy	
Chittleford	72/75	(Hennesbury) Gate	74/76
Higher Dunstone	71/75	Seven Lords' Lands	74/76
Lower Dunstone	71/75	Whittaburrow	73/75
Tunhill Farm	72/75	Hay (Hey) Tor	75/77
Blackslade Farm	72/75		

THE THIEF OF VIRTUE

Postbridge	65/79	South Teign River	67/85
General Store and P.O.,		Broad Down	62/80
Postbridge	65/79	Arch (Archerton) Tor	63/78
Hartland Tor	64/79	Bellever (Bellaford) Tor	64/76
Hartland Farm	64/79	West Dart River	61/78
East Dart River	64/79	Brown's House (ruin)	61/79
Merripit Hill	65/80	Crow Tor	60/78
Stannon Farm	65/80	Wistman's Wood	61/77
Warren House Inn	67/80	Saracen's Head Inn—	
Grey Wethers (stone		later Two Bridges	
circles)	63/83	Hotel ('Ring o' Bells')	60/75
Sittaford (Siddaford) Tor	63/83	Fur Tor	58/83
Teign Head Farm	63/84	River Tavy	56/83

225

THE RIVER

Two Bridges	60/75	River Cowsic	60/75
Saracen's Head Inn—		Devil's Tor	59/79
later Two Bridges		Cut Hill	59/82
Hotel ('Ring o' Bells')	60/75	Rough (Row) Tor	60/79
West Dart River	61/78	Crow Tor	60/78
Crockern Tor	61/75	Bellever (Bellaford) Tor	64/76
Wistman's Wood	61/77	Laughter (Laugh) Tor	65/75
Wistman's Warren	61/77	Prince Hall	62/74
Warrener's hut (site)	61/77	Prince Hall Avenue	
Longaford Tor	61/77	entrance (site of	
Higher White Tor	61/78	Chugg's cottage)	62/74
Cherrybrook	62/77	Postbridge	65/79
Powder Mills ('Cross		Pixies' Holt	66/73
Ways') Farm	62/76	Dartmeet	67/73
Smith Hill		Eagle Rock	72/72
('Cherrybrook') Farm	63/75	Princetown	58/73
Beardown ('Bray') Farm	60/75	Moretonhampstead	75/86
Beardown Lodge (Mark		Ashburton	75/69
Trout's cottage at)	60/75	Cross Ways	
Beardown (Bair Down)		Powder Mills	62/76
Hill	60/76	Cherrybrook	62/77
Beardown (Bair Down)			
Tors	60/77	The Judge's Chair	
Beardown (Bair Down)		Laughter Tor	65/75
Man	59/79	Dunnabridge Pound	64/74

MISER'S MONEY

White Works	61/71	Nun's Cross Farm	60/69
Black Houses	61/71	North Hessary Tor	57/74
River Swincombe	63/72	South Hessary Tor	59/72
Strane River	61/71	Tor Royal	60/73
Count House (ruin)		Princetown	58/73
('Strane Steps')	61/71	Prince Hall	62/74
Cater's Beam	63/69	Two Bridges	60/75
Fox Tor Mire	61/70	Devil's Bridge	58/72
Fox Tor Farm (ruin)	62/70	Moor Shop	51/74
Childe's Tomb	62/70	Staple Tors	54/75
Nun's (Siward's) Cross	60/69	Yelverton	51/67

LIST OF TOPOGRAPHICAL FEATURES AND PLACE-NAMES

THE VIRGIN IN JUDGMENT

Sheep's Tor	56/68	Cramber Tor	58/71
Sheepstor	56/67	Crazywell Pool	58/70
Bull Ring, Sheepstor	56/67	Norsworthy Bridge	56/69
Ringmoor Down	56/66	Down Tor	58/69
Yennadon Down	54/68	Combeshead Tor	58/68
River Meavy	53/67	Combeshead Farm (ruin)	58/68
Leather (Lether) Tor	56/70	Eylesbarrow	59/68
Sharpitor (Sharp Tor)	55/70	Ditsworthy Warren	58/67
Black Tor	57/71	River Plym	56/65
Hart Tor (Harter)	58/73	Shell Top	59/63
Dean Combe		Pen Beacon	59/62
(Dennycombe)	58/68		

THE THREE BROTHERS

Shaugh Prior	54/63	Collard Tor Cottage	
White Thorn Inn,		('Hawk House')	55/62
Shaugh	54/63	Coldstone Farm	55/61
St Edward's, Shaugh	54/63	Dewerstone	53/63
Cadover (Cadworthy)		North Wood	54/63
Bridge	55/64	River Plym	56/65
Cadworthy Farm	54/64	Trowlesworthy Warren	56/64
Nethershaw		Great Trowlesworthy Tor	57/64
('Undershaugh') Farm	53/62	Pen Beacon	59/62
Shaugh Bridge	53/63	Blackaton	
Wigford Down	54/64	(St Rumon's) Cross	57/63
Shaugh Moor	55/63	Devil's Bridge	58/72
Hen Tor	59/65	Princetown	58/73
Hawk Tor	55/62	Cornwood	60/59

THE MOTHER

Merivale	54/75	Windystone	53/74
Dartmoor Inn, Merivale		Moorshop	51/74
('The Jolly Huntsmen')	54/75	Cox (Cock's) Tor	53/76
Vixen Tor	54/74	Roos (Roose) Tor	54/76
Vixen Tor Farm	54/74	Staple Tors	54/75
River Walkham (Walla)	55/75	Shillapark ('Stone Park')	55/75
Sampford Spiney	53/72	Langstone Moor	55/78
Ward Bridge	54/72	Lone Stones (stone circle)	55/78
Pew (Pu) Tor	53/73	Great Mis Tor	56/76
Feather Tor	53/74	King Tor	55/73

THE WHIRLWIND

Lydford	50/84	Amicombe Hill	57/86
St Petrock's, Lydford	50/84	Hunt (Hunter) Tor	55/87
Lydford Castle	50/84	Watern (Wattern) Oke	56/83
Castle Inn, Lydford	50/84	Ger Tor	54/83
White Hill	53/83	River Tavy	54/82
Redford ('Ruddyford')		Tavy Cleave	55/83
Farm	53/83	River Lyd	52/84
Great Links Tor	55/86	Kit's—or Skit—Steps	51/84
Rattlebrook	55/85	Brat (Bra) Tor	54/85
Dunnagoat	55/86	Doe Tor	54/84

THE PORTREEVE

Bridestowe		Black Tor	56/89
(Bridgetstowe)	51/89	Black Tor Copse	56/89
St Bridget's, Bridestowe	51/89	Fordsland Ledge	57/88
Royal Oak Inn,		Lints Tor	58/87
Bridestowe	51/89	Dinger Tor	58/88
Sourton	53/90	Amicombe Hill	57/86
Corn Ridge	55/89	Blackavon Brook	59/89
Shilstone Tor	55/89	Curtory (Curters)	
Meldon Viaduct	56/92	Clitters	59/89
Higher Bowden Farm	55/91	High Willhayes	58/89
South Down	55/91	Yes Tor	58/90
Fishcombe Head Water	56/91	Cranmere Pool	60/85
West Okement River	57/88	Okehampton	58/95
Homerton Hill	56/90	Halstock Hill	60/93

THE SECRET WOMAN

Belstone	61/93	East Okement ('Oke')	
St Mary's, Belstone	61/93	River	60/92
River Taw	61/91	East Okement ('Harter')	
Belstone Tors	61/92	Farm	60/91
Watchet Hill	61/93	Okehampton	58/95
Watchet Hill Cottage		Taw Marsh	61/90
('Farm')	61/93	Row (Rough) Tor	59/91
Cullever Steps	60/92	Steeperton Tor	61/88
Nine Stones (stone circle)	61/92	Mill Tor (West)	58/90
Halstock Hill	60/93	Yes Tor	58/90
Halstock Wood	60/93	Cosdon Beacon	63/91
		Church Hill Cross	62/96

THE BEACON

Cosdon (O.S. Cawsand)		Spitlar Farm ('North	
Beacon	63/91	Combe Farm')	66/95
Raybarrow Pool	63/90	South Tawton Common	64/91
South Zeal	65/93	Taw Green	65/96
Oxenham Arms, South		Clannaborough Farm	66/91
Zeal	65/93	River Taw	61/91
South Tawton	65/94	Belstone Tors	61/92
St Andrew's, South		Steeperton Tor	61/88
Tawton	65/94	Okehampton	58/95
Seven Stars Inn, South		Yeoford	65/96
Tawton	65/94		

SONS OF THE MORNING

Gidleigh ('Little Silver')	67/88	East Dart River	62/81
Berrydown ('Beardown')	66/87	Watern Tor	62/86
Scor Hill Down	65/87	Cranmere Pool	60/85
Scor Hill Circle (stone		Great Kneeset	58/85
circle)	65/87	Little Kneeset	58/84
Chagford	70/87	Cut Hill	59/82
River Teign	70/88	Fur Tor	58/83
Kes Tor	66/86	Cosdon Beacon	63/91
Sittaford Tor	63/83		

CHILDREN OF THE MIST

Chagford	70/87	Metherall ('Newtake')	
Rushford Bridge	70/88	Farm	67/83
Rushford Mill Farm		Scor Hill Down	65/87
('Monk's Barton')	70/88	Watern Tor	62/86
River Teign	70/88	Cranmere Pool	60/85
Pixies' Parlour (Combe		Wallabrook	63/87
Farm)	72/89	Steeperton Tor	61/88
Whiddon Park	72/89	Taw Marsh	61/90
Natterdown	70/86	Cosdon Beacon	63/91
Middledown (Meldon		Belstone Tors	61/92
Hill)	69/86	Oke Tor	61/89
Batworthy	66/86	East Okement River	60/92

LIST OF TOPOGRAPHICAL FEATURES AND PLACE-NAMES

THE FOREST ON THE HILL

Ilsington	78/76	Rippon Tor	74/75
Yarner Wood	77/78	Middlecott	78/76
Dury, Postbridge	66/77	Hameldown	70/80
Hay (Hey) Tor	75/77	Grimspound	70/80

ORPHAN DINAH

Buckland in the Moor	72/73	Ashburton	75/69
St Peter's, Buckland	72/73	New Bridge, Dart	71/71
Lower Town	71/72	Lizwell Wood	71/74
Buckland Beacon	73/73	Hay (Hey) Tor	75/77
Beacon ('Falcon') Farm	73/72	Dean (Dene) Moor	67/65
Hazel Tor (Ausewell		Huntingdon	
Rocks)	73/71	('Shepherd's') Cross	66/66
Rippon Tor	74/75		

DEMETER'S DAUGHTER

Holne	70/69	Yar Tor	67/74
Church House Inn,		Sharp Tor	68/72
Holne	70/69	Bel Tor	69/72
Holne Moor	66/70	Mel Tor	69/72
Holne Ridge	66/69	Rowbrook	68/72
River Dart	67/72	Holne Chase	71/71
Rippon Tor	74/75	Buckland Beacon	73/73
Stoke Farm	69/70	Postbridge	65/79
Venford Brook	68/71	Merripit	65/79
Combestone Tor	67/71	Bellever (Bellaford) Farm	65/77

CHILDREN OF MEN

South Brent	69/60	Owley	67/59
Shipley Bridge	68/62	Glaze Brook	67/59
Shipley Farm	68/62	Ugborough Beacon	66/59
Shipley Tor	68/63	Three Barrows	65/62
River Avon (Auna)	68/61	Abbot's Way	67/65
Brent Moor House (ruin)		Huntingdon Cross	66/66
('Red House')	68/63	Huntingdon Warren	
Black Tor	68/63	House	66/66
Bullhornstone (Bullstone)		Ryder's Hill	65/69
Farm	67/60		

230

BRUNEL'S TOWER

River Erme	64/62	Shell Top	59/63
Erme Clay Pits	62/66	Pen Beacon	59/62
Piles Copse	64/62	Cornwood	60/59
Ugborough Moor	65/62	Harford	63/59
Sharp Tor	64/61	Harford Moor	64/63
Three Barrows	65/62		

(*Note* The narrative of this book is mainly set at Kingskerswell, Newton Abbot)

Dictionary of Characters

CHILDREN OF THE MIST (1898)

Bassett, Peter	Farm worker
Blanchard, Will (I)	Rushford Bridge, Chagford, under water-bailiff; subsequently 'Newtake', farmer, *m* Phoebe Lyddon
Blanchard, Damaris	Mother of Will Blanchard (I)
Blanchard, Chris	Sister of Will Blanchard (I), *m* Martin Grimbal
Blanchard, Phoebe	See Lyddon, Phoebe
Blanchard, Tim	Son of Chris Blanchard and Clement Hicks
Blanchard, Will (II)	Son of Will and Phoebe Blanchard
Blee, Billy	'Monk's Barton', Miller Lyddon's right-hand man
Bonus, Sam	'Newtake', farm worker
Chapple, Mr	Chagford, village patriarch
Chown, Abraham	Chagford, police-officer
Chown, Ted	'Newtake', farm worker
Coomstock, Mary	Chagford, widowed aunt of Clement Hicks
Coomstock, Charles	Chagford, nephew of Mary Coomstock
Ford, Joel	Newton Abbot, attorney
Grimbal, John	Chagford, diamond miner, retired
Grimbal, Martin	Brother of John Grimbal, *m* Chris Blanchard
Hicks, Clement	Chagford, bee-keeper
Hicks, Mrs	Mother of Clement Hicks
Lezzard, Gaffer	Chagford, village patriarch
Lyddon, Vincent	'Monk's Barton', Chagford, miller
Lyddon, Phoebe	Daughter of Vincent Lyddon, *m* Will Blanchard (I)
Parsons, Dr	Chagford, medical practitioner

Shorto-Champernowne, Rev James	Chagford, vicar
Tremayne, Major	Okehampton Camp, artillery officer
Vogwell, Mr	Duchy of Cornwall's representative

SONS OF THE MORNING (1900)

Ash, Churdles	'Bear Down' Farm, farm worker
Bates, Tommy	'Bear Down' Farm, farm worker
Brimblecombe, Noah	'Little Silver', sexton
Brimblecombe, Mrs	Wife of Noah Brimblecombe
Clack, Dr Courteney	Medical practitioner
Collins, Henry	'Bear Down' Farm, farm worker
Cramphorn, Jonah	'Bear Down' Farm, head man
Cramphorn, Sally Cramphorn, Margery	} Daughters of Jonah Cramphorn
Endicott, Honor	'Bear Down' Farm, farmer, m (i) Myles Stapledon (ii) Christopher Yeoland
Endicott, Mark	Bachelor uncle of Honor Endicott
Grepe, Charity (Cherry)	'Little Silver', wise woman
Libby, Gregory	'Little Silver', hedge tacker
Loveys, Mrs	'Bear Down' Farm, housekeeper, widow
Mathers, Dr	Medical practitioner, successor to Dr Clack
Pinsent, Samuel	'Bear Down' Farm, farm worker
Scobel, Mr	'Little Silver', vicar
Stapledon, Myles	Tavistock, kinsman of and m Honor Endicott (also referred to in *The River*, Book I, Chap. IV)
Stapledon, Honor	See Endicott, Honor
Yeoland, Christopher	'Godleigh Manor', landowner, m Honor Stapledon
Yeoland, Honor	See Endicott, Honor

THE RIVER (1902)

Axworthy, Albert	'Bray' Farm, farm worker
Barker, John	Two Bridges, hedge tacker
Bradridge, Betty	'Ring o' Bells', landlady, widow
Bradridge, Hannah	Daughter of Betty Bradridge, m Timothy Oldrieve

Chugg, Merryweather	Prince Hall Lodge, water-bailiff
Chugg, Mrs	Wife of Merryweather Chugg
Chugg, Jenny	Daughter of Merryweather Chugg
Delve, Samuel	Two Bridges, farm worker
Edgecombe, Nicholas	Wistman's Wood, warrener (also referred to in *The Thief of Virtue*, Book IV, Chaps. IX and XVI; and in *Sons of the Morning*, Book III, Chap. XII)
Light, Dr	Princetown, medical practitioner
Merle, Mrs	'Bray' Farm, farmer, widow
Merle, Mary	Daughter of Mrs Merle
Merle, Teddy	Son of Mrs Merle
Oldreive, Timothy	'Cherrybrook' Farm, farmer, *m* Hannah Bradridge
Oldreive, Hannah	See Bradridge, Hannah
Sage, Mrs	'Ring o' Bells', mother of Betty Bradridge
Scobhull, Sorrow	Two Bridges, stonebreaker; 'Cherrybrook' Farm, farm worker
Snow, Mr	'Cross Ways' Farm, farmer
Snow, Mrs	Wife of Mr Snow
Trout, Mark	'Ring o' Bells, stableman; 'Bray' Farm, farm worker
Trout, Tom	
Trout, Rupert	
Trout, Jane	Children of Mark Trout
Trout, Ethel	(11 children in all)
Trout, Minnie	
Trout, Albert Victor	
Vosper, Jacob	'Bray' Farm, head man
Wade, Walter	Two Bridges, farm worker
Wood, Jane	'Ring o' Bells', maid to Betty Bradridge

THE SECRET WOMAN (1905)

Arscott, William	Belstone granite works, owner
Bloom, Joshua	Belstone, quarry worker
Hannaford, Toby	'Hearty Welcome', Belstone, landlord
Haycraft, Mrs	Watchett Hill Farm

234

Lethbridge, Paul	Watchett Hill Farm, farm boy
Pearn, Ned	Belstone, stone cutter
Redvers, Anthony	'Harter' Farm, farmer
Redvers, Ann	Wife of Anthony Redvers
Redvers, Jesse Redvers, Michael }	Sons of Anthony and Ann Redvers
Tapp, Nathaniel	'Harter' Farm, farm worker
Tapp, Sarah	Wife of Nathaniel Tapp
Westaway, Joseph	Watchett Hill Farm, farmer
Westaway, Barbara Westaway, Salome }	Daughters of Joseph Westaway

THE PORTREEVE (1906)

Ball, John Ball, Thomas }	Cousins of Abel Pierce
Barkell, Abner	Meldon, retired railway worker
Barkell, Richard	Railway signalman (LSWR), son of Abner Barkell
Horn, Alexander	Bowden Farm, farmer
Horn, Mrs	Wife of Alexander Horn
Horn, Primrose	Daughter of Alexander Horn, *m* Orlando Slanning
Perryman, Ned	Sourton, shepherd
Perryman, Jane	Granddaughter of Ned Perryman
Pierce, Abel	Homerton Hill, general worker, *m* Ilet Yelland
Pierce, Henny	Widowed mother of Abel Pierce
Pierce, Ilet	See Yelland, Ilet
Pierce, Henny Ilet	Daughter of Abel and Ilet Pierce
Slanning, Orlando	Bridgetstowe, miller's son, Master of North Devon Foxhounds, *m* Primrose Horn
Slanning, Primrose	See Horn, Primrose
Sim, Mr	Bridgetstowe, curate
Thatcher, Mr	Okehampton, landowner
Wolferstan, Dod	Bridgetstowe, market gardener, vicar's churchwarden and Portreeve, *m* Ilet Pierce

235

Wolferstan, Ilet	See Yelland, Ilet
Yelland, Ilet	Sourton, *m* (i) Abel Pierce (ii) Dod Wolferstan
Yelland, Susan	Aunt of Ilet Yelland

THE WHIRLWIND (1907)

Agg, Walter	'Ruddyford', farm worker
Brendon, Daniel	'Ruddyford', cattleman, *m* Sarah Jane Friend
Brendon, Sarah Jane	See Friend, Sarah Jane
Brendon, Gregory Daniel	Son of Daniel and Sarah Jane Brendon
Churchward, Adam	Lydford, schoolmaster
Churchward, William	Son of Adam Churchward
Churchward, Mary	Daughter of Adam Churchward, *m* Jarrett Weekes
Friend, Gregory	Dunnagoat, caretaker Amicombe Peat Works
Friend, Sarah Jane	Daughter of Gregory Friend, *m* Daniel Brendon
Huggins, Valentine	Lydford, oldest inhabitant
Lethbridge, Peter	'Ruddyford', farm worker
Norseman, Henry	Lydford, factor and churchwarden
Pearn, Noah	Lydford, Castle Inn, landlord
Prout, John	'Ruddyford', head man
Prout, Tabitha	Sister of John Prout
Spry, Nathaniel	Lydford, postmaster
"Susan"	Lydford, maid to Hephzibah Weekes, surname unknown
Tapson, Joe	'Ruddyford', ploughman
Taverner, Jacob	Lydford, miller
Weekes, Philip	Lydford, huckster
Weekes, Hephzibah	Wife of Philip Weekes
Weekes, Jarrett	Son of Philip and Hephzibah Weekes, Lydford Castle keeper, *m* Mary Churchward
Weekes, Mary	See Churchward, Mary
Woodrow, Hilary	'Ruddyford', farmer

THE MOTHER (1908)

Bachelor, Inspector	Police-officer
Bolt, Samuel	Merivale, steam-roller driver, *m* Jill Wickett
Bolt, Rachel	Widowed mother of Samuel Bolt
Bolt, Jill	See Wickett, Jill
Brown, Arthur	Sampford Spiney, schoolmaster, *m* Lizzie Pomeroy
Cawker, William ('Moleskin')	Merivale, poacher
Cawker, Mrs	Wife of William Cawker
Cawker, Mary	Daughter of William Cawker, *m* Rupert Johnson
Codd, Emmanuel	Vixen Tor Farm, farm worker
Johnson, Rupert	Vixen Tor Farm, farm worker, *m* Mary Cawker
Johnson, Mary	See Cawker, Mary
'Moleskin'	See Cawker, William
Northmore, Matthew	'Stone Park', farmer
Pomeroy, Avisa	Vixen Tor Farm, widow
Pomeroy, Ives	Son of Avisa Pomeroy, *m* Ruth Rendle
Pomeroy, Lizzie	Daughter of Avisa Pomeroy, *m* Arthur Brown
Pomeroy, Jane	Widowed mother of Avisa Pomeroy
Pomeroy, Ruth	See Rendle, Ruth
Rendle, Ruth	Merivale, cousin of the brothers Toop, barmaid at 'The Jolly Huntsmen', *m* Ives Pomeroy
Toop, Peter	Publican, undertaker ⎫ Brothers, proprietors of 'The
Toop, Joel	Publican, pigs and poultry ⎬ Jolly Huntsmen'
Warren, Nicholas	Police-officer
Wickett, Jill	Merivale, *m* Samuel Bolt

237

THE VIRGIN IN JUDGMENT (1908)

Bowden, Elias	Ditsworthy Warren, warrener and farmer
Bowden, Sarah	Wife of Elias Bowden
Bowden, David	*m* Margaret Stanbury
Bowden, Joshua	
Bowden, Sophia	Widow, married name unknown
Bowden, Rhoda	
Bowden, Dorcas	*m* William Screech
Bowden, Wellington	
Bowden, Napoleon	
Bowden, Samson	
Bowden, Richard	

Children of Elias and Sarah Bowden

Bowden, Margaret	See Stanbury, Margaret
Crocker, Bartley	Sheepstor, smallholder
Crocker, Nanny	Widowed mother of Bartley Crocker
Elford, Mr	Good-a-Meavy, farmer
Fogo, 'Frosty-faced'	London, prize-fighting sportsman
Mattacott, Timothy	Sheepstor, farm worker
Maunder, Ernest	Sheepstor, police-officer
Merle, Parson	Sheepstor, vicar
Moses, Job	Sheepstor, shoemaker and vicar's churchwarden
Saunders, Susan	Sheepstor, widowed aunt of Bartley Crocker
Screech, William (Billy)	Lowery, *m* Dorcas Bowden
Screech, Eliza	Widowed mother of William Screech
Screech, Dorcas	See Bowden, Dorcas
Shillabeer, Reuben	Sheepstor, 'Corner House', landlord
Snell, Simon	Lowery, leat man
Stanbury, Bartholomew	Coombeshead, farmer
Stanbury, Constance	Wife of Bartholomew Stanbury
Stanbury, Bart	
Stanbury, Margaret	*m* David Bowden

Children of Bartholomew and Constance Stanbury

West, Jane	Norsworthy, courted by Bart Stanbury and Timothy Mattacott

THE THREE BROTHERS (1909)

Baskerville, Humphrey (I)	'Hawk House', farmer (also referred to in *The Thief of Virtue*, Book I, Chap. XI)
Baskerville, Mark	Son of Humphrey Baskerville I (also referred to in *The Thief of Virtue*, Book II, Chap. V)
Baskerville, Nathan (I)	Shaugh Prior, White Thorn Inn, landlord, widower, brother of Humphrey Baskerville (I)
Baskerville, Vivian	Cadworthy Farm, farmer, brother of Humphrey Baskerville (I)
Baskerville, Hester	Wife of Vivian Baskerville
Baskerville, Ned	
Baskerville, Rupert	*m* Milly Luscombe
Baskerville, Nathan (II)	Sailor
Baskerville, May	
Baskerville, Polly	*m* Nicholas Bassett
Baskerville, Humphrey (II)	

Children of Vivian and Hester Baskerville

Baskerville, Milly	See Luscombe, Milly
Bassett, Nicholas	*m* Polly Baskerville
Bassett, Polly	See Baskerville, Polly
Elford, Abraham	Shaugh Prior, White Thorn Inn, landlord, successor to Nathan Baskerville (I)
Gollop, Thomas	Shaugh Prior, parish clerk and sexton
Gollop, Eliza	Sister of Thomas Gollop
Hacker, Susan	'Hawk House', widowed housekeeper to Humphrey Baskerville (I)
Head, Jack	Trowlesworthy Farm, head man
Lintern, Priscilla	'Undershaw' Farm, farmer
Lintern, Heathman	
Lintern, Cora	
Lintern, Phyllis	

Children of Priscilla Lintern and Nathan Baskerville (I)

Luscombe, Saul	Trowlesworthy Farm, farmer
Luscombe, Milly	Niece of Saul Luscombe, *m* Rupert Baskerville
Masterman, Rev Dennis	Shaugh Prior, vicar
Masterman, Alice	Sister of Dennis Masterman

Voysey, Joseph	Shaugh Prior, vicarage gardener
Waite, Timothy	Coldstone Farm, farmer

THE THIEF OF VIRTUE (1910)

Birdwood, Henry	Teign Head Farm, shepherd
Coaker, James	Stannon Farm, farm worker
Crymes, Quinton	Stannon Farm, farmer
Crymes, Gertrude	Wife of Quinton Crymes
Crymes, Maggie	⎫ Children of
Crymes, Jackie	⎬ Quinton and
Crymes, Samuel	⎪ Gertrude
Crymes, Minnie	*m* Martin Ouldsbroom ⎭ Crymes
Crymes, Unity	Sister of Quinton Crymes, *m* Philip Ouldsbroom
Culme, Peter	Postbridge, water keeper
Dury, Betty	Postbridge, washerwoman and sick nurse
French, Jonathan	Teign Head Farm, shepherd, successor to Henry Birdwood
French, Mary	Sister of Jonathan French, *m* 'Tiger'
Hext, Barbara	Postbridge, post office and general store
Hext, Saul	Nephew of Barbara Hext
Lyd, Pancras ('Tiger')	Workhouse boy; Hartland Farm, head man, *m* Mary French
Ouldsbroom, Philip	Hartland Farm, farmer, *m* Unity Crymes
Ouldsbroom, Unity	See Crymes, Unity
Ouldsbroom, (Philip) Martin	Son of Unity Ouldsbroom by Henry Birdwood
Ouldsbroom, Minnie	See Crymes, Minnie
Ouldsbroom, Wesley	Son of Martin and Minnie Ouldsbroom
Sleep, Ned	Teign Head Farm, assistant shepherd
'Tiger'	See Lyd, Pancras
Twigg, Gregory	Warren House Inn, landlord
Twigg, Mrs	Wife of Gregory Twigg
Twigg, Millicent Mary	Daughter of Gregory Twigg
White, Martha	Hartland Farm, housekeeper
Woodley, Nat	Postbridge, ancient man

240

DEMETER'S DAUGHTER (1911)

Angel, Samuel ('Hay-corn-roots')	Holne, farm worker
Bright, Mr	Holne, curate
Cleave, Aaron	Holne, thatcher
Cleave, Alison	Wife of Aaron Cleave
Cleave, Giles	Farm worker
Cleave, Frank	Stone breaker
Cleave, Joyce	*m* Timothy Sheldon
Cleave, Dick	
Cleave, Polly	

Cleave, Giles — Farm worker
Cleave, Frank — Stone breaker
Cleave, Joyce — *m* Timothy Sheldon
Cleave, Dick
Cleave, Polly
} Children of Aaron and Alison Cleave

Coneybeare, Matthew	Stoke Farm, head man
Coneybeare, Jenny	Daughter of Matthew Coneybeare
Cottle, William	Holne, Church House Inn, landlord
Godolphin, Mr	Holne, vicar
Grills, Teddy	Holne, baker
Hamlyn, Uriah	Stoke Farm, farmer
Hatch, Lavinia	Holne, 'shop of all sorts'
Sheldon, Timothy	Hairdresser, *m* Joyce Cleave
Tolchard, Dr	Holne, one-time employer of Alison Cleave
Tolchard, Mrs	Wife of Dr Tolchard
White, Drusilla	Affianced to Frank Cleave

THE BEACON (1911)

Bolt, Susan	Widowed sister of Frank Madders
Burgoyne, Minnie	*m* Tom Underhill
Cann, Fanny	Aunt of Tom Underhill
Denshaw, Elizabeth	Zeal, Oxenham Arms, barmaid, *m* Charles Trevail
Dunning, Reynold	Clannaboro' Farm, farmer
Jope, Jack	Zeal, shoemaker
Jope, Nelly	Zeal, Oxenham Arms, maid, *m* Ned Startup
Jope, Emma	Eloped with Tom Underhill
Knapman, Ned	Zeal, sportsman

Jope, Nelly — Zeal, Oxenham Arms, maid, *m* Ned Startup
Jope, Emma — Eloped with Tom Underhill
} Daughters of Jack Jope

Madders, Frank
('Lucky')   South Tawton Quarry, kiln master
Pike, Abraham ('Iron') South Tawton Quarry, owner, uncle of
                       Charles Trevail
Startup, Ned   Zeal, Oxenham Arms, first driver,
                       m Nelly Jope
Startup, Nelly   See Jope, Nelly
Trevail, Charles   'North Combe', farmer, nephew of
                       Abraham Pike, m Elisabeth Densham
Trevail, Elisabeth   See Densham, Elisabeth
Underhill, Tom   Zeal, Oxenham Arms, landlord,
                       m Minnie Burgoyne
Underhill, Minnie   See Burgoyne, Minnie
Vallance, Noah   Clannaboro' Farm, head man
Vallance, Mercy   Clannaboro' Farm, housekeeper, wife of
                       Noah Vallance

THE FOREST ON THE HILL (1912) retitled THE FOREST (1927)

Blackaller, Ned   Ilsington, 'Coach and Horses', landlord
Butt, Saul   Yarner, woodman
Campion, Seth   Middlecot, farm worker
Champernowne, Eustace Yarner, heir-presumptive, m Audrey
                       Leaman
French, Mercy   Postbridge, sister of John Redstone
Kingdon, Amos   Yarner, head keeper
Leaman, Willes   Middlecot, farmer
Leaman, Audrey   Daughter of Willes Leaman, m Eustace
                       Champernowne
Moyle, Frederick   Ilsington, police-officer
Redstone, John   Dury, farmer, m Drusilla Whyddon
Redstone, Jacob   Grandfather of John Redstone
Redstone, Drusilla   See Whyddon, Drusilla
Snow, Timothy   Yarner, under-keeper
Snow, Sarah   Mother of Timothy Snow
Snow, Lot   Ilsington, uncle of Timothy Snow
Snow, Sibella   Sister of Lot Snow
Turtle, Thomas   Ilsington, carrier
Whyddon, Drusilla   Yarner, m John Redstone
Widger, Jenny   Aunt of Drusilla Whyddon

WIDECOMBE FAIR (1913)

Bell, Gaffer	Widecombe, almshouses resident
Blake, Sandy	Blackslade, farm worker
Blake, Joan	Wife of Sandy Blake
Blatchford, Mr	Exeter, lawyer
Brown, Mr	Widecombe, vicar
Cann, Rebecca	Widecombe, parish nurse
Chave, Ernest	Widecombe, police-officer
Coaker, William	Southcombe, farmer
Coaker, Grace	Wife of William Coaker
Coaker, Elias	Son of William and Grace Coaker, betrothed to Petronell Shillingford
Cobleigh, Uncle Tom	Venton, farmer
Cobleigh, Christian	Son of Uncle Tom Cobleigh
Dench, Araminta	Niece of Valiant Dunnybrig, *m* Samuel Sweetland
Dunnybrig, Valiant	Chittleford, farmer
Dunnybrig, Jane	Wife of Valiant Dunnybrig
Gay, Milly	Venton, widowed daughter of Uncle Tom Cobleigh
Glubb, Nicky	Widecombe, blind accordion player
Glubb, Nanny	Wife of Nicky Glubb
Grenville, Dr Hugh	'Woodhayes', medical practitioner
Gurney, Abel	Dunstone, farmer
Gurney, Bassett	Son of Abel Gurney
Gurney, Nelly	Daughter of Abel Gurney
Gurney, Sarah	Second wife of Abel Gurney
Gurney, Tom	Widecombe, blacksmith, *m* Mabel Pierce
Gurney, Mabel	See Pierce, Mabel
Harvey, Tryphena	Southcombe, niece of Grace Coaker
Hawke, Old Harry	'Woodhayes', farmer
Hawke, Young Harry	'Woodhayes', farmer
Hawke, Emma	Wife of Young Harry Hawke, daughter of Peter and Martha Smerdon
Hearn, Mary	Widecombe, post office
Hearn, Mrs	Mother of Mary Hearn
Johnson, Birkett	Tunhill, head man
Leyman, Patience	Widecombe, schoolmistress

243

Mogridge, Alfred	Bone Hill Cottages, sexton and jobbing gardener
Mogridge, Jack	Son of Alfred Mogridge, *m* Margery Reep
Mogridge, Margery	See Reep, Margery
Pierce, Arthur	Widecombe, Old Inn, landlord
Pierce, Mabel	Wife of Arthur Pierce, divorced, *m* Tom Gurney
Reep, Daniel	Bone Hill Cottages, poacher
Reep, Joyce	Wife of Daniel Reep
Reep, Margery	Daughter of Daniel and Joyce Reep, *m* Jack Mogridge
Saunders, Adam	Widecombe, police-officer
Shillingford, Gabriel	Blackslade, farmer
Shillingford, Sibley	*m* Whitelock Smerdon ⎫ Daughters
Shillingford, Petronell	Betrothed to Elias ⎬ of Gabriel
	Coaker ⎭ Shillingford
Smerdon, Peter	Bone Hill, farmer
Smerdon, Martha	Wife of Peter Smerdon
Smerdon, Whitelock	Son of Peter and Martha Smerdon, *m* Sibley Shillingford
Smerdon, Sibley	See Shillingford, Sibley
Sweetland, Samuel	Tunhill, farmer, widower, *m* Araminta Dench
Sweetland, Harriet	Sister of Samuel Sweetland
Sweetland, Araminta	See Dench, Araminta
Tapper, Thirza	'Genoa Villa', spinster
Turtle, Timothy	Widecombe, Rugglestone Inn, landlord
Turtle, Sally	Kingshead, maid to Louisa Windeatt, daughter of Timothy Turtle, betrothed to Pancras Widecombe
Widecombe, Pancras	Rugglestone Inn, stonemason, betrothed to Sally Turtle
Windeatt, Louisa	Kingshead, farmer, widow

BRUNEL'S TOWER (1915)

Appleby, Alice	Betrothed to Rupert Marsland
Body, Thomas	Brunel's Tower, thrower
Coysh, Timothy	Brunel's Tower, teapot spout moulder

Coysh, Charlie	Nephew of Timothy Coysh
Crispin, Luther	Erme Clay Pits, partner of Anthony Fincher
Easterbrook, George	Brunel's Tower, partner 'Easterbrook & Pitts'
Easterbrook, Joanna	Daughter of George Easterbrook
Ede, Christopher	Brunel's Tower, oven placer
Ede, Jack	Younger brother of Christopher Ede
Fincher, Anthony	Erme Clay Pits, partner of Luther Crispin
Fincher, Amy	Wife of Anthony Fincher
Fincher, Mary	
Fincher, John	} Children of Anthony and Amy Fincher
Fincher, Wilfred	
Godbeer, William	Brunel's Tower, turner
Godbeer, Billy	Son of William Godbeer
Greenslade, William	Brunel's Tower, boy
Luke, Davy	Brunel's Tower, wedger
Marsland, Rupert	Brunel's Tower, handler and painter, betrothed to Alice Appleby
Masters, James	Todd's Pottery, fireman
Medway, Sophia	Brunel's Tower, painter, aunt of George Easterbrook
Porter, Harvey (Hockin, Lee)	Reformatory boy, protégé of George Easterbrook
Pitts, Paul	Brunel's Tower, partner 'Easterbrook & Pitts'
Punchard, Samuel	Brunel's Tower, master fireman
Todd, Wilberforce	Todd's Pottery, owner
Todd, Nelly	Daughter of Wilberforce Todd
Tolley, Jeremiah	Brunel's Tower, engineman
Tolley, Mrs	Wife of Jeremiah Tolley
Zachary, Adam	Brunel's Tower, second thrower

MISER'S MONEY (1920)

Baird, Robert	Two Bridges, kinsman of Marian Dennis
Bascombe, John	Nun's Cross Farm, head man
Bascombe, Jenny	Wife of John Bascombe

Bascombe, 'Little' Jack	Son of John and Jenny Bascombe, m Jane Bond
Bascombe, Jane	See Bond, Jane
Bascombe, Johnny	Son of Little Jack and Jane Bascombe
Bond, Jane	Maid to Sarah Mortimer, m Little Jack Bascombe
Dennis, Marian	Princetown, "Plume of Feathers", barmaid, m Barry Worth
Edwards, Mr	Princetown, general stores, owner
Edwards, Sophia	Daughter of Mr Edwards, m Charles Pascoe (I)
Halfyard, Benjamin	Princetown, shoesmith, m Damaris Worth
Halfyard, Damaris	See Worth, Damaris
Mortimer, David	Nun's Cross Farm, farmer (also referred to in *The Three Brothers*, Chap. XXXIX)
Mortimer, Nathan	White Works, farmer, brother of David Mortimer
Mortimer, May	Wife of Nathan Mortimer
Mortimer, Anstice	Daughter of Nathan and May Mortimer, m Charles Pascoe (I)
Mortimer, Sarah	White Works, spinster, sister of David Mortimer
Pascoe, Charles (I)	White Works, farmer, m (i) Anstice Mortimer (ii) Sophia Edwards
Pascoe, Rebecca	Sister of Charles Pascoe (I)
Pascoe, Anstice (I)	See Mortimer, Anstice
Pascoe, Anstice (II)	Daughter of Charles and Anstice Pascoe
Pascoe, Sophia	See Edwards, Sophia
Pascoe, Charles (II) Pascoe, Rupert	} Sons of Charles and Sophia Pascoe
Square, Mr	Lawyer
Worth, Mary	White Works, widowed sister of David Mortimer
Worth, James	Assistant, Edward's Stores
Worth, Barry	Nun's Cross Farm, farmer, successor to David Mortimer, m Marian Dennis

Worth, James — Worth, Barry: Children of Mary Worth

Worth, Damaris   *m* Benjamin Halfyard
Worth, David   ⎱
Worth, Mary Ann ⎰ Children of Barry and Marian Worth

ORPHAN DINAH (1920)

Bamsey, Benjamin	Lower Town, Buckland, farmer
Bamsey, Faith	Wife of Benjamin Bamsey
Bamsey, John	Water-bailiff ⎱ Children of Benjamin
Bamsey, Jane	⎰ and Faith Bamsey
Chaffe, Arthur	Lower Town, Buckland, carpenter
Ford, Harry	Buckland, gardener, *m* Melinda Honeysett
Ford, Melinda	See Honeysett, Melinda
Honeysett, Melinda	Buckland, widowed daughter of Enoch Withycombe, *m* Harry Ford
Maynard, Lawrence (Courtier, Gilbert)	'Falcon' Farm, cowhand, betrothed to Dinah Waycott
Palk, Thomas	'Falcon' Farm, horseman, *m* Susan Stockman
Palk, Susan	See Stockman, Susan
Stockman, Joseph	'Falcon' Farm, farmer
Stockman, Susan	Daughter of Joseph Stockman, *m* Thomas Palk
Tutt, Neddy	'Falcon' Farm, farm worker
Waycott, Dinah	Lower Town, Buckland, step-daughter of Benjamin Bamsey, betrothed to Lawrence Maynard
Withycombe, Enoch	Buckland, bedridden widower, huntsman

Withycombe, Jerry   ⎱
Withycombe, Robert ⎰ Sons of Enoch Withycombe

CHILDREN OF MEN (1923)

Bullstone, Jacob	'Red House', farmer, breeder of red Irish terriers, *m* Margery Huxam
Bullstone, Mrs	Widowed mother of Jacob Bullstone
Bullstone, Margery	See Huxam, Margery

Bullstone, Peter	} Children of Jacob
Bullstone, John Henry	} and Margery
Bullstone, Auna	} Bullstone
Bullstohe, Avis	*m* Robert Elvin
Catt, Matthew	Bullstone Farm, farmer
Cousins, Dr	Medical practitioner
Elvin, Joe	Owley Farm, farmer
Elvin, Mrs	Wife of Joe Elvin
Elvin, Robert	Son of Joe Elvin, *m* Avis Bullstone
Gill, Barton	'Red House', head kennelman
Elvin, Avis	See Bullstone; Avis
Huxam, Barlow	Brent, draper and postmaster
Huxam, Judith	Wife of Barlow Huxam
Huxam, Margery	Daughter of Barlow and Judith Huxam, *m* Jacob Bullstone
Huxam, Jeremy	Owley Cot, son of Barlow and Judith Huxam
Huxam, Jane	Wife of Jeremy Huxam, daughter of Milly Parsons
Marydrew, William	Shipley, octogenarian
Middleweek, George	'Red House', kennelman, successor to Barton Gill
Parsons, Milly	Bullstone Farm, widowed daughter of Matthew Catt
Veale, Frederick	Huntingdon Warren, warrener
Veale, Benjamin (Benny)	Warrener, son of Frederick Veale
Veale, Sally	Wife of Benny Veale
Winter, Adam	Shipley Farm, farmer
Winter, Amelia	Aunt of Adam Winter
Winter, Samuel	Elder brother of Adam Winter, farm worker
Woolcombe, Nurse	Brent, district nurse